Theoretical Issues in Stuttering

Although there is now a large body of research into the nature and treatment of stuttering, little is understood about its underlying mechanisms. As a result, until now there has been no comprehensive review of the numerous theories and models that have been proposed to explain stuttering.

Theoretical Issues in Stuttering provides a comprehensive account of the contribution of theory to understanding and managing stuttering. It covers an impressive range of topics including a description of both past and current theories of stuttering, placing each within the relevant historical context. In addition, the authors evaluate the explanatory power of such models and provide a detailed exploration of the implications of these models for the practitioner.

Theoretical Issues in Stuttering aims to fill a gap in the literature on the subject of stuttering theory and to act as an invaluable resource for speech-language pathologists, lecturers, and advanced students of speech and language pathology.

Ann Packman is Senior Research Officer at the Australian Stuttering Research Centre at the University of Sydney.

Joseph S. Attanasio is a Professor in the Department of Communication Sciences and Disorders at Montclair State University, New Jersey, USA.

Theoretical Issues in Stuttering

Ann Packman and
Joseph S. Attanasio

Ψ Psychology Press
Taylor & Francis Group
HOVE AND NEW YORK

First published 2004
by Psychology Press
27 Church Road, Hove, East Sussex BN3 2FA

Simultaneously published in the USA and Canada
by Psychology Press
270 Madison Avenue, New York NY 10016

Psychology Press is a part of the Taylor & Francis Group

Copyright © 2004 Psychology Press

Typeset in Times by RefineCatch Limited, Bungay, Suffolk
Printed and bound in Great Britain by
TJ International Ltd, Padstow, Cornwall
Cover design by Hybert Design

This publication has been produced with paper manufactured to
strict environmental standards and with pulp derived from
sustainable forests.

British Library Cataloguing in Publication Data
A catalogue record for this book is available from the British Library

Library of Congress Cataloging-in-Publication Data
Packman, Ann.
  Theoretical issues in stuttering /
    by Ann Packman and Joseph S. Attanasio.—1st ed. p. cm
  Includes bibliographical reference and index.
  ISBN 1-84169-303-0 (hardcover)
  1. Stuttering. I. Attanasio, Joseph S.   II. Title.

  RC424.P33 2004
  616.85′54–dc22   2004015195

  ISBN 1–84169–303–0 (hbk)

To Marie and Brian

Contents

11 Theories and treatment   143

12 Final comments   157

List of figures and tables

Preface

The impetus for this book comes from our conviction that theorists and their theories must be held accountable, by clinicians and researchers, for what they propose and offer for consideration. The large number of theories of stuttering, often conflicting and incompatible with one another, makes the task of critically considering them a daunting one. Nevertheless, it is a task that must be faced if our profession and those of us interested in stuttering are to sort out what we believe to be the nature and cause of the disorder and the most effective ways to treat it.

This book, then, is not a book of theories of stuttering. Rather, it is a book that offers ways to think about theories of stuttering. Our primary purpose in the pages that follow is to provide information and guidelines that clinicians and researchers can use to evaluate the merits and usefulness of current and future theories of stuttering. We place the guidelines within the framework of science – its history, philosophy, purpose, methodology, and application – and seek to bring a scientific frame of mind into our reflections on theory. The first four chapters establish the context for thinking about theories, specifically theories of stuttering. Chapter 5 describes what a theory of stuttering ought to explain about the disorder. The subsequent five chapters present theories we have selected for the purpose of critical analysis by the application of the guidelines we have chosen. Our intent in those chapters is to exemplify a process by which the merits of theories may be assessed. In the two concluding chapters we invstigate how theory relates to treatment in stuttering and report our final musings. It is our hope that the text provides interesting and stimulating issues to think about. Most of all, we hope that readers of the text will find it useful.

We would like to thank Terence McMullen for his considerable contribution to our thinking about causality. We also extend our gratitude to our friends and colleagues Mark Onslow, Jerry Siegel, and John van Borsel for their support, encouragement, and helpful comments on earlier versions of the book.

Ann Packman and Joseph S. Attanasio

Theory helps us to bear our ignorance of fact
George Santayana

Chapter 1

The search for understanding

In his now classic text on the nature of stuttering, Charles van Riper (1971) described stuttering as "a puzzle, the pieces of which lie scattered on the tables of speech pathology, psychiatry, neurophysiology, genetics, and many other disciplines ... we suspect that some of the essential pieces are not merely misplaced but still missing" (p. 2). Van Riper's words might aptly be applied to the difficulties we continue to face in understanding stuttering in the early part of the 21st century. Stuttering has probably existed from the time humans began to speak, it exists in all cultures, and is present in around 1% of the population at any one time (see Bloodstein, 1995). Yet, despite the fact that stuttering has been studied extensively, elements of its puzzling and enigmatic nature continue to challenge many contemporary students, clinicians, and researchers.

What kind of disorder is it that unexplainably manifests itself in children after a period of apparently normal speech development? Why does stuttering take the form, at least in its early presentation, of the repetition of speech sounds and syllables? How is it that a child who stutters can speak without stuttering for hours, days, weeks – even months and possibly years – only to experience a return of the disorder? Why do some children who start to stutter continue to do so into adulthood, while others recover naturally within one or two years? What mechanisms lie behind the fluency-inducing effects of singing and choral speaking or reading; of speaking along with the rhythmic beat of a metronome; of delaying, altering, or masking the auditory feedback of the stutterer's own voice; or of prolonging speech or reducing its rate? Does one mechanism account for these fluency-inducing effects or are there a number of mechanisms that come into play? Why does the person who stutters say some words fluently but not others?

The foregoing questions and others like them continue to capture the attention of professionals and laypersons alike and they underscore the puzzle that is stuttering. Nevertheless, while much is unknown about the disorder, there is an extensive body of scientific research that gives hope for our ultimate ability to unwrap the nature of stuttering, divest it of its mysteriousness, and develop ways to treat it effectively. Indeed, a great deal of progress in those directions has been made.

Despite the progress, the questions posed above continue to prompt much theorizing about stuttering. The discussions that follow in this text are designed to organize, make sense of, and evaluate a number of theories of stuttering and to place theorizing about stuttering into the broader framework of the nature and philosophy of science. This would seem to be a necessary context for thinking critically about the nature of stuttering, and for questioning the logic of our propositions about stuttering.

SEEKING EXPLANATION

Humans crave explanation. We become uneasy when we are faced with things or happenings that we do not understand. This need for explanation develops early in life, as can be seen in the well-known "Why . . . ?" questions of 2–3-year-old children. The need for explanation was also clearly evident in primitive humans, who presumed that the gods caused events such as the eruption of volcanoes, for which they could see no other cause. This eased their discomfort at being unable to explain or control natural phenomena and led to various ritualistic practices such as dancing for rain or offering sacrifices to appease the gods (van Hooft, Gillam, & Byrnes, 1995).

We now know that many of these ancient beliefs and explanations about the natural world are not necessarily true. We now understand a great deal about why volcanoes erupt and why it rains. Yet the truth of a belief, even today, is not always of paramount importance in everyday life. In the face of lack of understanding, humans may find it preferable to have a plausible explanation rather than live with uncertainty. As we shall see later, this is certainly the case with stuttering.

Attempts to explain the unknown reflect the human need to impose order on the world and seek logical connections between events or phenomena. In modern times, of course, science has played an enormous role in explaining the natural world. Science, through observation and experimentation, has provided explanations for many of the things that were previously attributed to supernatural forces. The scientific method also enables systematic refining of the nature of natural phenomena and uncovering logical connections between events.

Theorizing about possible connections between events is an integral part of science. The theories of Galileo and Darwin are two of the most revolutionary and probably the most well-known in the history of science. Not that such revolutionary theories are always accepted without question, particularly when they contradict prevailing belief systems. It was more than 300 years before the Roman Catholic church gave credence to Galileo's theory that the earth moved around the sun. That seems a noncontroversial explanation of the universe today, but at the time it flew in the face of the orthodox belief that the opposite was the case. To be fair, this explanation also flew in the face of common sense. We see the sun rise in the eastern sky and set in the western sky, and there is no bodily sensation to support the idea that the earth is moving. Likewise Darwin's theory of natural selection has met with opposition since the publication of his treatise *The Origin of Species* in 1859. Opposition to this theory is apparent even today, primarily because it is at odds with certain religious beliefs.

The point here is that the need for a plausible explanation remains uppermost in humans, whether those explanations be religious or scientific. However, an explanation or belief that is plausible to one person is not necessarily plausible to another. Sometimes it takes an almost overwhelming body of evidence before a new and more plausible explanation is accepted over an older and deeply ingrained one. This, also, has been the case in stuttering. As will be seen later when we talk about the history of theories of stuttering, Johnson's view that parents caused stuttering remained viable for decades, despite a growing body of evidence to the contrary.

This is not to say that science is free of beliefs. On the contrary, Kuhn (1996) suggested that all observations in science are theory-laden. We will return to this later in our discussion of how theories develop. Yet the scientific method, with a reliance on replication of findings, establishes laws about nature, at least in the physical sciences. This may be quite different in the social and behavioural sciences, where human beings are the object of study. We return to this later also.

The puzzling nature of stuttering, combined with the fact that its cause is unknown, has provided fertile ground for the propagation of theoretical explanations about the disorder. Theories about the cause of stuttering have been around for centuries and have proliferated in the last three decades or so, prompted by an increase in scientific investigation into the disorder. Yet, as far as causal factors are concerned, we are not a lot closer now to understanding the mechanisms underpinning stuttering than we were centuries ago. The best that can be said is that we now know much more about the nature of stuttering, and we now know that many things once thought to cause stuttering do not in fact cause it.

CAUSALITY AND STUTTERING

Causality is not a simple matter. Causality may be explained at different levels and people will differ in their perspectives of what is required of a causal explanation (Siegel, 1989). Take the example of Bill, a young man who stutters, who is waiting in a fast-food outlet. When he finally reaches the head of the queue and is asked what he wants, Bill stutters severely on the word "burger". The search for understanding leads us to ask why Bill stuttered.

Why did he breathe in quickly and audibly, hold his lips together in the position for /b/ for around 2 seconds, and then release that lip posture with increased loudness on the following /ur/ sound? If one asked Bill why he stuttered, he may identify situational factors (for a discussion of attribution of cause see Einhorn & Hogarth, 1986). For example, he may say that he stuttered because the sales assistant was an attractive young female; or that he stuttered because he became aware that other customers in the shop were watching him; or because he felt that he had to give his order quickly in order not to hold up the queue.

The person behind Bill in the queue may be more inclined to attribute Bill's stuttering to constitutional causes. He may say that Bill stuttered because he was nervous or shy; or because he wasn't sure what to order.

Bill's speech clinician, when asked why he stuttered when ordering a burger, might say that he stuttered because he did not use the fluency skills that he had acquired in therapy; or because he anticipated that he would stutter; or because he became anxious in that particular situation.

A scientist conducting research in the area of stuttering may suggest that Bill stuttered because when he spoke there was interference between the left and right hemispheres of his brain; or that his control over his breathing muscles was inadequate for fluent speech; or that he had difficulty processing the motor plans for the production of the word "burger"; or that he did not coordinate the articulatory and phonatory systems involved in speech production sufficiently well to say the word fluently.

All these explanations for Bill's stuttering appear plausible. At the very least, they would be plausible to the person offering them. Each of the explanations provides an answer, at some level, to the question of why Bill stuttered. Some of them are causal explanations, and some of the explanations amounted to no more than descriptions of the mechanisms thought to underpin stuttering. The speech clinician's explanation that Bill was not using his learned fluency techniques was a reason rather than a cause, as it implied agency (Robinson, 1985) on Bill's part.

Of course the individuals in this scenario all had different associations and experiences with stuttering. Bill knows his stuttering first-hand, with all the bodily sensations and mental and emotional experiences associated with it. The observer in the fast-food outlet may never have seen someone stutter before and so had no frame of reference for understanding it. The speech clinician had a particular interest in whether Bill was able to put the skills he had learned in therapy into practice. The scientist explained Bill's stuttering by reducing his behaviour to a more basic, physiological level.

Of course, while each of the explanations in this scenario provides a reasonable explanation for Bill's stuttering, they may not be correct. Establishing the correctness of an explanation, or a causal theory, is quite another matter. This can only be addressed in the empirical world; that is, through hypothesis, experimentation, and the accumulations of evidence. We will address this in

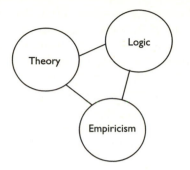

Figure 1.1 The three domains of inquiry.

subsequent sections on theory and hypothesis testing. For the moment, we are concerned with another – albeit highly related – level of thinking; namely, with the logic of causal explanations.

At this point, clarification is needed regarding the three domains of inquiry across which the discussions in this book range. They are the domains of theory, logic, and empiricism. The three are interconnected, as depicted in Figure 1.1 and, as may have become clear already, discussions in this text at times slip seamlessly among the three.

The theoretical domain is concerned with propositions; in this text we are concerned particularly with theories that propose possible causes of stuttering. The logical domain is concerned with the logic of the arguments contained in such propositions. The empirical domain is concerned with scientific observation and experimentation – evidence from the real world that might support or weaken a proposition under consideration. Terminology may change across domains. In the theoretical domain, hypothetical causes may be referred to as factors. In the logical domain, cause is defined as the necessary and sufficient condition that must pertain for stuttering to occur. In the empirical domain, hypothetical causes may be referred to as variables, because they can vary across experimental conditions (van Hooft et al., 1995).

The theoretical and empirical domains are addressed later in this text. For the remainder of this chapter, however, we are concerned mainly with the domain of logic. In particular, we address here some issues of logic that arise in causal arguments. The aim of this is to provide guidelines for evaluating the logic of the propositions contained in causal theories of stuttering. We draw largely from the writings of philosophers and illustrate with examples from stuttering where possible.

CAUSALITY: ISSUES OF LOGIC

A causal explanation indicates the mechanism by which something occurs. However, there is considerable disagreement among authorities about what constitutes a cause (Einhorn & Hogarth, 1986; White, 1990). For example, there is usually more than one factor that can be said to contribute to an event or state of affairs, and that might therefore be regarded as causal. Indeed, it has been argued that there is always more than one cause (Place, 1996). While some philosophers refer to causes as events, others maintain, "omissions (contrasted to commissions), standing conditions, material substances, and properties of things, may be causes" (White, 1990, p. 3). It has also been argued that things caused also cause other things, and in this sense causality has been described as the cement of the universe (see Mackie, 1974).

Although a detailed treatment of the philosophical thinking on the nature of cause or causation is beyond the scope of this book, the present discussion will benefit from a brief digression into selected aspects of that thinking. At first blush, it may seem odd to enter into a somewhat philosophical discussion of cause and cause–effect relationships. After all, who would doubt that events have causes or that causes produce effects? Certainly, a world without cause–effect relationships would be chaotic and unpredictable. In fact we conduct our daily lives, and scientists conduct their science, believing that there are causes and effects. If we want a glass of water, we turn on the cold-water tap in the sink and water pours out into the glass. Obviously, it was necessary for the tap to be opened in order to obtain the water, but was it sufficient? What chain of events or circumstances might need to be considered in a fuller description of the cause of water flowing from the tap? The tap must be connected to pipes, for water to reach the house and there must be sufficient pressure in the pipes for the water to flow.

Of course, one needs to be careful here, as this process could go on and on. When explanation is sought, one needs to decide what level of explanation is required by, or will satisfy, the inquiry at hand. For an everyday explanation it would be sufficient to say that the flow of water was caused by turning the tap. In this context, the pipes and the water pressure could be seen as background conditions (van Hooft et al., 1995) that are taken for granted.

A REALIST VIEW OF CAUSALITY

Despite the fact that we may settle on the reasonable explanation that turning a tap causes water to flow, Hume suggested that cause and effect cannot be observed directly, nor proved on either logical or empirical grounds (Osborne, 1992; Thompson, 1995). Hume said that we *assume* a cause–effect relationship between what very well may be separate events. An example of Hume's thinking, based on one given by Osborne (1992, p. 85), illustrates this. In a sequence of events during which an object A is struck and in turn strikes object B and there follows movement or displacement of the object B, we cannot be *certain* that what happened to and with object A caused object B to move or be displaced, despite the fact that we saw object A strike object

B. All that is observed is a conjunction of events. Furthermore, we cannot – through inductive reasoning – be certain that every time object A acts upon object B in the manner just described, object B will move or be displaced, unless of course we are able to observe every instance of A acting on B in exactly the same way.

Kant's resolution (see Osborne, 1992, pp. 101–106) to such problems with induction and causality was to reconcile empiricism (wherein knowledge is based on experience and not on innate ideas or logic) with rationalism (wherein knowledge is based on logical deduction, reason, and *a priori* knowledge and intuition). Kant (see Menand, 2001, p. 357; Osborne, 1992, pp. 101–106; Thompson, 1995, pp. 144–146) believed that innate categories of thought enable us to make sense of and structure experience. The categories are imposed upon experience and knowledge is possible only through them. For Kant, this is a reflection of how the mind works. Causality is one of those categories. Returning to the sequence given above of the conjunction of events concerning objects A and B, Kant's view would allow a causal statement to be made – object A, by striking object B, caused object B to move. We impose the category of causality on our experience of the sequence and conclude, or act as though, A was the cause of B (Menand, 2001; Osborne, 1992; Thompson, 1995). Nonetheless, there are many instances, and stuttering is one of them, where causality is a much more complex state of affairs and where fallacious reasoning can lead to quite extraordinary propositions about causal relationships.

In the discussions to follow later in this text, the view is taken that cause is a legitimate and necessary component of the structure of theories. We take this realist view because we believe, as do others (for example Blalock, 1964), that there is heuristic value in doing so. Reasoning and behaving from cause, or thinking causally, makes science, theory construction, and the scientific method itself more fruitful and productive than they would be if the construct of cause were not adopted. The proposition that thinking causally has heuristic value is not far from James's thinking on how we adopt certain mental structures. James (1981) suggested that if experience teaches us that a belief in causation helps to clarify our understanding of the relationships between events, then we must be correct in thinking that way; there is benefit in thinking causally. For James, the spokesman for pragmatism, experience eventually tells us if it is correct to think causally because we are able to assess the benefit of doing so. In other words, we determine if thinking a given way (in the present case, causally) results in what we are after. Experience verifies our belief (Menand, 2001). James (1981, p. 1264) writes:

> We have no definite idea of what we mean by cause, or of what causality consists in. But the principle expresses a demand for *some* deeper sort of inward connection between phenomena than their merely habitual time-sequence seems to us to be. The word "cause" is, in short, an altar to an

unknown god; a pedestal still marking the place of a hoped-for statue. *Any* really inward belonging-together of the sequent terms, if discovered, would be accepted as what the word cause was meant to stand for.

The belief that thinking causally has heuristic value is not to be taken as an assertion that causality can be proven beyond all doubt. According to Blalock, no amount or kind of empirical evidence can prove causal laws. This view echoes Hume. For Blalock, causal thinking belongs to the realm and language of theory; however, the implications of causal relationships are couched in operational language and can be indirectly tested, an issue we turn to later. In order to construct causal hypotheses, certain simplifying assumptions about the nature of reality have to be made and scientists have to act as if those assumptions are correct. If the assumptions are not considered to be correct and if scientists do not act as if they are, Blalock states that science could not be done and generalizations beyond the single case or event could not be made. Examples of these simplifying assumptions are: (1) events are repeated and (2) objects have properties that remain constant over a period of time. Because simplifying assumptions are not testable, the correctness of a causal theory cannot be demonstrated by correct empirical predictions made from it but, as stated above, the implications of the theory can be indirectly tested (Blalock, 1964).

ESTABLISHING CAUSE: NECESSARY AND SUFFICIENT CONDITIONS

In order to attribute causality to a condition, the condition must be both necessary and sufficient for the effect to occur (see Mill, 1967). A condition is described as *sufficient* when it alone always leads to a certain effect, and a condition is described as *necessary* when it is always present prior to the effect. Thus, we could say that exposure to the measles virus is *necessary* for the development of measles. However, exposure is not a *sufficient* condition for the development of the disease because many people are immune to the virus as a result of previous contact or immunization. Thus, to contract measles the person must be exposed to the virus *and* not be immune. These two factors together constitute the necessary and sufficient condition for the contraction of measles. An example of a simple cause, where a single factor constitutes a necessary and sufficient condition, would be the genetic abnormality that causes Down syndrome. *Every* child who has this abnormality will have Down syndrome and *only* children who have this genetic abnormality will have Down syndrome.

So how do we go about addressing, in the logical domain, the question "What causes stuttering?" As we will see below, the complex and poorly understood nature of stuttering means that attributing cause in stuttering is not nearly as straightforward as it is in measles or Down syndrome. In discussing causal theories of stuttering, Bloodstein (1995) maintained that a theory must not only explain why people stutter, in general, but must also explain each individual stuttering event. While this is a sensible suggestion, it should not be interpreted to mean that there are two different sets of causal factors operating in stuttering, one that explains stuttering in general and another that explains each instance of stuttering. We suggest that the general question "What causes stuttering?" is in fact a question about the *necessary* condition for stuttering (at the theoretical level it might be referred to as a risk factor). One straightforward, albeit hypothetical, answer to such a question might be that people who stutter have a deficit in lexical retrieval. Since in this proposal this deficit is a necessary condition for stuttering it is, *by necessity*, operating at the time of each stuttering event (moment of stuttering). We use the term "condition" here at the logical level, but this does not imply that the necessary condition for stuttering consists of only one factor. To take the hypothetical example above further, it might be that this deficit only results in stuttering in children who demonstrate slow didokokinetic articulation rates. In this proposal, then, together these two factors constitute the condition that is necessary and sufficient for stuttering to occur. Both are necessary but neither *on its own* is sufficient for stuttering to occur.

The importance of establishing the logic of causal arguments is very important when studying causal theories in stuttering. The prior decade has seen the rise of objections to the idea that there is in fact a necessary and sufficient condition for stuttering. It has been argued that proposals that involve a necessary and sufficient condition are simplistic and an offshoot of the medical model where stuttering is explained as the response of the organism to an underlying physical pathology, possibly a deficit or processing inefficiency (Smith & Kelly, 1997). The reaction to this idea of a necessary condition has taken the form of multifactorial models of stuttering. In their strongest form, multifactorial models posit that there is no *one* cause of stuttering; rather, stuttering is caused by different combinations of factors in different individuals and there need not be any constitutional deficit in the person who stutters. Multifactorial models are discussed in considerable detail in Chapter 9. Suffice it to say here that at the logical level this multifactorial view posits that there is no necessary and sufficient condition for stuttering (see Packman, Onslow, & Attanasio, 2004).

We return now to Bloodstein's statement that not only should a theory explain why people stutter (a general explanation of what causes stuttering) but it must also explain individual stutters. One of the problems with proposals that there is a necessary and sufficient condition for stuttering is that they do not appear to do this. They do not explain, for example, why Bill stuttered on "burger" in the fast-food store but had said the word quite fluently only 5 minutes previously when discussing with his friend what they might order. This brings up the possibility that certain factors that are neither necessary nor sufficient for stuttering to occur may "trigger" stuttering. This is addressed in the following section.

The causal field

So far, we have been discussing cause in general terms, with universal statements, such as the cause of measles. However, determining cause – namely the conditions that are necessary and sufficient for an effect – is not so straightforward when talking about causality in specific instances; namely, when making singular causal statements (Mackie, 1975). Many philosophers use fire as an example of this, and we shall continue that here, using the specific example of bushfires. The immediate cause of any fire is the application of heat of sufficient temperature to flammable material. This condition is both necessary and sufficient to cause fire. However, this explanation would be considered trivial in attempting to determine the cause of a particular bushfire that destroyed, for example, large amounts of property. Rather, we would want to know what particular event or set of conditions caused this particular fire. Was it caused by a lightning strike? Or by a smouldering cigarette butt discarded from a passing car? Or by the striking of a match by an arsonist? Any of these could have caused the particular bushfire, yet none in itself would be considered both necessary and sufficient to cause a bushfire. To take the example of the lightning strike, clearly lightning might cause a bushfire in some circumstances but not others. The circumstances (context) in which the effect occurred (in this case this particular bushfire) are known as the causal field. In other words, lightning may cause a fire in a particular forest in one causal field (on a very hot dry day, when there is thick undergrowth) but not in another (when it is raining, and when the undergrowth has been cleared).

The idea of the causal field was proposed by Anderson (see Anderson, 1962; Baker, 1986; White, 1990). Anderson argued for a *three-term* view of causality, as opposed to the two-term (simple cause and effect) views described above. As stated by Baker (1986, p. 112) in his account of Anderson's work:

> Ordinary accounts of causes and effects or of conditions necessary and sufficient for the occurrence of certain phenomena usually ignore and fail to specify what it is that is subjected to causal influence and comes to undergo change.

According to Anderson, when we consider causality we are considering what causes one thing to become another. We do not ask simply what causes Y, but we ask what causes Z to become Y. We can say, then, that lightning may cause a quiet forest to become an inferno in one causal field but not in another. The three-term view of causality, and the notion of the causal field, introduces the idea that a causal relationship always involves change.

Using the bushfire scenario again, lightning is neither a necessary or sufficient condition for a bushfire to occur. Yet, in practical terms, it is perfectly acceptable to say that the fire in the example given *was caused by* a lightning strike. To accommodate this, Mackie proposed what is known as the INUS condition (for discussions see Mackie, 1975; White, 1990). While neither necessary nor sufficient for bushfires, in this particular fire the lightning strike was an Insufficient (I) but Necessary (N) part of this particular scenario that is, however, Unnecessary (U) but Sufficient (S) for a fire to occur. The lightning strike was necessary for this particular bushfire to start, but not necessary or even sufficient for other bushfires (that is, in other causal fields) to start.

We believe that the logic of the causal field and INUS conditions helps to clarify our thinking about stuttering, in particular about understanding cause in relation to individual moments of stuttering. The three-term view of causality prompts us to ask what causes the word "burger" to be stuttered in one situation and spoken quite fluently in another. In other words, in the scenario we have used, what caused a potentially fluent word (Z) to become a stuttered word (Y) in the fast-food shop – that is, in that particular causal field?

One possible explanation is that the word "burger" was uttered with hesitations and explosive release of air – in the causal field of the fast-food shop – because Bill became anxious in that situation. High anxiety is, in itself, insufficient to cause stuttering; after all, almost everyone gets anxious at times but only a few people stutter when they are anxious. But in Bill's case it could be said that anxiety "triggered" stuttering; that is, anxiety was a necessary condition for stuttering to occur *in this particular scenario*. In this scenario, then, anxiety is an INUS condition. Anxiety does not cause stuttering but was necessary to the occurrence of stuttering *on this occasion*. Of course, the "general" cause (in Bloodstein's causal model), whatever it may be, was also operating at that time. In lay terms one might say that Bill stuttered because he was anxious, but we cannot say that anxiety is a cause of stuttering because it is neither necessary nor sufficient for stuttering to occur. This way of looking at cause – invoking the causal field and the INUS condition – is helpful in trying to isolate causal and triggering factors and identify factors that appear to be influencing variability in stuttering. This is helpful in critically appraising any causal theory of stuttering, but is particularly so in the case of multifactorial models that propose no necessary and/or sufficient condition.

Interestingly, the idea of the causal field can also be used to attempt to understand the variation in stuttering across words in an utterance. Why, for example, does a person not stutter on every word? Why did Bill stutter on "burger" but not on the preceding part of the utterance, "I want a . . ."? At the logical level, one could view every word, or syllable, as a causal field and attempt to determine the INUS condition (triggering factor or factors) that causes stuttering to occur on some and not others. Indeed, many attempts have been made at both the theoretical and the empirical level to explain this feature of stuttering (Bloodstein, 1995).

DISTAL AND PROXIMAL CAUSE

As well as considering necessary and sufficient conditions in relation to causality, it is also possible to consider causes as *proximal* (near) and *distal* (far removed). The proximal and distal causes of an effect are separated by necessary steps. Van Hooft et al. (1995) provide a good illustration of this. They offer the scenario of a man who complains to his doctor of headaches. The man has attributed the headaches to work-induced stress; however, on further questioning it becomes apparent that the man meets with his friends and has a few beers each night after work in order to relieve the stress, and that this is what is causing the headaches. In this scenario, the stress is the distal cause of the headaches and the drinking is the proximal cause. In other words, the stress causes the drinking which in turn causes the headaches. Given our example of the bushfire, it could also be said that the proximal cause of the bushfire was the application of heat to the dry bush, whereas the distal cause was the lightning strike. In other words, the lightning was necessary for the generation of heat, which was necessary for the bush to ignite.

Philosophers have criticized the proximal/distal dichotomization of cause, however, as being pragmatic, since a single event always has multiple and interdependent causes. However, at the empirical level, distinguishing between distal and proximal cause can be critical, *depending on the level of interest*. For example, failure to distinguish between proximal and distal cause could jeopardize successful management of the problem at hand, as in the scenario of headaches described above. A possible management strategy for the distal cause of the headaches could be counselling to find a less stressful job. However, the man may very well enjoy his job, and not want to leave it despite the stress. Addressing the proximal cause, such as finding ways other than drinking beer to counter stress, may lead to a much more acceptable outcome. The man keeps his job and no longer has headaches.

Determining cause as being proximal or distal is also critical in adjudicating legal cases. Proximal cause is defined as "the cause immediately preceding an event, and therefore, if that event constitutes a crime or private wrong, a point of exposure to legal liability" (Menand, 2001, p. 223). Remote cause (distal) is "a cause farther back in the chain, and therefore a point generally exempt from liability" (Menand, 2001, p. 223).

Clarification is needed in the use of the terms "distal" and "proximal" when talking about cause in stuttering. If we accept the definition of these terms proposed by van Hooft et al. (1995), then the proximal cause of stuttering consists of those conditions operating at the time of a stuttering moment. A distal cause would be, by definition, factors that are removed by necessary steps from the proximal cause. We discuss the logic of attributing distal and proximal cause in stuttering later in this chapter.

DEFINITIONS

Any discussion of logic must take into account the matter of definition. As we discuss in Chapter 2 accurate terminology is a critical feature of scientific theories. Defining "definition", however, is not as simple as it seems (Borsodi, 1967; O'Neil, 1962; Webster, 1977). In general terms, a definition is the meaning of a word. More specifically, an Aristotelian definition consists of stipulating those features that identify members of a group and that at the same time differentiate them from those things that are not part of the group (O'Neil, 1962). As outlined by Borsodi (1967), a definition should be adequate, it should differentiate the referent sufficiently to avoid confusion, it should be impartial, and it should be complete. Borsodi tells how in ancient Athens the definition of "man" was given as a *featherless animal with two feet*. The philosopher Diogenes, on hearing this, plucked the feathers off a rooster and declared it "Plato's man". Whereupon the members of the Academy considered the matter carefully and added "without claws" to the definition. This story illustrates how interested parties might continue to refine a definition until it meets Borsodi's criterion of differentiating the referent from all others.

However, other ways of defining have been suggested. It has been argued, for example, that the most useful definition for science is an operational definition (see O'Neil, 1962; Webster, 1977). According to Webster (1977, p. 70), in operational definitions concepts are defined according to their relationship to actual events:

> The meaning of a construct is tied directly to the operations that generate the observable conditions necessary for the inference of that concept. The rigor with which constructs are tied to empirical events is a determinant of the concept's adequacy. In the early stages of scientific development, definitions of constructs may be rather diffuse. However, in order for successful development to occur, ties between concepts and operations must be strengthened. The requirement of operational definitions in scientific concepts assures us that we are dealing with palpable events and not mere fictions.

As we see in later chapters on theories of stuttering, lack of operational definition is one of the reasons that some theories cannot be tested. We refer not only to the fact that stuttering cannot be defined satisfactorily, but also to the lack of operational definitions for the sorts of scientific concepts referred to by Webster.

FALLACIES OF CAUSAL REASONING

Before leaving this very brief discussion on causality, it may be instructive to examine some faulty reasoning related to causal relationships. We are interested here in the logic of arguments proposed in the theoretical domain. There are many examples of such faulty reasoning (see Damer, 1987; van Hooft et al., 1995) and we describe only those that are relevant to evaluating theories of stuttering. The ones covered here are the post hoc fallacy, confusing necessary and sufficient conditions, confusing distal and proximal cause, confusing cause and effect, causal oversimplification, failure to separate cause and effect, and ignoring a common cause. An understanding of fallacious causal reasoning helps us appreciate Hume's view, which was discussed earlier in this chapter, that attributing cause involves assuming unobservable links between events. We conclude this section with an example of fallacious reasoning from the logical domain; namely *affirming the consequent*.

The *post hoc fallacy* (after this, therefore because of it) is perhaps the most well-known causal fallacy. Put simply, an event A is thought to cause another event B, simply because B followed A. Although a temporal relationship is one indication of a causal link, and although the related notion that effects come after causes and not before them is a working assumption of scientific thinking, establishing cause requires more. Thinking that only a temporal relationship is needed to establish a causal relationship may give rise to such clearly fallacious reasoning as "night is caused by day because night always follows day or because day always precedes night".

As previously discussed, a necessary condition of an event is one that must be present in order for the event to occur; without the necessary condition, the event cannot occur. On the other hand, an event will occur in the presence of a sufficient condition. *Confusing necessary and sufficient conditions* may lead to the erroneous belief that the presence of a necessary condition is all that is needed for a condition to occur. Some explanations of the cause of stuttering, for example, suggest that a genetic predisposition to stutter is a necessary condition for the disorder to develop. The genetic predisposition, however, may not be sufficient; it may be that one or more other conditions are also required. If that is the case, then not every individual with a genetic or constitutional predisposition to stutter will stutter, if the other conditions are not present. On the other hand, if the predisposition is necessary, then no one who does *not* have it will stutter, despite the presence of those other conditions. Of course, as alluded to above, unless the construct "predisposition to stutter" can be defined operationally, the truth or falsity of these propositions cannot be demonstrated empirically.

The term "distal" is sometimes used in human disorders such as stuttering to refer to a necessary condition, while the term "proximal" is used to refer to triggering conditions. This is a case of *confusing distal and proximal cause*. In much thinking about stuttering, it is proposed that the necessary condition is a constitutional factor, such as a deficit in linguistic processing or inefficiency in respiratory control, or any number of others. However, such a condition must be operating at the time of each stuttering event and so cannot be considered to be distal from it. Parents sometimes report that they think that their child's stuttering was caused by a traumatic event, such as the birth of a sibling or being bitten by a dog. However, such an event cannot be considered a distal cause because there are no necessary steps linking it to subsequent stuttering moments. For such an event to be considered a distal cause, it would need to be explained how the event is logically connected with stuttering events occurring, say, a year later.

Taking an effect as a cause, or failing to realize that there may be a reciprocal causal relationship between two factors, are cases of *confusing cause and effect*. This issue was canvassed by Packman and Onslow (2000) in relation to stuttering, and also by Onslow (1996). Onslow, for example, suggests that differences seen in stutterers (anomalous hemispheric processing, EMG activity, or voice reaction times) when compared to non-stutterers may be the result of stuttering rather than its cause. Attanasio, Onslow, and Packman (1998) expanded Onslow's statement, "The features of a disorder are not necessarily related to its cause" (p. 128) into a discussion of the representative heuristic. Put simply, reasoning based on the representative heuristic holds that the causes of events or phenomena are to be seen in their effects; it is reasoning back from effects to cause. The representative heuristic can be, and often is, a helpful problem-solving strategy for reasoning about cause. However, because such reasoning can lead to faulty conclusions Attanasio et al. (1998) caution against its uncritical use in the search for causes of stuttering.

The fallacy of *causal oversimplification* occurs when a very obvious antecedent of an event is thought to be the cause or sufficient condition of the event when, in fact, the cause of the event can be traced to a collection of antecedents that work together or together are sufficient to cause the event.

Failure to separate cause and effect occurs when cause is not identified separately from effect. This occurs in circular reasoning. An example of circular reasoning is contained in the proposition that stuttering is caused by a deficit in fluency skills. Cause and effect are not identified separately because stuttering can be defined as a deficit in fluency skills.

Finally, attributing cause to one of two factors that covary when in fact both factors are the result of a third factor is the fallacy of *ignoring a common cause*. It was suggested above that certain variables are sometimes thought of as a cause of stuttering when in fact they may be a result of stuttering. It might also be the case that they are not causally related at all and are in fact both the result of some other factor.

The preceding examples of fallacious reasoning come from the theoretical domain, in that they refer to arguments about possible causal factors. The fallacy of *affirming the consequent*, however, comes from the logic domain, and has to do with the structure of arguments. It is included here because of its importance in relation to testing theories. The following is an example of affirming the consequent:

If A (antecedent) then B (consequent)
B, therefore A.

As discussed in the following chapter, a theory may be tested by testing predictions arising from it. A prediction could, for example, involve the argument that if theory A is true (antecedent), then B will result (consequent). In this example, B could refer to the findings of an empirical investigation such as an experiment. If the results of the experiment are as predicted (B), then theory A is said to be confirmed. However, the reasoning here is fallacious because it involves affirming the consequent. On the other hand, if the experiment does *not* result in B, the consequent is denied, which is a valid argument. In other words, if a prediction arising from a theory is *not* supported, then the theory cannot logically be true.

Interestingly, despite the fact that affirming the consequent is fallacious, this form of reasoning underpins much scientific inquiry (Sidman, 1960). Indeed, as we discuss in Chapter 3, one of the features of a scientific theory is that it yields predictions that are testable in precisely the way we have illustrated above. We suggest that this state of affairs is a good example of the way the domains of logic, theory, and empiricism interact in science. We return to the implications of affirming the consequent in science a number of times in this text.

Chapter 2

The role of theory in the sciences

In this chapter we investigate the purpose of theorizing in science. We believe that a distinction needs to be drawn here between the physical and the human sciences, as has been proposed by a number of writers. We use the term human sciences here to refer to the behavioural and social sciences. In the first section we look at the work of some of the prominent writers in the history and philosophy of science. In the second section we look at how some of the propositions put forward vary somewhat when it comes to the human sciences. In this second section, then, we draw more on the writings in the history and philosophy of psychology, the discipline from which much of our understanding of stuttering is drawn. We do this in the full understanding that this area is fraught with controversy. This is not intended to be a comprehensive coverage of the area, indeed it is very brief. Our aim is simply to draw the reader's attention to some of the most salient issues that can be followed up at will.

THEORY IN THE PHYSICAL SCIENCES

Theorizing is attempts to organize or make sense of observations and data, as opposed to experimental investigation. Theories are "speculative and tentative conjectures or guesses freely created by the human intellect in an attempt to overcome problems encountered by previous theories to give an adequate account of some aspects of the world or universe" (Chalmers, 1999, p. 60).

Although it may be that a theory, in its initial state, is a speculative conjecture or guess, it cannot remain as such if it is to be considered scientific. Scientific theories are not uninformed guesses, musings, or mere notions, speculations, or guesswork. They are not based on personal preference or prejudice nor are they dogmatic statements in the form of unverifiable assertions. This is not to suggest that scientists and researchers do not have personal preferences in regard to what they choose to investigate, or that they do not begin their work after having speculated on the nature of the phenomenon of interest. It would be erroneous to suggest that the personal curiosity of the scientist or researcher plays no part in undertaking a research project. A scientist who is not curious or who does not speculate is obviously in the wrong line of work, and it would be a sad state of affairs if scientists found no personal joy or satisfaction in what they do. It is when scientists put their theories to the test and attempt to validate those theories that personal preferences and prejudices must be put aside and the data or findings be allowed to speak for themselves.

The beginnings of a theory, then, may come from the personal speculation and curiosity of the scientist, but even then the formulation of a theory is guided by modes of scientific thinking and is often influenced or prompted by the scientific climate of its day. For example, evolution as an explanation of the origin and variety of species did not start with Charles Darwin; the scientific community of which he was a part was considering it before he formulated his own version – evolution was "in the air". Darwin was searching for an explanation of how evolution worked, an explanation that did not require the role of intelligent design or a supreme being. His search (and that of Alfred Russell Wallace) ended in the adoption of natural selection as the explanation.

Although there may be times when the two agree or overlap, scientific explanations are not synonymous with common-sense notions of how the world works. It may be common sense to get in from being out in the rain for many reasons, but science tells us that viruses, not the rain, cause colds. Indeed, the function of science is to uncover relationships between variables that are not apparent through common sense.

In their developed form, scientific theories are explanations supported by a sufficient amount of factual evidence (Newton, 1997). They are constructs of how things work and they generate testable hypotheses or predictions that, if borne out, provide support for the theory and contribute to its validity. Results from hypothesis testing or the predictions made must be observable. A scientific theory is one that is able to describe and predict future states and extend research by generating new ideas (Dunbar, 1995) or problems to investigate and solve.

Theories, then, are not simply descriptions or catalogues of current states. Rather, they explain or predict by generating testable hypotheses that are able to yield empirical data or observable results. Theories, therefore, lead to experimentation. The enterprise has a built-in self-correcting mechanism: If the hypotheses or predictions are not upheld, then the theory must be revised, modified, or ultimately abandoned. Indeed, theories must fit the facts and the comment that we have all heard, that "it works in theory but not in practice" can be seen as being illogical in light of this self-correcting mechanism. Theories provide a conceptual framework within which facts are made intelligible. In so doing, theories are organizing statements that make connections among what might mistakenly be viewed as isolated facts.

Research, however, may be undertaken in the absence of a theory to guide it. In the early stages of investigation, researchers may be involved in gathering and organizing facts or data, prompted by the need or desire to know or understand more about what interests them. In some instances, observations or facts may come to researchers unbidden by them. As the facts or data accumulate, theories to explain them and connect them to one another may emerge. Indeed, without the emergence of theory, researchers do not have a mechanism to explain the accumulated facts, nor do they have a vision to guide them or a clear path to take for continued investigation.

Wynn and Wiggins (1997) describe the following sequence as being characteristic of the scientific method. As repeated observations are made of a specific phenomenon or event, an assertion is made, through a process of inductive reasoning, that casts those observations into a statement or *hypothesis* that describes the general nature of the observed event or phenomenon. The hypothesis is then used to make *predictions* that are consistent with the hypothesis. Reasoning from the hypothesis to the prediction is by deduction rather than by induction. The prediction is then tested through *experimentation* designed to determine if the prediction is correct or if what is predicted actually occurs. If the prediction is correct, the hypothesis is upheld. If the experiment fails to yield results that support the prediction, the hypothesis is not upheld and must either be modified or abandoned. Wynn and Wiggins view hypotheses as tentative and without a sufficient amount of experimentally confirmed predictions or evidence to allow firm statements to be made. This process of induction and deduction is shown in Figure 2.1.

Once a body of evidence is developed, the data may be summarized in the form of a *law*. A scientific law is a statement, confirmed by repeated observation or experimentation, of how a given aspect of nature works. "[A law] is a statement of some kind of regularity in nature" (Wynn & Wiggins, 1997, p. 3). A theory may next be developed to explain the "underlying causes of the law's regularities" (Wynn & Wiggins, 1997, p. 113). We stated previously that hypotheses are derived from theories yet here we report that, according to Wynn and Wiggins (1997), theories are developed some time after corroborated hypotheses have been gathered. Which comes first, hypotheses or

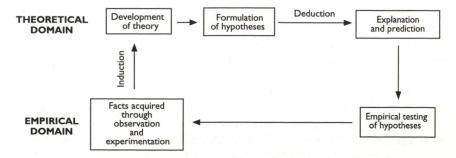

Figure 2.1 The process of induction, deduction, and experimentation in science.

theories? Not quite the "chicken/egg" problem, but the answer to the question is problematic and not straightforward. One finds in the literature on the philosophy of science that the two terms are used interchangeably by the same writer or are used to mean the same thing by different writers or are used to show a specific progression (i.e., from theory to hypothesis). This seeming confusion or inconsistency in the use of the terms will be seen later in the text where at least one of the theories of stuttering we review is designated as a hypothesis by its originators. It may very well be the case, however, that the empirical and theoretical domains overlap, to the extent that it is possible to have theories generating hypotheses in certain stages of scientific investigations and to have hypotheses leading to theories in other stages. Figure 2.1 suggests such a possibility. In the end, careful reading of a given author's intended use of either term is required.

A few words are needed here about modelling. A model is a form of theorizing. One of the functions of models in science is to "describe and help us to understand complex systems" (Chapanis, 1963, p. 113). They do this by "replacing intricate and complex systems with simpler and more familiar analogies" (Chapanis, 1963, p. 114). They can also help us to see new relationships between variables or help us see relationships in new ways. There are many types of modelling in the various sciences, and indeed the term model is used quite loosely, often being used interchangeably with the term *theory*. According to Chapanis, there are two main categories of models: replica models and symbolic models. Replica models are tangible, whereas symbolic models make use of ideas, concepts, and abstract symbols, such as boxes and arrows. They are typically schematic. We return to the use of modelling in more detail in the following section on Theory in the Human Sciences.

Kuhn and scientific revolutions

In his discussion on the emergence of scientific theories, Kuhn (1996) outlines a process that begins with the occurrence of an anomaly and ends with a paradigm shift. Kuhn (1996) applied the word paradigm to ". . . the legitimate problems and methods of a research field . . ." that have two primary characteristics: The achievements of the research field are ". . . sufficiently unprecedented to attract an enduring group of adherents away from competing modes of scientific activity. Simultaneously, [they are] sufficiently open-ended to leave all sorts of problems for the redefined group of practitioners to resolve" (p. 10). A paradigm includes a theory, but also research questions that are seen as the appropriate ones for investigation, the vocabulary and symbol system that scientists use to describe their research field, and agreed-to research methods and instruments. An anomaly is an event, observation, occurrence, or phenomenon that is unexpected within the context of an existing received paradigm; it is a violation of what would be expected under the existing paradigm. Normal science, in Kuhn's terms, proceeds under an accepted paradigm and is quite successful in building knowledge. Kuhn defines normal science as ". . . research firmly based upon one or more past scientific achievements, achievements that some particular scientific community acknowledges for a time as supplying the foundation for its further practice" (Kuhn, 1996, p. 10). It encompasses a body of accepted theory and its applications and experiments. It does not seek novel facts or theories. Eventually, however, novelty or the unexpected does occur; something anomalous is encountered. For Kuhn, this is the first step to scientific discovery.

The scientific community's response to the anomaly takes the form of a crisis. That is, a period of professional insecurity follows the occurrence of the anomaly. The existing paradigm is threatened and unable to adequately account for the anomaly.

The next step in the chain of events that leads to a paradigm shift is the scientific community's response to the crisis. Initially, the existing paradigm is not abandoned because scientists do not view the anomaly as a contradiction of the existing theory and they acknowledge that there are always discrepancies between theory and observation. According to Kuhn, scientists will attempt to reconcile the anomaly and the existing theory by qualifying or modifying the theory. For a full-blown crisis to develop, the anomaly must be seen as something fundamental or extraordinary. Then, the anomaly comes to be recognized by more and more scientists as requiring attention.

Finally, a paradigm shift takes place; a new paradigm becomes necessary to accommodate what was anomalous under the former one. Kuhn makes the point that a theory is abandoned only when there is another to take its place and that falsification by direct comparison to nature is not a sufficient reason to reject an existing theory. The decision to reject one paradigm is always dependent on the decision to accept another paradigm. Both paradigms are compared to each other and to nature (Kuhn, 1996). For Kuhn, paradigm choice is not based on logic and experimentation alone. Debate, persuasion, and finally "the assent of the relevant community" (Kuhn, 1996, p. 94) – the community of scientists – are very much a part of the acceptance of a new paradigm. These last criteria for paradigm choice are most likely what Kuhn's critics have called his relativism and subjectivism.

We have spent some time investigating the contribution of Kuhn to the discussions about the role of theory in science. However, Kuhn's position here has not gone unchallenged. Popper is another of the 20th century's most influential thinkers on the nature of science and the role of scientific theories. Popper's primary contribution to the area was his theory of refutation. In short, Popper proposed that the science is not concerned with proving theories but with disproving them. We return to this in Chapter 3, when we discuss evaluating theories.

Popper's views are often contrasted with those of Kuhn. In fact, Popper himself made the contrast. Popper believed that he and Kuhn agreed on the notion of falsifiability and on the "impossibility of conclusive proofs of falsi-fication" (Popper, 1999) and their role in scientific revolutions. Popper asserted that whereas he was committed to the ancient theory of proof, Kuhn was affected by relativism and subjectivism.

Both Popper (1999) and Kuhn (1996) hold that the choice of a theory cannot be based on the kind of proof used in mathematics or logic. Still, there do appear to be major differences between these two philosophers. Popper suggested that, when two competing theories present themselves, sci-entists would choose the better one, the one that is able to survive the most rigorous crucial tests. Kuhn rejected this notion of Popper's by proposing the view that shifts in paradigms are drastic and cause major alterations of per-ception that make agreement on what constitutes a valid test impossible. An essential element of a paradigm is the theory, but Kuhn meant something broader. Included in the notion of paradigm are a scientific community's shared and accepted vision of the way things work, an agreed-upon set of problems or puzzles that provide scientists with the opportunity to conduct research, and agreed-upon rules and standards for the practice of science (Kuhn, 1996).

Furthermore, Kuhn did not believe, as Popper did, that a better, deeper theory takes the place of one that fails to pass a falsifying test or that science proceeds by revolutionary changes that overturn existing theories. Instead, Kuhn suggested that when new theories are constructed to explain anomalies that cannot be accounted for by the existing theory, the new theories compete with one another for acceptance while adherents to the existing theory struggle to retain it.

The salient similarities and differences between Popper and Kuhn may be highlighted in the following way. Conjecture, test, and refutation are central elements of Popper's views on how science works. These elements are also a part of Kuhn's position, but only present during what Kuhn (1996) called normal science – the work scientists do within the context of an existing and received paradigm. Popper gave a prominent place to conjecture, but main-tained that the introduction of a new conjecture is not based on a given rationale. Attempts to falsify the conjecture or hypothesis are, however. Kuhn argued similarly that the introduction of a new paradigm is not based on a given rationale but that scientists do have rationales for the work they do within the paradigm; that is, as they proceed with the tasks of normal science. The major difference between Popper and Kuhn concerns the nature of a scientific revolution or the manner in which science moves or shifts from one theory or paradigm to another. For Popper, the move is rational and logical; scientists accept the better theory, the one that withstands falsification. For Kuhn, the shift is characterized by profound alterations of perception that give rise to new and different ways of seeing, of new and different scientific problems to solve, and of new and different ways to solve those problems. When the paradigm shift is complete, "the profession will have changed its view of the field, its methods, and its goals" (Kuhn, 1996, p. 85). A fundamental change in orientation and in the framework for normal science is the result of the paradigm shift.

THEORY IN THE HUMAN SCIENCES

We now turn our attention to the role of theory in the human sciences and explore some of the differences between the physical and the human sciences, in the empirical as well as the theoretical domains. Indeed, the two domains are in symbiosis here. In this section we draw primarily on the literature in the history and philosophy of psychology, using examples from stuttering where possible.

As alluded to earlier, the methods and standards used in the hard sciences, in particular physics, are not necessarily appropriate in the human sciences. According to Chalmers (1999, p. 147):

> Physics can, and often does, proceed by isolating individual mechanisms . . . in the artificial circumstances of a controlled experiment. People and societies cannot in general be treated this way without destroying what is being investigated.

The point here is that it is not possible to control for all possible variables when studying, for example, human behaviour. When control *is* exerted it changes the context and may well change the behaviour of interest as well. According to Rakover (1990), as a science psychology is fragmented and not unified, due to a discrepancy between a commitment to the methods of science and consideration of the complexities of the human condition.

That certainly applies in the case in stuttering. Being a disturbance of human communication, stuttering typically occurs in the context of verbal exchanges, and altering the nature of communicative contexts in order to gain experimental control may in fact change the nature of the stuttering.

Nonetheless, experimentation is as important in the behavioural sciences as it is in, say, physics. It is the methods of experimentation, however, that vary, "One cannot capture (that is describe and explain) human behavior by means of the categories of the natural sciences" (Rakover, 1990, p. 23). Further, in physics it may take only one experiment to show the relationship between two variables. To use a very simple example, one only needs to heat a particular metal once to determine at what temperature it starts to expand, providing of course that potentially confounding variables are controlled. While replication is required, the experiment does not need to be repeated many times to verify the finding. When complex human behaviour is the object of study, however, the effects of a variable may not be the same for each person. Rather, the experiment needs to be performed with many human subjects to determine if the finding occurs in a sufficient number of subjects to be considered a meaningful effect. Even in descriptive studies in the human sciences, where behaviour is not the dependent variable, a particular anomaly may be observed in all experimental subjects but may still vary in extent across subjects and may even be apparent in some control subjects.

As we shall see later, one of the problems with theory building in stuttering is that this type of replication of findings is rarely undertaken, whereas in psychology:

> Theoretical propositions are tested not only under directly replicated conditions but also under a variety of different conditions, and it is only after a considerable amount of empirical support has been amassed that very serious attention can be accorded a theoretical proposition.
>
> (Marx, 1976a, p. 260)

We now look in more detail at the following issues as in the human sciences: paradigms, laws, theories, hypotheses, and models. We conclude the chapter with a brief discussion of pseudoscience.

Paradigms

In the previous section on the physical sciences we discussed Kuhn's contribution of the idea of the paradigm. A paradigm is a way of looking at things. It is a set of assumptions, beliefs, and theories shared by scientists working in a particular field. According to Kuhn "When the individual scientist can take a paradigm for granted, he need no longer, in his major works, attempt to build his field anew, starting from first principles and justifying the use of each concept introduced" (Kuhn, 1996, pp. 19–20).

Kuhn was referring here to the physical sciences and the paradigms he was referring to were indeed large, such as Copernican astronomy and Newtonian dynamics. Kuhn did not believe that the behavioural and social sciences operate under paradigms, as there are no completely accepted laws and theories in these fields of study. Rather, Kuhn referred to these sciences as passing through the preparadigm stage.

Nonetheless, the term paradigm is still used to refer to passing fads in research focus in the human sciences (Ingham, 1984) including the study of stuttering (see Ingham, 1984; Siegel, 1998). As we explore more fully later, the study of stuttering has changed over the years in response to the influence of developments in the various sciences that support that study. One of the most striking influences was that of behaviour therapy, which occurred in the 1960s and 1970s (see Ingham, 1984). In more recent times, however, the study of stuttering as an operant has fallen out of favour (Siegel, 1998) and there has been an almost paradigmatic shift towards researching stuttering as a disorder of speech motor control (see Ingham, 1998). However, this is not the only approach currently in favour (Siegel, 1998), with, as we see later, theories of stuttering arising out of a variety of epistemological perspectives. While this may be seen as faddishness, there is of course value in broadening the scope of experimental approaches (Marx, 1976b).

There have been calls for the establishment of a unifying framework or theory of stuttering (for example see Fox et al., 1996; Smith & Weber, 1988). However, as yet, no such framework or theory exists (Siegel, 1998) which could provide socially sanctioned guidelines for those engaged in research into stuttering.

Laws

Wynn and Wiggins (1997) define a law as "a verbal or mathematical statement of a relationship between phenomena" (p. 113). An example of a law in the physical sciences is that the sun always rises in the east. This is a statement about a relationship between the rising sun and the eastern sky that always occurs. The use of the term "law" does not imply that nature somehow obeys laws. Laws simply describe universals in nature. In terms of logic, we can say that an event is lawful once we have established the conditions that are necessary and sufficient for its occurrence (O'Neil, 1962). In the physical sciences, a law is "a statement of a regular predictable relationship among empirical variables" (Marx, 1963, p. 7).

Logically, laws are generally stated in terms of functional relationships. This means, at a theoretical level, that a law states the way one factor varies in relation to another. However, it has been said that there are no laws in the social and behavioural sciences (Robinson, 1985), although Bothamley (1993) has suggested some.[1] In reference to psychology, O'Neil (1962) stated that laws might in fact apply, but that their forms are masked by the influence of other variables. In other words, relationships between variables in the social and behavioural sciences may be obscured by the presence of other variables. In regard to functional relationships in psychology, O'Neil (1962) stated, "our evidence does not enable us to state much more than the direction (positive or inverse) of the concomitance" (p. 115). Thus, in psychology at least, a law may be described as a "tendency" (O'Neil, 1962, p. 115).

O'Neil's discussion on the use of the term "law" in psychology is of particular interest in the study of stuttering. Wingate once stated that the rhythm effect is probably the only law in stuttering (Wingate, 1976). The rhythm effect refers to the widely demonstrated phenomenon that stuttering tends to disappear when people speak in time to a rhythmic stimulus. However, the effect is not universal, and one possible reason for this is that some people apparently cannot speak rhythmically, regardless of whether or not they stutter (see Packman, Onslow, & van Doorn, 1997). If the reason for this inability to speak rhythmically were known, it could be argued that a law is indeed operating here, with the reasons for exceptions understood. If we accept O'Neil's proposition that statements of tendency are admissible as laws in psychology, then we can say that statements such as "more males stutter than females" and "70–90% of children who start to stutter recover naturally" are also laws. Of course, for statements to be considered laws, they must be supported by reliable scientific evidence.

Theories

We discussed the role of theories in the physical sciences earlier in this chapter, and in fact the role of theories is much the same in the human sciences as it is in the physical sciences. In psychology, for example, theory has been defined as "a provisional explanatory proposition, or set of propositions, concerning some natural phenomena" (Marx, 1976a, p. 237).

However, where human behaviour is the subject of the theorizing, there will be obvious differences. In discussing the role of theory in the behavioural sciences, Robey and Schultz (1993) stated that every theory has five components, the first four of which they consider to be elemental: (1) populations; (2) constructs; (3) environments; (4) parameters; and (5) cause. Although they are listed separately, there are obvious connections between and among the five components and they overlap to form a complete theory statement. *Populations* are the units of observation that are of experimental interest and share a common feature or set of features that may be described generally (e.g., people, clinic populations) or specifically (e.g., 3-year-old male children who stutter). *Constructs* are those characteristics or attributes of the population that are of experimental interest and are common to each and every member of the population. Robey and Schultz (1993) list such characteristics as hearing loss, reaction time, and communicative style as examples of constructs. Stuttering, of course, may be included in a list of attributes. *Environments* is the element that describes the setting or context within which population members exist for the purpose of the experiment – schools, clinics, stressful situations, and the like. Examples of the fourth element, *parameters*, given by Robey and Schultz (1993) include such measures of populations as the mean, variance, correlation coefficient, and proportion. The search for *cause*, the fifth component, is the *raison d'être* of theory and experimentation. Eventually, as a scientific discipline matures and its research methods become more sophisticated, attempts to explain why things are as they are become the focus of the scientific enterprise. The component of cause in Robey and Schultz's (1993) view explains the relationships among the four elements of theory and the changes in those relationships. Robey and Schultz (1993) maintain that all five components are necessary for a complete theory statement.

Hypotheses

As we have noted, *hypothesis* is sometimes used interchangeably with *theory*. However, while theories and hypotheses are both propositions, a theory is typically supported by more evidence than a hypothesis. A hypothesis, then, is a "conjecture or surmise that states a relationship among variables" (Marx, 1963, p. 7) and is considered to be tentative, or conditional, in that it is a provisional explanation or proposition that makes predictions about data.

According to Marx, hypotheses may be experimental, which means they can be tested, or they may be more abstract, which may lead in turn to the development of testable hypotheses. In informal usage, a hypothesis may even simply state a position. For example, someone may say, "My hypothesis is that she catches so many colds because she works in an air-conditioned office." There is no suggestion in such a statement that this will be put to the test. In scientific usage, however, an experimenter formulates a hypothesis, which is then tested. In this case, the terminology of the hypothesis must be operational, allowing it to be confirmed or rejected by the experiment. Given the complexity of the human systems (see above), experimental hypotheses in the behavioural sciences are frequently couched in relative terms. For example, in an investigation into the nature of the communication styles of children who stutter and their parents for possible triggering factors, a hypothesis might be: *Parents of children who stutter use questions more often when talking with their children than do parents of normally fluent children*. At the empirical level, the investigators would be estimating the probability of a difference between the two groups – parents of children who stutter and parents of the control group – that is sufficiently great to be deemed statistically significant, or clinically significant, or both. There is no suggestion in the hypothesis that every parent of a stuttering child will ask more questions than every parent of a normally fluent child. This is in contrast to hypotheses in the physical sciences where nature is considered to be lawful and where replication (i.e., repetition of the experiment) rather than probability statistics would be used to confirm a result – for example, the outcome of mixing certain chemicals together.

Models

As discussed earlier, models in science are a way of understanding complex systems. A model is a scientific tool. Writing in the psychology literature, Marx (1976a, p. 244) argues for a more specific use of the term modelling:

> A model is a conceptual analogue that is used to suggest how empirical research on a problem might be pursued. That is, the model is a conceptual framework or structure that has been successfully developed

in one field and is now applied, primarily as a guide to research and thinking, in some other, usually less well-developed field.

For example, in the human sciences the computer has long been used as a model for attempting to understand how the brain processes language (Lieberman, 2000). Another example of conceptual modelling, this time in physiology, is to describe the heart as a pump. The heuristic value in modelling is that the process generates hypotheses and once the relevant experiments have been conducted, one can evaluate the appropriateness of the model. In what ways, if any, does the brain function like a computer? Is the heart really like a pump, or does it function so differently that the analogy of the pump is inappropriate?

According to Marx (1976a), the critical difference between a theory and a model, at least in psychology, is that a model is not modified in response to experimental findings in the way that a theory might be. A model cannot be true or false; rather it is judged according to how useful it is in understanding the behaviour or phenomenon being modelled. If the findings of a study suggest that the heart does not function like a pump in some particular way, the model is not altered to accommodate those findings, as a theory might be. It is simply regarded as inadequate. Being an analogy, a model does not necessarily represent the phenomena of interest accurately (Chapanis, 1963).

Marx acknowledges that not everyone adheres to this view of modelling, and that over time modelling has become almost synonymous with theorizing, thus erasing the critical distinction between the two. One of the dangers in this is that it can give investigators a false sense of security, and frees them from checking the adequacy of the propositions involved in the model.

Modelling can play an important role in the development of theories (Rakover, 1990) by enhancing understanding. Models can also be used to test out certain facets of theories by generating hypotheses. However, models are open to – as are predictions of theories – the logical fallacy of affirming the consequent. Theories are never proved, but this axiom is even more important in models (Chapanis, 1963).

Chapanis (1963) proposed that the main functions of models are that they help us to understand complex systems, see new relationships between variables, and predict when experiments are impossible, and can amuse and engage our interest. By the same token, models invite overgeneralization, fallacious reasoning, and unwarranted assumptions about constants and about relationships between variables. Finally, they are too often not validated.

One useful role of modelling in the human sciences is to help us understand causality, given the often complex relationships between human beings and their environment – often referred to as in lay terms as the question of nature and nurture. We now look in detail at models that have been used in the human sciences to describe complex causal relationships involving both constitutional and environmental factors (cf. Hubbell, 1981). These models are particularly relevant to stuttering, which is widely thought of as being influenced by constitutional and environmental factors. The four models we describe here are the simple linear cause–effect model, the complex linear cause–effect model, the interactional model, and the transactional model. The models are symbolic in nature and they provide good examples of some of the characteristics of models that are discussed above. For example, variables and relationships between them are depicted with boxes and arrows.

The *simple linear cause–effect* model posits a one-to-one relationship between cause and effect. In such a model, a given cause has a given effect and a given effect can be traced back to a given cause. Versions of the model incorporate the notion of nature versus nurture, namely whether cause rests in the person's genetic and neurophysiologic make-up or in the person's environment. Some models place cause within the individual and others place cause within the environment. The simple linear cause–effect model has been used in medicine and found to be helpful in understanding the cause of and treatment for certain diseases. The simple linear cause–effect model is shown in Figure 2.2.

The *complex linear cause–effect* model implicates both the constitution and the environment in explaining cause. These models are sometimes erroneously referred to as interactional (Attanasio, 2003). Complex linear cause–effect models are more comprehensive and complex than simple linear cause–effect models and they reject single variable or single factor explanations of cause. However, while these models combine both nature and nurture, the two do not act on each other. The complex linear cause–effect model is shown in Figure 2.3.

An example of a model in which constitution and environment truly interact is the *interactional* model. In this model, one or both act on the other and cause an effect. A version of an interactional model is shown in Figure 2.4.

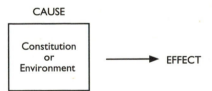

Figure 2.2 Simple linear cause–effect model.

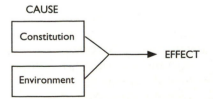

Figure 2.3 Complex linear cause–effect model.

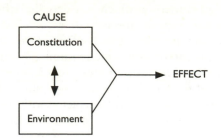

Figure 2.4 Interactional model.

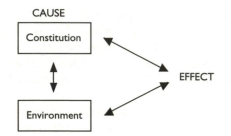

Figure 2.5 Transactional model.

The models we have presented so far are unidirectional. An interactional model in which the thing caused may, over time, influence both constitution and environment in reciprocal fashion, is the *transactional* model (see Hubbell, 1981). Such a model would be described as bidirectional. It is depicted in Figure 2.5.

We stress that there are many ways in which relationships between variables in the human sciences can be modelled; more examples can be found in the discussion on the relationship between temperament and child development in Rothbart and Bates (1998). We choose to present these four causal models because they are relevant to later discussions of causality in stuttering.

Pseudoscience

We conclude this section on the role of theory in the human sciences with a brief comment on the misuse of science. While it is the case that theories function to explain, we are faced with the counterintuitive proposition, often recited without attribution but derived from the writings of Polanyi (1958) and Popper (1959), that a theory that explains everything explains nothing. Theories claiming to be scientific, but which in fact do not conform to scientific principles, are referred to as pseudoscience.

The issue of pseudoscience is particularly relevant, and of concern, in the human sciences because of the possible risks of practices or procedures that are purported to have therapeutic or healing qualities but may not, in fact, have them. The problem is one of pseudoscience if such practices claim, erroneously, to be based on scientific principles. Such practices are not grounded in scientific concepts but are supported by claims of effectiveness based on novel or pseudoscientific explanations (see Herbert et al., 2000).

A psychotherapist friend of one of the authors once teased about his psychoanalytic orientation. He placed his patients into three categories: those who arrived exactly on time for their appointments were obsessive-compulsive; those who arrived late were passive-aggressive; and those who arrived early were neurotically dependent. "You see," he said, "psychoanalytic psychology can explain everything!" We are not certain if the anecdote originated with this particular psychotherapist, but we are certain that it is clear that in fact nothing was explained here. In the anecdote, every possible behaviour provided evidence for the "truth" of psychoanalytic psychology. Thus, "since everything can serve as evidence for it, nothing in particular can" (*Supernaturalism*, 14 January 2003). Science cannot be done in situations of that kind. Such explanations as the one indicated in the anecdote are impervious to testing or validation and can never be wrong.

In contrast to science, pseudoscience is not self-correcting, with advocates interpreting "every failure as confirmation and every criticism as attack" (Herbert et al., 2000, p. 957). Also, advocates market their practices, and promote and persuade rather than think sceptically which is the way of the scientist. This includes dismissal of critical independent evaluations as erroneous or incompetent. The real indication of pseudoscience, however, is that it is not possible to refute the soundness of practices on logical grounds. In the face of disconfirmation, "advocates typically perform a strategic retreat" (Herbert et al., 2000, p. 957) and modify the postulates underpinning the theory in order to explain away the troubling evidence. In the following chapter we explore ways in which the scientific soundness of theories can be established.

NOTE

1 These are the Laws of Association, for example, "similarity, where two similar memory contents are linked; contrast, where two contrasted elements are linked; and contiguity in space and time, where two simultaneous or immediately successive elements are linked together" (Bothamley 1993, p. 35); the Law of Closure ". . . a tendency to perceive incomplete objects as complete by filling or closing the gaps in sensory inputs . . ." (p. 95); and the Law of Effect, ". . . the law of effect postulates that one learns or retains responses which are followed by satisfiers, and refrains from responses followed by annoyers" (p. 168).

Chapter 3

Evaluating theories

We have spent some time in the previous chapter looking at the role of theories in the physical and the human sciences. We have suggested that the main function of scientific theories is to interpret facts in a new way, by suggesting new links that had not previously been contemplated. In this way, theories make predictions and so prompt new research. In summary, if the findings of this research support the predictions, then they are said to confirm the theory. If they do not support the predictions, they are said to be inconsistent, or even to falsify, the theory. When a theory is no longer considered tenable it may be adjusted, in which case new predictions should arise, or it may be rejected, in which case a new theory will supplant it.

It is frequently the case, particularly in the human sciences, that a number of theories may coexist. In psychology, for example, there are many theories that have not been critically tested and which languish in the literature unassailed (Lundin, 1972). This is also the case in stuttering (Webster, 1977), as we will see later in this text. Indeed the proliferation of untested theories in stuttering was one of the reasons for the writing of this text. There are so many theories and models of stuttering that one wonders how they can all coexist, why they continue to attract interest, and why many continue to spawn therapies (Webster, 1977). Surely some must be better in some way than others. More plausible perhaps? Or more scientific?

The aim of this section is to provide some guidelines for critically evaluating theories. Critical thinking is essential if we are to establish whether a theory is in fact scientific. We acknowledge that there are many other types of theory, particularly in the social sciences, that are not scientific or causal in nature. For example, critical theory is a theoretical framework for understanding the effects of social change, and linguistic theories provide different frameworks for studying language. We stress here that we are prompted in the writing of this text by the need to evaluate *causal* theories of stuttering.

Many texts on the history and philosophy of science and psychology have proposed the critical features of scientific theories (in particular see Goodson & Morgan, 1976) and, indeed, the criteria for scientific theories apply equally in both branches of the sciences. We now present a set of guidelines that incorporate those ideas into what seems to us to be a logical and manageable set of principles.

Before getting down to specifics, however, we suggest that theories should be appreciated in light of the cultural, historical, and social setting in which they emerged. We address this idea in detail in relation to stuttering in Chapter 4. Students of stuttering will be only too aware of how perspectives on stuttering change in relatively short periods. Interestingly, these changes depend largely on advances in other disciplines. In the end, although theories should be appreciated within the context of the prevailing Zeitgeist (see Chapter 4), they must be evaluated according to scientific principles.

We now go on to suggest that theories can be evaluated against the following four criteria: testability and falsifiability, explanatory power, parsimony, and heuristic value.

TESTABILITY AND FALSIFIABILITY

Almost all philosophers of science and psychology agree that testability is the most important criterion to consider when judging the worth of a theory. Testability refers in the main to the capacity of the theory to generate predictions or hypotheses. Most importantly, as proposed by Popper (1959, 1979, 1999), a theory must be falsifiable, or be able to be shown to be false. In other words, it must be possible to conceive a way in which the theory – and more specifically predictions or hypotheses arising from the theory – could be shown to be false. According to Chalmers (1999), a hypothesis is falsifiable "if there exists a logically possible observation statement or set of observation statements that are inconsistent with it, that is, which, if established as true, would falsify the hypothesis" (p. 62).

According to Popper, then, science is not concerned with proving theories but with disproving them. To meet this criterion, a theory must be constructed in a way that enables researchers to show that it is wrong. If a theory withstands the test, that is, if it is correct in its predictions, it is according to Popper corroborated rather than proved. Although multiple instances of corroboration keep the theory viable, one instance of falsification – failure to pass a crucial test – requires that the theory be put aside. A new and better theory is then developed. Popper's conceptualization of theory in this way, and of falsifiability, was his attempt to deal with what is known as the problem of induction, as explicated in the work of the philosopher David Hume (1711–1776), and with the problem of demarcation (Popper, 1959, 1979); that is, to find a criterion that distinguishes scientific empirical theories from statements that are pseudoscientific, metaphysical, and the like.

Induction proceeds from a series of observations of specific events to a general conclusion. If, for example, feelings of hunger go away each time food is eaten, the expectation is that if food is eaten the next time hunger is felt, the

sensation of hunger will be eliminated. The generalization is that eating satis-
fies hunger. Predictions of future events, then, are based on past observations
or experiences. It will immediately be seen that inductive reasoning is not
foolproof; there is no guarantee that the next observation or event will match
past ones. An illustration of the problem of induction in science makes the
point (O'Neil, 1962). Prior to the 19th century it was thought that all swans
are white. With English settlement of Australia, however, it became known
that black swans are plentiful in Australia. This news of the existence of black
swans in the New World was greeted with awe in the Old, for the sighting of
even one black swan was sufficient to destroy the long-held general statement
that all swans are white. Even though ten thousand swans may have been
observed and seen to be white, the theory or hypothesis was corroborated but
not proved and additional observations of white swans had not brought
proof closer to being achieved. Despite the fact that reasoning or predicting
by induction in this way has risks and may not be fully justified, it appears to
work fairly well in day-to-day living and in science (Warburton, 1999). However, Popper felt that the problem of induction meant that theories cannot be
proved but only corroborated and that they must be structured in ways that
allow them to be falsified through testing.

Popper's view of scientific theories may itself be called a theory of refutation. He did not believe that a criterion of proof is possible or that an empirical scientific theory can be proved false conclusively. According to Popper,
valid and positive reasons for the truth of a theory cannot be offered. Indeed,
even if a prediction arising from a theory is confirmed, it cannot be said to
prove the theory.

We see that Popper's argument draws on elements of the logical fallacy of
affirming the consequent. We discussed this fallacy in Chapter 1, and now
provide another hypothetical example. Consider the hypothesis that a given
linguistic deficit is the cause of stuttering: If a linguistic deficit is the cause of
stuttering (A), then children with the deficit will stutter (B). A group of
children who stutter is found to have the deficit (B); therefore the linguistic
deficit is the cause of stuttering (A). Placing the hypothesis within the structure of affirming the consequent, we have: If A is true (the linguistic deficit is
the cause of stuttering), then B is true (children with the deficit will stutter). A
group of children with the linguistic deficit is found to stutter (B is true).
From the observation that these children stutter, we conclude that (A) is true
(the linguistic deficit is the cause of stuttering) – we accept the truth of our
hypothesis. Of course that is false on logical grounds because the truth of (A)
– linguistic deficit is the cause of stuttering – was not given as necessary and
sufficient for the truth of (B) – the children with the deficit will stutter. Agents
other than linguistic deficit may cause stuttering or it may be that children
who stutter and who also have the linguistic deficit may stutter for some
reason other than having the linguistic deficit; that is, (B) may be true –
children with the linguistic deficit stutter – but (A) may be false – the deficit

caused the stuttering. Perhaps a simple example other than stuttering will help to clarify the logical fallacy. We know that measles makes people ill. Thus, if a person has measles (A), then that person is ill (B). We observe an ill person (B), and conclude that the person has measles (A). Again, agents or conditions other than measles make people ill. In sum, there is no logical connection between the truth of (B) and inferences that can be made about (A) (Sidman, 1960).

Sidman (1960), while acknowledging the pitfalls of reasoning by affirming the consequent, states that affirming the consequent ". . . is very nearly the life blood of science. There is, in other words, a discrepancy between logical rules and laboratory practice" (p. 127). With what we believe are Popperian overtones, Sidman (1960, pp. 127–128) states:

> But the establishment of the truth of B does tell him [the scientist] something about A. For one thing, he has eliminated one of the conditions which could have proved A to be false. If B had turned out false, then the truth of A could not be upheld. His confidence in the truth of A is, therefore, increased by a small unquantified bit.

Returning to our example of the linguistic deficit and stuttering, finding a group of children who stutter and who have the linguistic deficit would increase our confidence in the hypothesis that stuttering and the linguistic deficit are somehow related to one another.

One need not entirely accept Popper's views in order to agree to the widely held position in the scientific community that a distinguishing characteristic of a scientific theory is its openness to testing and empirical verification, and to the related belief that scientific findings are best seen as tentative. We are talking here in the logical domain; that is, about the reasoning contained in the arguments. However, when considered from an empirical or experimental perspective, the situation is not so clear-cut. It may be that a theory cannot be tested *at the present time* because of, say, limitations in technology. But it must be logically possible to test it. An experiment that is logically, although not logistically, possible to conduct may be referred to as a thought experiment.

So, still in the logic domain, what makes a theory testable? We suggest two factors that contribute to testability: internal consistency and operationism. *Internal consistency* refers to the logic of the proposition contained in the theory; in other words, the reasoning. A theory should not contradict itself (Rakover, 1990) in the sense that predictions should be consistent with each other. Testable hypotheses are generated from theories inferentially, and so must adhere to the rules of deduction. In other words, the predictions and hypotheses arising from the theory must be derived logically and not simply be ad hoc propositions.

Consider a hypothetical theory that states, in essence, that children start to stutter because they have a predisposition to do so. This proposition is not falsifiable because the reasoning in it is circular. Every child who stutters presumably has a predisposition to stutter. The fallacy of reasoning here is *failure to separate cause and effect* (see Chapter 1).

Of course, this proposition would be come testable if *predisposition to stutter* were defined operationally. *Operationism* means that the empirical bases of the terms and theoretical constructs used are stated clearly (Marx, 1976b; Webster, 1977). In other words, terms and constructs must be stated in such a way that they can be identified and measured reliably. For example, predisposition to stutter in the scenario above would be operational if it were defined as a certain genetic condition, because children who stutter could then be tested for the presence of this condition.

The implications of lack of testability are summarized by Marx (1976a, p. 249):

> If there is no way of testing a theory it is scientifically worthless, no matter how plausible, imaginative, or innovative it might be. This proposition is sometimes hard for the layman to swallow. As a matter of fact, it may also sometimes be hard for the scientist to accept. But there does not seem to be any alternative to its acceptance.

EXPLANATORY POWER

Explanatory power refers to the extent to which a theory subsumes the phenomena, or facts, relating to the area of interest. One needs to consider the extent of phenomena explained. Does the theory explain only a few of the known facts about a puzzling state of affairs, or condition, or does it explain many or even all the known facts?

It needs to be said, however, that a theory with greater explanatory power is not necessarily superior to one that has less explanatory power. A theory of stuttering, for example, may seek to explain one aspect of stuttering only, and yet still be useful. A theory that explains only a few phenomena may be as enlightening and fruitful as one that explains all. The established facts of stuttering that call out for explanation are discussed in detail in Chapter 5.

Another way in which explanatory power of a theory can be assessed is in terms of the number of predictions or hypotheses generated (also see the discussion of "fruitfulness" below). It may be that a theory based on a single postulate may have the capacity to link, in the future, many phenomena considered at the time to be disparate and not interconnected.

So far, we have discussed the ability of a theory to explain phenomena. A distinction needs to be drawn, however, between explanation and description. Developing elaborate descriptions does not necessarily increase understanding or lead to an increase in explanatory power (Rakover, 1990).

It would seem that explanatory power is of particular importance in evaluating theories of stuttering. In the physical sciences a theory is developed only after considerable accumulation of supporting evidence. Darwin, for example, went to extraordinary lengths to gather support for his theory of natural selection before proposing it to the scientific community. However, this does not seem to be the case in stuttering. A study of the history of stuttering indicates that many of the causal theories proposed appear to be little more than good ideas, with little attempt to explain the phenomena of stuttering. We discuss the phenomena of stuttering that require explanation by a theory in Chapter 5.

PARSIMONY

The idea of parsimony is particularly important in light of the previous principle. For while a theory may subsume many of the known facts about stuttering, the principle of parsimony suggests that it is desirable that this be achieved with fewer rather than more postulates. In other words, a theory that proposes an overarching explanation is preferable to one that proposes a number of postulates to cover the known facts. Parsimony suggests that an explanation for a set of events should be simpler rather than more complex. As noted by Marx (1976a), "the more assumptions there are involved – or the more complex a theory – the greater likelihood there is of error" (p. 251). This time-honoured principle is referred to as Ockham's Razor, following the pronouncement of William of Ockham (1290–1349): "*Entia non sunt multiplicanda praeter necesitatem*".

However, complexity or proliferation of postulates does not necessarily mean that a theory is flawed. Nonetheless, on logical and empirical grounds, Ockham's Razor provides a useful guideline for evaluating theories. It is useful to apply Ockham's Razor in comparing competing theories, providing all of them satisfy the data to the same extent. In such a case, it is safer to come down on the side of the theory that explains more with less.

HEURISTIC VALUE

Heuristics are patterns of reasoning that are employed to ". . . assist and guide us in our search for answers or solutions and tell us how probable it is that we are on the right course" (Attanasio et al., 1998, p. 226). Correctly applied, heuristics ". . . allow us to make judgments accurately and efficiently" (Attanasio et al., 1998, p. 226). A theory can be evaluated according to its ability to function heuristically. This depends, to some extent at least, on its relevance. For example, a (hypothetical) theory concerning eye movements in stuttering is likely to be of little interest and concern to theoreticians, researchers, clinicians, and the general public, and in particular to people who stutter.

Also, a theory should be more than just an explanation. It should consolidate previous findings by incorporating deeper unobservable structures (Rakover, 1990). The heuristic value of a theory, then, rests to some extent on its explanatory power (see above). A theory should also provide new perspectives on the area of interest. If it prompts discussion and generates research, a theory can be described as fruitful (Rakover, 1990; Zuriff, 1985). According to Rakover, the more fruitful a theory is, "the greater our understanding of the phenomena to which it is addressed, and the greater the amount of scientific knowledge we acquire about those phenomena" (1990, p. 103).

The responsiveness of the theory to new information should also be considered. Can the theory be modified in response to emerging findings in other than an ad hoc manner, and without becoming too unwieldy or jeopardizing parsimony?

The heuristic value of a theory also depends to some extent on the clarity with which it is presented. The ability of a theory to inform is diminished if the formulation of the theory is complex, or if it is presented incoherently.

As will be clear from the above, theories provide explanation through suggesting unexpected links between phenomena, and enhance understanding of the area of interest. However, we need to be cautious here in our use of the terms "explanation" and "understanding". An explanation and the understanding it generates are not always correct. Feelings of satisfaction flowing from a sense of understanding may be misplaced, if it is in fact a *mis*understanding. Understanding is a subjective experience.

Plausibility can also be considered in assessing the heuristic value of a theory. One might ask, for example, whether a theory appeals to common sense. However, it must be remembered that a theory that is highly plausible may not be true. Likewise, a theory that is not plausible may in fact be true. The example discussed earlier of Galileo's theory that the earth revolves around the sun rather than vice versa is a good example. It was not plausible to many people at the time but it turned out to be true. Nonetheless, in the event that two theories are competing for acceptance, plausibility can be taken into account.

SUMMARY AND DISCUSSION

In this chapter we have considered four criteria against which to evaluate theories. These criteria were drawn from an extensive review of the literature on the history and philosophy of science and psychology. The four criteria and corresponding questions that can be asked of a theory are presented in Table 3.1. We believe these guidelines are as appropriate for evaluating theories of stuttering as they are for evaluating theories in other branches of

Table 3.1 Criteria for evaluating theories and questions to be asked of theories

Criterion	Questions to ask of a theory
Testability and falsifiability	• Does it lead to testable hypotheses? • Is the logic of the argument contained in the theory valid? • Are the terms in the argument defined operationally; that is, can the constructs be measured?
Explanatory power	• Is it supported by evidence? • How much of what we know about the phenomenon of interest does it explain?
Parsimony	• Does it provide one overarching explanation for what we know?
Heuristic value	• Does it provide new insights or understanding by proposing previously unreported connections between phenomena? • Has it been fruitful in terms of generating research? • Is it plausible?

science. Indeed, we use them when we come to reviewing current theories of stuttering later in this text.

These guidelines are in no way intended as a checklist, with some sort of weighting system, with which one can tally the pros and cons and determine whether one theory "wins". That would not be a productive approach, in our view. Rather, these principles are meant as a guide, to suggest features to look for in theories that help one come to some sort of position as to a theory's merit – so that reasons can be offered for preferring one theory to others. A theory that is seen as being closer to the truth, for example, or one that generates hypotheses that if true would solve given problems, is the preferred theory. In place of attempting to justify a theory by making positive statements about it, Popper offers the idea that reason and criticism are grounds for believing that a theory is true or a closer approximation to the truth. To prefer one theory to another or to say that one theory is better than another is not to say that the theory is true. Popper saw the acceptance of a theory as the problem of justification versus criticism. Preference for a given theory is not based on justification but is always conjectural and open to criticism through a process of critical debate.

Popper was a realist and a rationalist who believed that nature is knowable – although probably never fully understandable – if it is probed by bold assertions or conjectures and thus prompted to reveal itself. Science advances rationally and critically. He believed that once an existing theory is falsified, a better and richer theory could emerge to replace it. For Popper the aim of science is to achieve "better and better explanations" (Popper, 1999, p. xxv). The new theory allows scientists to get closer to the explanations they seek.

Popper (1999, p. 25), however, did not believe that ultimate explanations are possible:

> Truth – absolute truth – remains our aim; and it remains the standard of our criticism; almost all criticism is an attempt to refute the theory criticized; that is to say, to show that it is *not true*. (An important exception is criticism attempting to show that a theory is not relevant – that it does not solve the problem it was designed to solve.) Thus we are always searching for *a true theory* (a true and relevant theory), even though we can never give reasons (positive reasons) to show that we have actually found the true theory we have been searching for. At the same time we may have good reasons – that is, good *critical* reasons – for thinking that we have learned something important; that we have progressed towards the truth.

We have talked in general terms here, but later in this text we will apply these guidelines to the evaluation of prominent theories in stuttering. One of our main goals in writing this text is that the reader will be able to apply these guidelines in the future, as new theories emerge.

Chapter 4

Historical perspectives on selected past and present theories of stuttering

Influences of the Zeitgeist

Casti, in 1989, published a delightful book entitled *Paradigms Lost* with the subtitle *Images of Man in the Mirror of Science*. With that subtitle, Casti was suggesting that science holds up a looking glass in which we, women and men, see who and what we are, who and what we were, and who and what we may become. Some tinkering with that subtitle provides us with a looking glass that reflects a somewhat different point of view, one that is the theme of this discussion on historical perspectives: *Images of Science in the Mirror of Man* (read Humankind). By this we repeat what was stated earlier in this text – science is a human undertaking and thus influenced by historical, social, and cultural factors. We hold up a looking glass to science so that it can be seen as part of the human drama that was, is, and is yet to be. Unlike any other member of the animal kingdom, humans are a theory-making species. It is people who make theories, not the other way around.

Ideas, including scientific theories, have histories. Indeed, one of the authors each year suggests to his students that one reason to read the speech-language pathology research journals (once it has been made clear that questions based on information obtained from the assigned readings will appear in the final exam) is to develop a sense of where ideas in the communication sciences and disorders have come from, how they have evolved (or haven't), and what have been the influences that have shaped them. In short, he tells his students that our research journals are the discipline's history books. Ideas on, and theories of, stuttering are no less affected by historical, social, and cultural factors than are the ideas and theories of any other intellectual enterprise. We offer the view that at any given time in the history of stuttering theories, the advocacy or acceptance of a particular set of theories is to be understood as part of a larger socio-cultural outlook extant at that time. The German word *Zeitgeist* nicely captures the idea: "The general intellectual, moral, and cultural climate of an era" (Mish, 1993, p. 1375).

For this discussion of historical perspectives on stuttering theories, we have chosen to look through the lens of the history of psychology and, to some extent, the history of the physical and social sciences in order to understand historical, social, and cultural factors that have influenced theories of stuttering. We do so because we believe, as we stated earlier, that psychology and those sciences that bear upon human behaviour have informed and continue to inform our theory construction in stuttering. It is also the case that the histories of these disciplines reflect the very same socio-cultural factors that influence the history of theories of stuttering: the intellectual, social, economic, and political climates of the day (Schultz & Schultz, 2000).

We do not intend this chapter to be a complete history of ideas or theories in stuttering, for that would take an entire book unto itself. The thorough and insightful treatments of the history of ideas and theories in stuttering in Bloodstein (1993) and Wingate (1997) will provide the reader with interesting and more detailed information on the history of the study of stuttering. Our intent, rather, is to give a brief glimpse of how theorizing on stuttering is influenced by the Zeitgeist within which ideas develop. We do this by using examples of several past and current theories. A number of theories have been omitted from this discussion (there are, for example, explanations of stuttering that are based on learning theory). We have purposely selected theories that we believe suit our purpose for this chapter of the text. We start with a very brief outline of some of the early developments in psychology that set the scene for subsequent theory building in stuttering.

PSYCHOLOGY: A VERY BRIEF HISTORY

Psychology became an experimentally oriented discipline in Germany during the late 19th century. The experimental direction that psychology took was largely the result of the work of Johannes Müller, a German physiologist and professor of anatomy and physiology at the University of Berlin. Müller published his *Handbook of the Physiology of Mankind* in a number of volumes between 1833 and 1840 and he developed a theory of nerve energies that, in turn, encouraged research into the localization of functions within the nervous system (Schultz & Schultz, 2000). In 1870, Gustav Fritsch and Edward Hitzig conducted research on the cerebral cortex. They studied motor responses in rabbits and dogs by stimulating the cortex with electrical currents. By the middle of the 19th century, the electrical nature of nerve impulses was a scientifically accepted fact. During this time, research was also done on the anatomy of the nervous system (Schultz & Schultz, 2000).

The work that was being done by Müller, Fritsch, Hitzig, and others, combined with a focus on the related ideas that mechanisms underlie mental phenomena and that the principles of physics could explain all phenomena, provided the foundation for the beginning of experimental psychology (Schultz & Schultz, 2000). In a real sense, in the beginning physiology and psychology were the same discipline (Thompson, 1967). Experimental psychology in the 19th century was essentially mechanistic, deterministic, and positivistic. That orientation guided much of the research in psychology and influenced early theories of stuttering. Mechanistic psychology recognizes the complexity of human behaviours but posits that the behaviours can be understood in mechanical terms, especially according to the basic principles of physics (Bothamley, 1993). Deterministic psychology states that all behaviours can ultimately be traced to specific causes – that there are causal chains that end in given behaviours. Ends are determined (Bothamley, 1993). Mechanistic psychology incorporates determinism. Positivism takes the scientific approach to the study of human behaviour and, because of its insistance on data, rejects metaphysical or mentalistic approaches (Bothamley, 1993). It is clear that these three doctrines – mechanism, determinism, and positivism – are linked together.

The differences between the German university system on the one hand, and the English university system on the other, played a large part in the fact that Germany was the country where experimental psychology was to have its beginnings. For example, the characteristics of the German university, compared to the university system in England, played a part in the acceptance of scientific inquiry. The principles of academic freedom that were part of the reform movement in German universities in the early 19th century allowed professors to decide the directions their work, research, and teaching would take. Likewise, German university students were able to select courses that were of interest to them; their studies were not constrained by a fixed curriculum. In England, however, the only two existing universities, Cambridge and Oxford, were much more conservative and resistant to change. Attitudes in France and in the United States were similar to those in England. The structure of the German university and the nature of German university professorships provided the context within which science could flourish (Schultz & Schultz, 2000). The Oxbridge point of view, however, essentially kept science, including experimental psychology, out of the academy. Then, too, the acceptance of experimental physiology was already higher in Germany than it was in either France or England, and the Germans were open to applying science to the study of the human mind, more so than the French and English (Schultz & Schultz, 2000). The new science of psychology soon spread, however, and was apparent in the United States in the late 19th and early 20th centuries (Schultz & Schultz, 2000).

Instrumental in the development of experimental psychology were Hermann von Helmholtz's researches into the neural impulse, vision, and audition; Gustav Fechner's work in psychophysics; and Wilhelm Wundt's work in conscious experience, and the laboratory he established in Leipzig where his focus was on the psychophysiology of the senses, reaction time, psychophysics, and association (Schultz & Schultz, 2000). Wundt is credited with establishing psychology as a formal academic discipline. Psychology had become a new science and its separation from philosophy had begun. Nevertheless, psychology remained a subspecialty of philosophy in the German universities into the early 1940s (Schultz & Schultz, 2000). The new psychology quickly became heterogeneous, with several movements in the discipline over-lapping or succeeding each other (Schultz & Schultz, 2000). Whatever the specific focus a particular movement or school-of-thought took, the objective measurement and description of behaviour were the hallmarks of the new science (Thompson, 1967).

Physiological psychology, as a branch of psychology, grew under the influ-ence of Karl Lashly, who in 1929 published *Brain Mechanisms and Intelli-gence* (see Thompson, 1967). Lashly continued his research until his death in 1954. The related discipline of neurophysiology saw the publication of a number of significant research papers during the late 19th and early to mid-20th centuries.

LEE EDWARD TRAVIS: CEREBRAL DOMINANCE AND STUTTERING

Given the developments in late 19th and early 20th century experimental psychology and physiology described above, it is not surprising that a theory of stuttering would develop in the first several decades of the 20th century that was experimental and neurophysiologic in nature. An additional factor may have operated to encourage neurophysiological research into stuttering; namely speech-language pathology's professional identification in its early years with the medical model (Culatta, 1976). According to Culatta (1976), this identification with the medical model was influenced by the need for speech-language pathology to "establish a viable identity" (p. 795). One of the central elements in the medical model is that symptoms – the observable signs of a disease, disorder, or behaviour – are indicators of an underlying cause or process that needs to be treated in order for the symptoms to be relieved. The symptoms themselves are not the disorder.

Lee Edward Travis, an American and the first person to be awarded a PhD with a specialty in what has become speech-language pathology (Bloodstein, 1993), is typically credited with developing what became known as the cerebral dominance theory of stuttering, although it was based on the work and observations of Samuel Orton, a German neurologist and neuro-psychiatrist with whom Travis was associated, and is thus also known as the Orton-Travis theory (Travis, 1978). The essential proposal of the theory is that stutterers have failed to develop cerebral dominance, that is, the dominance of one of the cerebral hemispheres over the other hemisphere so that motor acts that use both sides of the body in a simultaneously inte-grated fashion can be coordinated. The observation that some stutterers were left-handed may have been the impetus to examine cerebral dominance in stutterers (Wingate, 1997). It was thought that one effect of this lack of dominance would be that the midline, bilateral speech musculature, rather than acting in concert under the "neurologic pacing" provided by a dominant hemisphere during speech production in order for speech to be fluent, would be activated instead by each cerebral hemisphere independently, with stuttering being the result.

The decline and eventual abandonment of the Orton-Travis cerebral dominance theory resulted from problems with the research conducted into it (e.g., lack of availability of the research methodology and technology needed for such physiological-based investigations) (Moore, 1993) and the failure of Travis and his students to obtain, in their investigations, sufficient and unambiguous data to corroborate the theory (see Andrews, Craig, Feyer, Hoddinott, Howie, & Neilson, 1983).

Other neurophysiologic theories

In the 1950s, two theories, neurophysiological or medical in nature, gained some temporary attention. They were Robert West's idea that stuttering was a convulsive disorder related to pyknolepsy, a childhood form of epilepsy, and Jon Eisenson's view that stuttering was a perseverative disorder, in that stutterers had an abnormal constitutional tendency to persist in motoric and linguistic behaviours after the reasons for those behaviours had passed. Unlike the cerebral dominance theory, which has recently been revisited in altered formulations (see Chapter 6), neither West's nor Eisenson's theory has had any long-lasting effect.

An example of a possible paradigm shift in the related fields of psychology, philosophy, and anthropology also contributed to the decline of the Orton-Travis theory, and perhaps the theories of West and Eisenson. This shift and its impact on theories of stuttering are clearly seen in the development of Wendell Johnson's diagnosogenic/semantogenic theory, which will be discussed below.

PSYCHOANALYSIS AND STUTTERING

Another branch of psychology, again from Europe, was influencing stuttering theory during the early part of the 20th century (1930s and 1940s) – Sigmund Freud's psychoanalytic movement (Culatta, 1976). Soon after Freud received his MD in 1881 and began a practice in clinical neurology, he developed a friendship with the physician Josef Breuer who was using hypnosis and catharsis to treat hysterical patients (Schultz & Schultz, 2000). Breuer discussed his patients with Freud, among them the person identified as Anna O. The case of Anna O. was to become significant in the development of Freud's psychoanalytic theories.

In 1885, Freud studied hypnosis for the treatment of hysteria with Charcot in Paris and learned from him the role of sex in hysteria. Freud returned to Vienna and after trying Breuer's methods of hypnosis and catharsis in his own practice, found hypnosis to be of little lasting value. He stopped using it, but continued to employ catharsis and added the technique of free association to his methods (Schultz & Schultz, 2000). By this time, Freud had become convinced that sex was the sole cause of neuroses. Breuer was unconvinced that sex was the only factor and decided not to publish with Freud until more evidence could be gathered. Freud, concerned that any delay in publication might allow others to publish on sex in neurosis first and thus relegate him to a secondary position, was unwilling to wait for additional evidence. With some later modification, Freud continued to believe that sex was the cause of neuroses (Schultz & Schultz, 2000).

It should be noted that, to a large extent, Freud worked within the context of 19th-century science, embracing whenever he could the mechanistic, deterministic, and positivistic concepts of experimental psychology referred to in the discussions above, and consequently he never did abandon his belief in the biological determinism of personality (Schultz & Schultz, 2000). Psychoanalytic thinking can be seen as an example of the application of the medical model (see above) to understanding and treating psychological or emotional disorders (Onslow, 1996). Freud's initial training, after all, was in medicine and he established the medical profession as the context within which analysts were to receive their training. Individuals who eventually trained and practised outside medicine were referred to as "lay analysts".

According to Schultz and Schultz (2000), the American public in the 1930s and 1940s took notice of psychoanalysis because, "The combination of sex, violence, and hidden motives, and the promise to cure a variety of emotional problems, proved attractive, almost irresistible" (p. 414). Quite the opposite view of psychoanalysis was taken by mainstream professional psychology at that time.

Freud expressed his thinking on stuttering in several case presentations and theoretical writings, beginning in 1888. In the early 1900s, other psychoanalysts followed him with interpretations of their own (Glauber, 1958). Basically, the psychoanalytic view ". . . regards stuttering broadly as a neurotic disorder in which personality disturbance is in part reflected in disturbances of speech" (Glauber, 1958, p. 73), with the symptom of stuttering being a reflection of the simultaneous and competing desires to talk and to remain silent (Glauber, 1958). Stuttering is driven by a number of unfulfilled or unresolved infantile psychosexual needs and conflicts that have been repressed. The psychosexual needs and conflicts centre on oral and anal erotic gratification, feelings of hostility and anger towards the parent (usually the mother), and aggression (see Bloodstein, 1995, for more information). The psychoanalytic view and treatment of stuttering did not catch hold in mainstream speech-language pathology, although Travis, for one, did adopt some psychoanalytic principles in his later thinking on stuttering (Travis, 1957). Even though Travis's adoption of psychoanalytic principles departed from the earlier Orton-Travis theory of stuttering, both sprang from the same positivistic, deterministic, and mechanistic Zeitgeist, the Zeitgeist that also influenced Freud's work.

There is one final note on Travis and the theory of cerebral dominance: In 1986, Travis combined the psychoanalytic principles he expressed in 1957 with his earlier work in cerebral dominance (see above) when he wrote that ". . . repressed thoughts and feelings . . . are caused by the stuttering, which results from a lack of the two cerebral hemispheres cooperating sufficiently in managing the bilaterally innervated peripheral speech mechanism" (Travis, 1986, p. 121). Thus, Travis clearly indicated that problems in cerebral dominance were the cause of stuttering and the repression of thoughts and feelings was the effect of stuttering.

WENDELL JOHNSON: CULTURE, LANGUAGE, AND STUTTERING

A number of years ago, in the 1970s, one of us presented a workshop on speech and language disorders to a group of early childhood teachers. The aim of the workshop was to give the teachers an overview of communication disorders in early childhood and to suggest what teachers could do in assisting children with those disorders. Stuttering was included and the presenter used the word *stuttering* when the topic was introduced. Almost immediately upon the utterance of the word, a sincere and well-meaning teacher, a member of the group at the workshop, asked if it was wise to use the word *stuttering* when referring to such young children. When asked the reason for the concern, the teacher said that they had been taught that using the "label" *stuttering* would cause a child to become a stutterer. When told that the presenter was talking about children who did indeed stutter, the teacher replied that they had also been taught that these children were experiencing "disfluencies", that they were not actually stuttering, and that the problem would worsen and they would become stutterers once they were labelled and treated as such. This concern was not allayed when it was pointed out that there were no children present at the workshop who could hear the accursed word. No matter, said the teacher, because to use the word is to bespeak an attitude towards children's speech that was fraught with negativity. There, in abbreviated and simple terms, was an expression of Wendell Johnson's diagnosogenic/semantogenic theory of stuttering and the power it had in shaping ways of thinking about early childhood stuttering. Despite the fact that the theory, at least to us, is part of the past, its influence continues to the present day. How did this view of stuttering come to be?

In the early 1940s, Wendell Johnson, although a student of Travis at the University of Iowa, formed a theory of the cause of stuttering that was quite different from the Orton-Travis cerebral dominance explanation. In brief, Johnson's diagnosogenic/semantogenic theory holds that stuttering begins when parents or other significant adults in the child's environment make the diagnosis of the disorder and use the word "stuttering" to describe the child's normal disfluencies (see for example Johnson 1956, 1957, 1961). It is important to understand that Johnson was saying that the adults who make the diagnosis of stuttering do so mistakenly, taking what are normal disruptions in the child's speech to be stuttering. Once the label "stuttering" is used, parents begin to treat the child as a stutterer and the child in turn attempts to avoid the normal disfluencies in response to parental admonitions to speak correctly or not stutter. It is the child's response to this kind of parental pressure that causes the child to begin to stutter and causes the stuttering to progressively worsen if the parents continue to pressure the child. Thus the meaning of diagnosogenic/semantogenic: caused by the diagnosis or caused by the use of the word or label. Obviously, the diagnosis, in Johnson's terms, is inseparable from the use of the label – the label is the diagnosis.

Johnson's theory is somewhat of an extension of the concepts of primary and secondary stuttering developed by Bluemel (1932). Bluemel described primary stuttering as unconscious repetitions made without effort or struggle that would eventually cease if the child's attention were not drawn to them. If, however, the child was made aware of the repetitions and make anxious about them, then secondary stuttering, or fully developed stuttering, would result. Johnson believed that what Bluemel was calling primary stuttering was actually the normal disfluencies typically produced by normally speaking children.

To understand Johnson's thinking about the cause of stuttering we need to return to the history of psychology. The direction psychology took in the United States was influenced by what was occurring in England. Darwin's theory concerning evolution and Francis Galton's work in the psychology of individual differences had significant influences on the developments in American psychology (Schultz & Schultz, 2000). So, too, did the branch of psychology known as functionalism. Functionalism, which originated in England and evolved from Darwin's and Galton's work, took hold in the United States by the late 19th and early 20th centuries and served as the forerunner of American psychology in the decades that followed. Essentially, functionalism focused on conscious processes and how they operated, including "memory, perception, feeling, imagination, judgment, and will" (Schultz & Schultz, 2000, p. 185). According to Schultz and Schultz (2000), functionalism took hold in the United States because of that country's Zeitgeist at the time: ". . . in the American temperament, in its unique social, economic, and political characteristics" (p. 160). The influence of functionalism can be seen in the works of John Dewey and is mirrored in the earlier works of C. S. Peirce and William James, all of whom are associated with the philosophy and psychology known as pragmatism (Thompson, 1995).

Other winds were also blowing through psychology by the end of the 19th century and the beginning of the 20th century that are pertinent to Johnson's theory. That period saw the emergence of social psychological theories (Schultz & Schultz, 2000). According to Schultz and Schultz (2000, p. 434):

> Research in anthropology, sociology, and social psychology supported the proposition that people are products of social forces and institutions and therefore should be studied in social rather than strictly biological terms. As anthropologists publicized their studies of various cultures, it became clear that some of the neurotic symptoms and taboos Freud described were not universal, as he proposed.

American philosophy also took a direction that was different from those taken in continental Europe. Language – the meaning of words, language as a part of culture, language and perception, and the uses and functions of language (e.g., expressing values and emotions) – occupied American philosophers for much of the 20th century (Thompson, 1995).

Johnson's association with Count Alfred Korzybski influenced his theorizing about stuttering. Korzybski, an engineer, established the General Semantics movement in 1933 (Pinker, 1995). Johnson became active in the General Semantics movement and it would be fair to say that he was, in addition to his other credentials, a semanticist. One of the central tenets of Korzybski's beliefs was that the structure and semantics of language were responsible for errors in the way we judge people and make decisions; the ways in which we think about people and their behaviours and respond to them are created and fixed by the semantic categories to which we put them (Pinker, 1995). That central tenet of Korzybski's seems to have informed Johnson's diagnosogenic/semantogenic theory of the cause of stuttering.

The work of the German-American anthropologist Franz Boas and his students, including the linguist Edward Sapir, and Benjamin Lee Whorf, who took a course from Sapir at Yale and was an amateur scholar of Native American languages (Pinker, 1995), are also relevant to Johnson's views. Boas led the way in the development of cultural relativism, the view which maintains that what were considered primitive cultures in comparison to what were thought to be more advanced societies are, in fact, rich and fully developed in their own right and have their own values and ways of viewing the world – each cultural or ethnic group is to be understood in its own cultural context (Bothamley, 1993; Pinker, 1995). Boas's related concept of cultural determinism held that cultural and social factors are primary in determining, shaping, and controlling human behaviour (Bothamley, 1993). Within the contexts of cultural relativism and cultural determinism established by Boas, Sapir and Whorf, focusing specifically on language in culture, were led to conclude what eventually became known as the Sapir-Whorf hypothesis, a form of linguistic determinism. The hypothesis, based on studies of Native American languages, stated that language determines the ways in which cultures and individuals within those cultures view the world;

language organizes the world and how the world is perceived, and directs thought. Furthermore, because different cultures speak different languages, cultural world-views therefore differ (Bothamley, 1993). It was the Sapir-Whorf hypothesis that Korzybski and his followers used to give scientific support to General Semantics (Pinker, 1995).

American philosophy's occupation with language, Boas's cultural relativism and cultural determinism, and Sapir's and Whorf's formulation of linguistic determinism can all be seen as integrated parts of the framework for Johnson's diagnosogenic/semantogenic theory of stuttering and his belief in the power of the word as semantic label.

The diagnosogenic/semantogenic theory lost its standing in the last decades of the 20th century (Onslow, 1996) as a result of the growing view that there is no scientific evidence to indicate that language significantly shapes thought (see Pinker, 1995, for a review) and because of the realization (perhaps the re-discovery) that every known culture has members who stutter and that every known language contains a word for the disorder. The following from Onslow (1996, p. 136) sums up a major reason for the theory's demise:

> Arguably, much of the theory's credibility once rested on Johnson's contention, based on anthropological surveys, that American Indians had no word for stuttering and that none of them experienced it [stuttering]. However, Bloodstein (1987) lists as one of the most significant revelations about the disorder in recent times that, "American Indians of the great plains do stutter and probably did stutter a generation ago, when they were reported not to".

There have also been studies in the speech-language pathology research literature that cast doubt on Johnson's contention that when parents make the initial diagnosis of stuttering in their children, they do so for children whose speech is entirely normal before the diagnosis is made (Onslow, 1996).

A re-examination of the role of punishment as a causal factor in stuttering may be added to the reasons for the demise of the diagnosogenic theory. Siegel's (1970) benchmark review of punishment studies in stuttering provided reassurances that punishing stuttering does not increase its frequency or severity. The "Puppet Study" (Martin, Kuhl, & Haroldson, 1972) indicated that time-out from talking (a form of punishment) could actually decrease the frequency of stuttering, albeit under experimental conditions. More recently, data from the Lidcombe Program – a behavioural programme for early stuttering that centres on reinforcement of stutter-free speech and punishment (in the operant sense) of stuttering – give strong indication that punishment of stutterings does not increase their frequency, but in fact works to decrease or eliminate stuttering when used in a carefully designed treatment regimen that is supportive of children and filled with praise for non-stuttered speech (Onslow, Packman, & Harrison, 2003).

CHAOS THEORY AND STUTTERING

The model of stuttering developed by Smith and Kelly (1997) (see Chapter 9) describes stuttering ". . . as an emergent, dynamic disorder" (p. 208) and proposes ". . . that stuttering refers to processes that change in time, rather than to compartmentalized, static events" (p. 208). The model is said to be multifactorial and interactional in nature and based on the principles of nonlinearity and dynamism (Smith & Kelly, 1997). Stuttering emerges from the dynamic, often changing, interaction of factors that reside both in the environment and the individual. The outcome of the interaction cannot be predicted fully because the relationship between the interacting factors and the results of those interactions is nonlinear. For example, small changes in initial conditions can lead to large effects; the large effects may be unexpected when the size of the change is considered. Although the effects may be unexpected or unpredictable, one major intent of such modelling is to detect order in what may appear to be random or chaotic phenomena (Newton, 1997; Wynn & Wiggins, 1997). These principles are part of the mathematical theory known as chaos theory, which became ascendant in the 1960s (Bothamley, 1993) and are similar to the holistic concepts of Gestalt psychology, developed in the early decades of the 20th century and given a voice by Wolfgang Kohler (Schultz & Schultz, 2000). The well-known mantra of holism and Gestalt psychology is that the whole is different from the sum of its individual parts. This reflects the notion of *synergism* and indeed the progenitor of chaos theory can be said to be holism. Smith and Kelly's model, then, has chaos theory as its basis and may be seen as a non-reductionistic approach to understanding stuttering – the opposite of reductionism or atomism, terms at times used in the pejorative by advocates of holism.

Smith and Kelly (1997) clearly state that their theory of stuttering ". . . has been strongly influenced by nonlinear dynamics" (p. 205). An examination of the sources in the scientific literature that they use to describe the nature of their thinking reveals the influence that chaos and complexity theories have had on their own theory construction (see Smith & Kelly, 1997). Principles of holism are seen in their position that in order to explain stuttering, both as the disorder itself and its manifestation in an individual, many levels of analysis are required and that ". . . a comprehensive theory of stuttering . . . should account for fluency failures in a multidimensional space that includes family history, social context, linguistic processes, emotional/autonomic factors, speech motor organization, and other factors" (p. 206). For Smith and Kelly (1997) stutters are not to be described as discrete, static, and isolated units or events. The following from Smith and Kelly (1997) may serve as a summary statement of their model: "The essence of our model, then, is that stuttering emerges from the complex, nonlinear interaction of many factors. No single factor can be identified as 'the cause' of stuttering" (p. 209).

Smith and Kelly's (1997) description of stuttering as an emergent disorder is patterned on the idea, from chaos and complexity, that ". . . many phenomena in nature are 'emergent'; they exhibit properties that cannot be predicted or understood simply by examining the system's parts" (Horgan, 1996, p. 192).

Arguably, such notions as "emergent", "nonlinear", and "dynamic" in a contemporary causal theory of stuttering would not have entered the lexicon of stuttering in the 1990s except for the appearance of chaos theory in the 1960s, with a number of publications for the non-professional mathematician appearing in the last decades of the 20th century (e.g., Briggs & Peat, 1989; Gleick, 1987; Stewart, 1996). Gleick's 1987 book, for one, became a best-seller and, according to Horgan (1996), reflected the pop-culture status of chaos theory. We do not mean to imply that Smith and Kelly (1997) have embraced pop-culture with the development of their theory, but only that the Zeitgeist was at work once again.

It may be, however, that causal models of stuttering that are based on chaos theory or similar theories may, in the end, not bear much fruit and be consigned to the archives of the history of stuttering, for it seems as though the soundness or useful applications of these theories have already been questioned by members of the scientific community, in that the anticipated benefits for understanding the phenomena studied through them or the acquisition of new insights into old problems have not been realized; little helpful information has been gained by adopting the theories (Newton, 1997). According to Newton (1997), chaos theory, catastrophe theory, and fractal theory – theories that were thought to hold promise for solving "a great variety of puzzles bedevilling scientists in many specialties" (pp. 108–109) – have turned out to be fads that in large measure have not lived up to their promises.

CONCLUSION

This section ends with the reminder, stated once again, that scientific theories are to be understood, at least in part, as products of their historical, cultural, and social milieus – the Zeitgeist. We hasten to add that these historical, cultural, and social influences do not necessarily make theories less scientific, worthy, or credible.

Chapter 5

What should a theory of stuttering explain?

In Chapter 3 we suggested that explanatory power is one of the important criteria against which to evaluate theories. In this chapter we explore features of stuttering that causal theories of stuttering should ideally explain.

As discussed in Chapter 1, there are a number of intriguing features of stuttering that are poorly understood. Although many writers have attempted to explain them, no overarching or parsimonious explanation for them all has so far been proposed. We suggest five phenomena that are supported by extensive evidence and that should feature in the explanatory power of any causal theory: the topography of the speech behaviour of stuttering, onset and development, natural recovery, genetics, and variability. There are of course other research findings in the literature that do not warrant the status of phenomena but that may still be explained by a theory. Caution is needed here, though, and it is suggested that the reader investigate the validity of such findings from original sources. However, before exploring the explicanda of stuttering – those features of stuttering that need to be explained – we address the vexed issue of the definition of stuttering. It is discussed here because stuttering itself is primarily what any causal theory must explain.

Two issues require clarification before we look specifically at recent definitions of stuttering. The first relates to what should be included in a definition of stuttering. The stuttering described in Chapter 1, where Bill had difficulty uttering the word "burger" in the fast-food shop, is known as *developmental* stuttering or, in the case of adults, *persistent developmental* stuttering. This widely recognized form starts in early childhood and a proportion of children continue to display it into adulthood. However, there is a group of late-onset speech disruptions that resemble developmental stuttering – to a greater or lesser extent – that are referred to as *acquired* stuttering (for a review see Bloodstein, 1995). The cause of acquired stuttering can be identified and is usually neurological or psychological, although stuttering-like speech disruptions can also be drug-induced. It has been suggested that in order to reduce confusion, late-onset stuttering-like speech disruptions should not be referred to as "stuttering" (Culatta & Leeper, 1988). Whatever it is called, late-onset stuttering of known origin is not included in the discussions of stuttering in this text.

The second issue is confusion in terminology. First, the terms "dysfluency/disfluency" and "disorder of fluency" are frequently used interchangeably with "stutter" and "stuttering". There is an interesting history to this (see Wingate, 1988). Stuttering is characterized by disruptions to the fluent production of speech. However, many factors contribute to speech fluency, and fluency disruptions – or dysfluencies – are thus not necessarily stutters (for a discussion of this issue see Finn & Ingham, 1989; Packman et al., 2004). Wingate is critical of the use of the term "dysfluency" for stuttering and argues that it is "an esoteric, special purpose word that has been promoted by advocates of the position that stuttering does not differ from normal speech" (Wingate, 1988, p. 7). This position is echoed much later (Wingate, 2001). Second, the terms "stammering" and "stuttering" are also used interchangeably. Perkins (1996) maintains, however, that there is a difference, stating that it is commonly accepted that "to stutter is to speak with repetitions and hesitations, to stammer is to speak with *involuntary* [our italics] repetitions and hesitations" (p. 52). However, this distinction has not been embraced or referred to since by other writers. It is also the case that for some who use the term "stammering" interchangeably with "stuttering" there is a caveat; disfluencies of early childhood that others may refer to as stammering (or stuttering) are sometimes not labelled as such until it is clear that they are not transient (Rustin, Cook, Botterill, Hughes, & Kelman, 2001).

It is not appropriate here to explore further the reasons for and the arguments supporting the use of varying terminologies. We simply draw attention to the lack of consensus on terminology and then state our position that in this text we use the term "stuttering" to refer to developmental stuttering and we use it regardless of whether the speech disruptions referred to are transient. We now move on to the vexed issue of defining stuttering.

THE PROBLEM OF DEFINITION

It has long been recognized that there is no adequate definition of stuttering (for recent discussions of this issue see Bloodstein, 1995; Culatta & Goldberg, 1995; Ingham, 1984; Onslow, 1996; Shapiro, 1999; Wingate, 1997, 2002). Indeed, it has been quipped that if ten speech-language pathologists were asked to define stuttering, they would come up with eleven definitions (Culatta & Goldberg, 1995).

This lack of consensus has considerable theoretical implications because, as discussed in Chapter 3, operational definitions are an integral part of what makes a theory testable. Theoretically at least, a lack of operational definition of stuttering could result in there being two competing theories that are supported by evidence but that offer quite different explanations of stuttering simply because they are in fact explaining two different phenomena. We now look at some of the recent and current definitions of stuttering.

According to the definition provided by the *International Classification of Diseases*, which draws on a definition offered some time earlier by Andrews and Harris (1964), stuttering consists of:

> disorders of the rhythm of speech, in which the individual knows precisely what he wishes to say, but at the same time is unable to say it because of an involuntary repetition, prolongation or cessation of a sound.
>
> (WHO, 1977, p. 202)

Wingate (1964, p. 488) defined stuttering as:

> (a) Disruption in the fluency of verbal expression, which is (b) characterized by involuntary, audible or silent, repetitions or prolongations in the utterance of short speech elements, namely: sounds, syllables, and words of one syllable. The disruptions (c) usually occur frequently or are marked in character, and (d) are not readily controllable.

For the sake of completeness, it should be said that Wingate's definition of stuttering included descriptions of accessory movements of the speech mechanism or other parts of the body. These accessory features of stuttering accompany the disruptions of verbal fluency and may be seen as being related to the struggle behaviours of stuttering. Wingate stated further that the individual who stutters often experiences alterations in emotion that may be as general as an increase in tension or excitement or as specifically negative as the occurrence of fear, embarrassment, or similar emotions.

The Microsoft Word (2001) definition is "to say something haltingly, repeating sounds frequently when attempting to pronounce them, either from nervousness or as the result of a speech disorder".

The above definitions fail to meet the criteria of definition discussed in Chapter 1. The most obvious problem is that they do not differentiate stuttering from other speech disruptions. For example, the Microsoft definition does not confine stuttering to speech disruptions that might be considered clinically significant. Other definitions implicitly restrict the use of "stuttering" to speech disruptions that would be clinically significant, but of course this in itself calls for a subjective judgement. Most speakers from time to time repeat sounds or words or syllables, or prolong sounds, or pause or hesitate while speaking.

According to Ingham (1984), the problem of definition revolves around the issue of frequency and form. In other words, the speech disruptions alluded to must occur excessively, and/or in a pronounced form, in order to be included. However, as Ingham (1984) points out, judgements of how frequent and in what form speech disruptions must be to qualify as stuttering are subjective. Nor do the definitions distinguish stuttering from other clinically recognized disorders such as dysarthria or aphasia, that may also include speech disruptions that could be judged to be excessive or marked, or uncontrollable, or that interfere with the speaker's ability to say what he or she wants to say. Nor are the attributes of stuttering in these definitions described in sufficient detail for them to be identified reliably.

Ingham (1984) suggested that since Wingate's definition is the most widely cited, it can probably be considered the closest we have to an acceptable definition of stuttering. Smith and Kelly (1997), however, disagree, stating that classical definitions of stuttering such as Wingate's "rely too heavily on perceptual/linguistic evaluation of the speech acoustic signal" (p. 205). We return to this below.

A number of writers in fact extend the definition of stuttering beyond just speech behaviours. For example, Cooper (1993) defines stuttering as "a diag-nostic label referring to a clinical syndrome characterized most frequently by abnormal and persistent dysfluencies in speech accompanied by characteristic affective, behavioral, and cognitive patterns" (p. 382). The same applies to the definition put forward by Peters and Guitar (1991), "A disorder of the neu-romotor control of speech, influenced by the interactive processes of language production, and intensified by complex learning processes" (p. 18). Sheehan (1970) described stuttering as "a disorder of the social presentation of the self. Basically stuttering is not a speech disorder but a conflict revolving around self and role, an identity problem" (p. 4). Definitions such as these do not describe the features of speech that constitute stuttering but rather incorporate partial allusions to the cause and nature of stuttering (Shapiro, 1999).

A more extreme example is the internal definition of stuttering. Perkins (1983, 1984) has argued that only the person who stutters knows when a stutter actually occurs. Based on this premise, Perkins (1984) defined stutter-ing as "temporary overt or covert loss of control of the ability to move forward fluently in the execution of linguistically formulated speech" (p. 431). One of the problems with this statement as a definition is that it is mentalistic and so renders stuttering a private event that is inaccessible to observation (see Martin & Haroldson, 1986).

As we have said, the fact that there is no adequate definition of stuttering is not new, and many have addressed the issue before this. While some have dismissed the problem as academic, or even trivial, others, such as Webster (1977, p. 65), have seen it as a serious obstacle to conducting science in stuttering:

> Faulty definitions of concepts and a preference for conceptual schemes that have been established largely through subjective judgment and rational analysis have led to a seriously reduced emphasis on the empirical aspects of stuttering.

Operationalizing stuttering

Since Webster's cautionary statement, there have in fact been a number of attempts to operationalize stuttering. At least an agreed-upon operational definition would mean that research into stuttering could be conducted with some agreement about what is being measured. However, again, consensus has not been reached.

One approach to operationalizing stuttering has been to look at groups of children judged to be stuttering and groups of children judged not to be stuttering, and to identify the types of speech disruptions that predominate in the speech of the first group as compared to the second. Based on this, children who display these speech disruptions in certain proportions or with sufficient frequency are then said to be stuttering. In the Stutter-like/Other Dysfluency taxonomy (see Yairi, 1997), for example, the types of speech disruptions known to be more common in the speech of children identified as stuttering have been labelled Stutter-like Dysfluencies (SLD). Three or more SLDs per 100 syllables is one criterion for labelling a child as stuttering. However, the problem here is that SLDs are not necessarily stuttering. Further, children already identified as stuttering may in fact display as few as one SLD per 100 syllables (see Yairi, 1997). Yairi has acknowledged that this procedure has problems (Yairi, 1997). One critic of the SLD/Other Dysfluency taxonomy is Wingate (2001, p. 382), who described it as:

> . . . another of those perennial confoundings that surface in the field of stuttering. It can be documented to reflect a position-driven bias that can be expected to keep the field moving in slow circles.

Here, Wingate is taking issue with the terminology. It must be said, however, that at the empirical level other indicators of stuttering, such as parental reports, are taken into account, along with SLD counts, before a child is identified as stuttering. Nonetheless, the SLD/Other Dysfluencies taxonomy is a taxonomy of dysfluencies, not stuttering.

Another procedure for operationalizing stuttering is the Within-word/ Between-word Dysfluency taxonomy (for example see Conture, 1990a; Zebrowski, 1991). Conture and colleagues proposed that stuttering occurs within words, and that dysfluencies that occur between words are not stuttering. Applying this taxonomy, then, provides a way to decide whether a speech disruption is a stutter. Children who display three or more Within-word Dysfluencies (WWD) per 100 syllables are labelled stutterers. The fact that this taxonomy is somewhat problematic has been discussed (Cordes & Ingham, 1995) and is acknowledged by Conture (1990a, 1990b). Conture acknowledges, for example, that although the repetition of single-syllable words may be stuttering, this speech disruption cannot, logically, occur *within words*. It also suffers from some of the problems of the SLD/Other Dysfluency taxonomy in that children who are considered to be stuttering may display only one WWD per 100 syllables. Conversely, we can be faced with the untenable situation where children who are not regarded as stutterers may be reported as in fact stuttering (see Luoko, Edwards, & Conture, 1990). An example of this is where Luoko et al. report: "One child in the normally fluent group exhibited an average of 3.6 stutterings/100 words" (p. 194).

Bloodstein (1995) proposed a way of operationalizing stuttering that involves consensus of experts. Bloodstein suggested that stuttering is "whatever is perceived as stuttering by a reliable observer who has relatively good agreement with others" (p. 10). This is sometimes referred to as the perceptual or consensus definition, and is widely used to identify moments of stuttering in research. However, despite being empirically useful, it is not strictly speaking a definition because it does not define stuttering objectively. Even more problematic is the fact that levels of agreement, both within and between observers, about the occurrence of instances of stuttering are not always high (for a discussion about the reliability of perceptual judgements of stuttering see Cordes & Ingham, 1994). Nonetheless, it is probably the most acceptable way of operationalizing stuttering for the purposes of empirical investigation.

So far, we have looked at attempts to operationalize stuttering by reference to perceptible speech disruptions. However, it has been argued that speech behaviour should not be the only basis for deciding that stuttering has occurred. The proposal here is that stuttering may at times be imperceptible. It has been argued that speech that is perceptually free of stuttering can be considered to be stuttered if physiological measures are aberrant in certain ways (for examples and criticisms of such arguments see Cordes & Ingham, 1997). The extreme position here is rejection of the idea that stuttering can be identified perceptually (Smith & Kelly, 1997). Smith and Kelly have argued that stuttering is not an event, and "units of stuttering are a convenient fiction that have no biological reality. They are fictive in time and space" (1997, p. 206). This position is countered, however, by Folkins' (1991) position that "movements and muscles are not disfluent, behaviors are" (p. 564). In other words, according to Folkins stuttering must be identified perceptually and not from the presence of aberrant physiological measures.

A final issue in operationalizing stuttering relates to the repetition of speech units. Historically, repeating speech sounds and syllables has been regarded as stuttering. Both Bluemel and Froeschels thought that the repetition of speech units in early stuttering is one of the well-known features of the disorder (Attanasio et al., 1998). Van Riper (1963) suggested that oscillations of the speech structures are basic to stuttering. Wingate (1964) stated that repetitions of single-unit speech elements and audible or silent prolongations are "kernel characteristics of stuttering speech [which] can be discriminated" (p. 487). Wingate (Hamre, 1992; Wingate, 1976) subsequently reaffirmed his view that audible and silent elemental repetitions are essential and universal speech features of stuttering. And Yairi (1997) stated,"the most common speech characteristics [of stuttering in early childhood] are repetitions of syllables and words . . ." (p. 56).

Yet, according to Starkweather (1997, p. 79):

> I don't consider these early behaviours to be stuttering, at least not in the sense that they are a disorder and a problem. I see the problem of stuttering as the extraneous effort, the reactions, and the struggles that can develop in response to those disfluencies. On the other hand, I don't believe that those early, easy repetitions are normal either.

The problem is apparent, more specifically, in relation to the repetition of single-syllable words. As stated earlier, Wingate (1964) included the repetition of single-syllable words in his definition of stuttering. This was echoed, less forcefully, in a later statement that a single-syllable repetition "may or may not actually mark a stutter event" (Wingate, 1988, p. 40). More recently, however, Wingate has argued (Wingate, 2001, 2002) that the repetition of single-syllable words is *not* stuttering. According to Wingate (2001) the repetition of a syllable may be a stutter if it is part of a multi-syllable word, but not if it is a word in its own right. Also, Conture (1990b) has said that the repetition of single-syllable words may reflect "pure expressive language delays" (p. 60) rather than stuttering.

However, there are no empirical grounds for asserting that the repetition of single-syllable words does not constitute stuttering. An example of such repetition was provided by Packman, Onslow, Richard, and van Doorn (1996) with an acoustic display. The young child's speech was recorded a few weeks after the onset of stuttering. The example consisted of "on . . . on . . . on . . . on . . . on . . . on a chair" and the utterance was the child's response to the question "Where is Big Bird?" There is no reason to think that these authors were wrong when they agreed that this speech disruption was stuttering.

In any event, there appears to be reasonable widespread agreement that the repetition of speech units, in general, can constitute stuttering. Packman and Onslow (1998) compiled descriptors of stuttering that were published by prominent scholars between 1959 and 1991. Of the 25 terms listed by Packman and Onslow, 10 (40%), describe the repetition of speech units, 3 (12%) describe prolongation of speech units, and the remaining 12 (48%) describe such behaviours as *broken words*, *hard vocal attack*, *tense pause*, and *disrhythmic phonation* (1998, p. 29). It is apparent, then, that the most commonly used terms summarized by Packman and Onslow (1998) describe the repetition of speech units.

In conclusion, however, this range of positions on how to operationalize stuttering is indeed extraordinary, given the large amount of research currently carried out into stuttering and the large number of reports in the current stuttering literature. While the problems of operationally defining stuttering have been readily acknowledged, it is surprising that students and teachers of stuttering, and researchers and clinicians working with people who stutter, have not, to date, been able or willing to reach some consensus here. Without agreement on such a basic issue as this, the study of stuttering clearly cannot be considered as occurring within a paradigm, or even, perhaps, within a preparadigmatic framework.

Having completed our preamble on stuttering, we go on now to dicuss the explicanda.

THE TOPOGRAPHY OF STUTTERING

A causal theory of stuttering needs to explain why people stutter. While this may seem a trivial statement, it is in fact a critical one. A theory needs to explain, for example, why Bill when uttering the word "burger" breathed in quickly and audibly, held his lips together in the position for /b/ for around 2 seconds, and then released that lip posture with increased loudness on the following /ur/ sound. A theory also needs to explain, for example, why the child reported above repeated the word "on" five times before going on to complete the intended utterance.

The Lidcombe Behavioural Data Language (Packman & Onslow, 1998; Teesson, Packman, & Onslow, 2003) is the only behaviourally based taxonomy of stuttering and so it provides an outline of the topography of the speech behaviours of stuttering. The taxonomy can be used to categorize stuttering at any age and its reliability has been demonstrated. As far as the verbal behaviours are concerned, there are two categories of activity related to speech production, namely *repeated movements* and *fixed postures*, both of which subsume more finely grained behavioural descriptors. The repetition of the word "on" described above is an example of *repeated movements*, while Bill holding his lips together on the /b/ sound is an example of *fixed posture*. The third category in the taxonomy is *superfluous behaviours*, which are the accompanying verbal and nonverbal behaviours that are not integral to the utterance. It is proposed, then, that these are the speech behaviours that need to be explained by any theory of stuttering.

ONSET AND DEVELOPMENT

It can be difficult to pinpoint the time and the nature of the onset of stuttering. Parents are usually the first to notice when stuttering is thought to have begun in their children. Parental reports may be flawed in a number of ways, however, most notably because parents may wait months before seeking out a speech-language pathologist or other professional to confirm the presence of stuttering (Yairi & Lewis, 1984) or parents might not even notice the stuttering until some time after onset (Onslow, 1996), particularly if onset is gradual.

Despite this, various reports in the professional literature on the age of stuttering onset tend to be consistent. Månsson (2000) found age of onset to range from 24 to 42 months with a mean age of onset of 34 months for boys and 31 months for girls. Yaruss, LaSalle, and Conture (1998) found the mean age of onset to be 36 months for boys and 30 months for girls. Yairi and Ambrose (1992b) reported that the greatest risk for the onset of stuttering is for children under 36 months of age, with 75% of the risk being prior to 3½ years of age for preschool children. Kloth, Kraaimaat, Janssen, and Brutten (1999) stated that stuttering is most likely to begin between the ages of 2 and 5 years, but can begin at any time during childhood. Onslow (1996) reported that the mean and median age of onset recalled by those who first notice the stuttering is generally below 5 years of age. His review of the literature on age of onset leads him to conclude that "stuttering begins mostly in the first few years of life" (p. 19).

A feature of stuttering that differentiates it from almost all other developmental communication disorders in childhood is that onset occurs after a period of apparently normal speech development. Children do not stutter when they babble, or first start to talk, but only once they start using two- or three-word utterances. The reason for this is not known, although it is commonly understood to be related in some way to the rapid development of language that is occurring at around this time. This feature calls out for explanation in any theory of stuttering.

Historically (for example, see Bloodstein, 1995), the onset of stuttering has been described as a gradual process, with severity at mild levels in the beginning but developing, if left untreated, into more severe or advanced stages as the months or years pass. Yairi and Lewis (1984), however, present data that cast doubt on this historical view. They were able to describe the disfluencies of young children within two months from the time the children were diagnosed by their parents as stuttering and to compare them to the disfluencies of a matched group of children who had been identified as normally fluent. Yairi and Lewis (1984) were thus able to observe disfluencies very close to the time of reported onset of stuttering. Analysis of the speech of the two groups indicated that the group of stuttering children was distinctly different from the group of normally speaking children, in that the stuttering children were three times more disfluent than the normally speaking children. Onslow (1996) reviewed a number of reports and studies which point to the real possibility that a significant number of children begin to stutter suddenly and quickly, and that the stuttering may be quite severe at onset or very soon thereafter.

Whether or not stuttering can be said to develop, therefore, is a matter for discussion and additional research rather than an issue that has been resolved. Yairi and Ambrose (1992a), for example, found questionable the historical or traditional view that stuttering tends to worsen with the passage of time. In fact they found, albeit in a small sample of subjects, that the development of stuttering may take the opposite direction – a decrease in disfluent speech as time passes (Yairi & Ambrose, 1992a). According to Wingate (1997) there is "very substantial evidence that stuttering typically does not 'develop' "(p. 157). Why does Wingate have to remind us of the existence of what he considers to be the well-documented case against the notion that stuttering develops? The answer lies in the history of the thinking on stuttering.

Bluemel (1932) and Froeschels (1915, 1933) noted that early stuttering is characterized by sound or syllable repetitions, and Bloodstein (1995) and van Riper (1982) noted that stuttering at onset is characterized by repetitions of speech elements typically located at the beginning of utterances. Attanasio et al. (1998) state that, in their experience, the repetitions of early stuttering are typically of word-initial syllables or of single-syllable words. According to van Riper (1982), Bluemel and Froeschels had gone further in their formulations by suggesting that stuttering severity developed from these early repetitions into more effortful, tense, and struggled speech. Bluemel used the terms "primary stuttering" and "secondary stuttering" to distinguish between the initial and advanced stages of the disorder, and Froeschels described seven stages of increased severity (van Riper, 1982). Van Riper (1982) described his own taxonomy in which he first listed three stages – primary, transitional, and secondary stuttering – with a fourth stage subsequently inserted between primary and transitional. Bloodstein (1995), in an attempt to describe the developmental progression of stuttering, delineated four phases of the disorder, with the implication that severity and complexity increase from one phase to the next.

Despite Wingate's (1997) statement that there is a considerable amount of evidence that stuttering does *not* develop in ways suggested by, among others, the taxonomies mentioned above; despite Bloodstein's (1995) statement that there are no developmental schemes that have gained general acceptance; and despite van Riper's (1982) criticisms of those taxonomies and the repudiation of his own, putative developmental phases of stuttering continue to be published in current textbooks. Unless consumers of those texts read carefully enough to understand the caveats given by the authors, the impression could be that stuttering does follow a developmental sequence.

What, then, is to be said about the development of stuttering? It seems that the progression of stuttering from mild to severe forms is not inevitable for every child who stutters, although particular children may indeed demonstrate such a developmental course. On the other hand, the stuttering of some children may fluctuate from mild to severe and back again on a daily, weekly, or monthly basis. Then, too, some children may start out stuttering severely but then progress to milder forms of the disorder. Onset may occur unambiguously and definitely in a short period of time or may occur gradually over time (Yairi & Ambrose, 1992b). Both the research literature and anecdotal clinical observation point to the possibilities of any one of these scenarios (Hamre, 1992; van Riper, 1982; Yairi & Ambrose, 1992a). Nonetheless, the repetition of syllables (repeated movements of the speech mechanism) appears to be, as we have said, the most common sign of stuttering at onset (see Yairi, 1997). So common is this finding that Attanasio et al. (1998) suggested that the repetition of syllables at onset may have causal implications. In any event, any theory of stuttering must account for this and for how other types of speech behaviours such as fixed postures come to be part of the topography of stuttering.

NATURAL RECOVERY

Discussions and debates in the literature indicate that it is not easy to know, with an acceptable degree of error, the percentage of children who recover naturally from early stuttering (see Finn, 1998). Equally difficult problems are apparent in attempting to uncover the course of natural recovery and the predictors of natural recovery for any given child who has begun to stutter (for a review see Onslow, 1996). Nevertheless, it is known from prospective research that a sizeable number of children who begin to stutter recover without clinical intervention within the early preschool years (for example see Månsson, 2000; Yairi & Ambrose, 1999). Drawing on data for 84 children, Yairi and Ambrose (1999) proposed a conservative recovery rate of 74%. A theory of the nature and cause of stuttering cannot ignore the phenomenon of natural recovery and should provide insights into this intriguing phenomenon.

One of the significant difficulties in theorizing about natural recovery is the possibility that it does not actually happen – the argument being that it is nearly impossible to demonstrate that a child has received no assistance from the environment (parents, siblings, teachers, caregivers, etc.) in dealing with stuttering or with the factors that might be implicated in the persistence of stuttering. That is, recovery that occurs without professional intervention may not necessarily be unaided (Attanasio, 1999). Theories of stuttering should take this possibility into account.

GENETICS

According to Drayna (1997), evidence for a genetically inherited predisposition to stutter has mounted over the last 30 years or so. The evidence comes from several sources: (1) stuttering runs or clusters in families in ways better explained by patterns of inheritance than by environmental factors; (2) concordance rates for stuttering are higher in monozygotic than in dizygotic twins; (3) adoption studies indicate that the clustering of stuttering is related to the presence of stuttering in biological rather than adoptive parents; (4) the identification of large families in which there is a high density of stuttering – in one large family investigated, stuttering is thought to follow a "simple, single-gene, Mendelian trait" (p. 237); and (5) studies indicate that the genetic epidemiology of stuttering is similar to that of a number of complex diseases known to have complex inheritance. Further evidence for the genetic inheritance of stuttering is seen in studies that point to a higher risk of stuttering for males, and in the research that suggests a genetic link to the persistence of, and the recovery from, stuttering (Yairi, Ambrose, & Cox, 1996).

For example, Ambrose, Cox, and Yairi (1997) found that there are families in which persistent stuttering is the pattern and families in which recovered stuttering is the pattern. Furthermore, Ambrose et al. (1997) found statistical evidence of a major locus and polygenic components that contribute to persistence and recovery. The authors stated that persistent and recovered stuttering are most likely not genetically separate and independent disorders and that recovery does not appear to be a milder form of persistent stuttering. It seems that persistent stuttering has genetic factors that are in addition to those genetic factors that are linked to the susceptibility to stutter. Thus the persistent stutterer is one who has both the genetically transmitted susceptibility to develop stuttering and the genetically transmitted factors that result in persistence.

Ambrose et al. (1997) also pointed to the issue of the interaction between environmental and genetic factors as being important to an understanding of the development of stuttering and to its persistence or recovery. Felsenfeld (1996) stated that the family and twin studies reviewed "provide the necessary foundation for future behavioral genetic investigations of stuttering" (p. 90) and more recently, Ingham and Bothe (2001) wrote, "There is currently no serious debate over the view that developmental stuttering emerges from a confluence of genetic, neurophysiological, and environmental factors" (p. 865). One recent indication that a genetic component to stuttering is not limited by geography or culture comes from a study by Månsson (2000) of the incidence and prevalence of stuttering in children on the Danish island of Bornholm. Månsson (2000) found that 67% of the children studied had stuttering relatives; 50% had first-degree relatives who stuttered and 17% had second-degree relatives who stuttered.

At the time this chapter was being written, long-term genetic studies of stuttering were underway. One major study in America, sponsored by the National Institute on Deafness and Other Communication Disorders, is a linkage study designed to collect DNA samples from stutterers and nonstutterers in stuttering families and to discover the "basic combination of genes (genotype) making up all of the participants' DNA" (NIH, 1997, p. 1). The focus of this second objective is to "map out and find areas or regions of

DNA that are linked to stuttering" (p. 1). Linkage studies use families that have a high number of members from several generations who stutter. The goal of linkage studies is to find genetic markers that are co-inherited with the disorder under investigation. Linkage studies in stuttering attempt to find the genetic markers that are co-inherited with stuttering. Finding the marker leads to identifying the gene or genes that cause the disorder or contribute to its cause, since the marker lies close to the gene or genes that are implicated in the disorder (Drayna, Online, 19 January 2003).

Knowing or believing that stuttering has an inheritable genetic component, whether it be the major component or not, does not tell us just what it is that is inherited. Likewise, knowing how the genetic defect is inherited does not tell us what the defect is or anything about the nature of stuttering (Yairi et al., 1996). Research into the nature of the defect that underlies stuttering runs parallel to genetic research. One line of research into a possible underlying defect is the investigation of differences in the brain anatomy of stutterers and nonstutterers. Foundas, Bollich, Corey, Hurley, and Heilman (2001), for example, found that their adult subjects with persistent developmental stuttering had anomalies in the perisylvian speech and language areas when compared to matched control subjects. Sommer, Koch, Paulus, Weiller, and Büchel (2002) also found evidence of structural anomalies in the speech-related areas of the brain. In both cases, the authors suggested that the anomalies they found may be risk factors for the development of stuttering.

While a considerable number of genetic studies have now been conducted in stuttering, the literature is not free from debate and disagreement, especially on issues of methodology (for example see Ingham & Bothe, 2001; Yairi & Ambrose, 2001) and perhaps a complete understanding of the role played by genetics in stuttering lies many years in the future. Nevertheless, a theory of stuttering must address the data we currently have and should hypothesize about the nature of inherited mechanisms thought to cause or contribute to stuttering.

VARIABILITY

An outstanding feature of stuttering is its natural variability. First, stuttering varies in rate and severity across individuals. In some people stuttering is so severe that the flow of speech may be arrested for 30 seconds or more, while in others stuttering may be barely perceptible. Second, stuttering severity varies within individual speakers. According to Yaruss (1997), "Variability is one of the hallmarks of stuttering in children and adults who stutter" (p. 187). Stuttering in young children tends to vary over time, and may even disappear for weeks or months and then reappear. This is not so much the case in older children, adolescents, and adults, where stuttering is more likely to vary in severity, and even in its actual appearance, from communicative context to communicative context.

Severity of stuttering also varies under certain artificial or experimental conditions. For example, stuttering rate reduces with response-contingent stimulation; that is, when certain environmental events are made contingent on stuttering and/or on intervals of stutter-free speech (see Ingham, 1984; Prins & Hubbard, 1988). Stuttering rate reduces in many speakers over repeated oral readings of a passage. This is known as the adaptation effect (see Bloodstein, 1995). Stuttering rate also reduces significantly or even disappears when people speak in time to a rhythmic stimulus or in a legato fashion, or when they speak in chorus with another person, or when the auditory feedback of the person's speech is altered in various ways (for reviews of these fluency-enhancing conditions see Bloodstein, 1995; Ingham, 1984). Fluency-inducing conditions have been the subject of much research over many years, and rhythmic and legato speech – known as novel speech patterns – have formed the basis of many behavioural speech-restructuring treatment programmes for stuttering (see Bloodstein, 1995; Ingham, 1984; Packman, Onslow, & Menzies, 2000b).

Due to the widespread use of novel speech patterns to induce fluent speech in treatments for stuttering, it may be appropriate to consider treatment effectiveness in this section on variability. However, we emphasize that positioning treatment effectiveness in this way indicates that we are considering here only those treatments that reduce the severity and/or rate of stuttering. Although a causal theory of stuttering is not obliged to speak directly to how stuttering should be treated, if the theory suggests that a given factor is implicated in the cause or maintenance of stuttering, then it ought to point to the ways in which that factor may be addressed in treatment. As we discuss in a later chapter, basing treatment on a theory does not mean that it will work. That can only be addressed empirically. Nonetheless, we suggest that the heuristic value of a causal theory is enhanced if it can explain why stuttering reduces with certain treatments, *providing that the treatment effectiveness has been adequately documented*. Consequently, in the chapters that follow, discussion of the capacity of a theory to explain treatment effectiveness is typically included in the section describing the theory's heuristic value.

The natural variability of stuttering remains one of its most puzzling and intriguing features, and can be seen as a reflection of the extraordinary complexity of living systems alluded to in Chapter 2. Similarly, the fact that stuttering is extensively reduced under certain speaking conditions and with various treatments is also of considerable interest in any discussion of cause in stuttering. Variability is one of the most important features of stuttering to be addressed by any causal theory.

Chapter 6

Theories of stuttering: Speech motor control

In this chapter and the following four chapters, we review some recent theories of stuttering. For the moment we use the term "theories" in the broadest sense, to mean theories, models, and hypotheses. Theories have been included according to four criteria. First, the theory has appeared in the professional and/or scientific literature in the last 15 years. The first publication of the theory may have been prior to this, but to be included the theory must have been alluded to or cited in the past 15 years. Second, the theory is causal in that it provides an explanation for the cause of stuttering. Third, it is referred to by the author or authors as a theory, a model, or a hypothesis. There are other theoretical musings about the cause of stuttering in the literature that we excluded because the author or authors have not labelled them, or developed them formally, as a theory. Wingate, for example, has written extensively on his view that stuttering is an intra-syllabic transition defect. However, as this view has not been presented as a formal theory, it was not included. The fourth criterion was that the theory has attracted interest in the stuttering literature. There was one other constraint in the selection of theories, which was that we drew only from the English-language literature. We acknowledge that influential theories from other cultures will have been omitted because of this.

In conducting this review, we have attempted as far as possible to remain objective. We realize that objectivity can never be achieved entirely, as every writer brings bias to the reviewing process. However, we have followed two guidelines in our attempts to maintain objectivity. First, we frequently quote directly from original reports. We do this in the hope that it minimizes misrepresentation. Second, we review each of the theories according to the criteria for scientific theories established in Chapter 3; namely testability and falsifiability, explanatory power, parsimony, and heuristic value. We outlined the features of stuttering that we think should be explained by a causal theory of stuttering in Chapter 5. These are the topography of stuttering, onset and development, natural recovery, genetics, and variability. We stress that in our report on the explanatory power of a theory, we present only those explanations put forward by the author or authors. A theory may have more explanatory power than this; however, if there is no discussion in this text of how a theory explains, say, the topography of stuttering, the reader should assume that the author or authors provided no such explanation. Before applying these criteria, we start each review with a statement of the arguments in the theory, and a brief outline of the background and development of the theory.

Our aim in reviewing these theories is threefold. First, we think there is heuristic value in providing, in one place, clear and comprehensive reports of the various theories that appear in the current literature. A number of the theories, and the research supporting them, are reported more than once in a variety of publications, some of which are not easily accessible. Second, we are interested in establishing the credentials of current theories, which has not been done before, at least not extensively. We stress, however, that this is not an exercise in scoring to see which theory comes out on top. This is simply an exercise in critique that we hope will be informative for readers. We actually consider our third aim to be the most important. This is to demonstrate how criteria may be used to establish the merits of theories presented to the professional community for its consideration. The task of judging theories is not one for academics or researchers alone. While it is true that theories may form the foundation for research, it is equally true that theories may influence the ways in which treatment is approached. We discuss the role of theory in treatment later in the text, but our point here is that clinicians need to be informed consumers of theory no less than do teachers and researchers. Indeed, when clinicians subscribe to a particular theory of stuttering they are, in effect, announcing their beliefs about the nature of the disorder and how it should be treated. We hope that after reading these reviews the reader will be well equipped to use the guidelines established in this book to critically evaluate for themselves new theories of stuttering as they appear in the literature.

We have attempted to categorize the theories and have placed them, accordingly, into five chapters. We stress that all theories are unique and that these categories are rather loose. In this chapter, we review a theory that explains the cause of stuttering in terms of speech motor control.

THE INTERHEMISPHERIC INTERFERENCE MODEL

This is a two-factor neuropsychological model. The two factors are (1) inefficiency in supplementary motor area (SMA) function, and (2) a labile system of hemispheric activation. Each factor alone is not sufficient for stuttering to occur, but together the factors are necessary and sufficient for stuttering to occur. The model is described in detail in a number of publications (see Webster, 1993, 1997, 1998). This is not a model in the classical sense of using an analogy from another discipline. However, it is a conceptual model in the sense that it provides an outline of how the neural processes underlying stuttering operate, without providing specific details of those processes. The model is depicted diagrammatically in the publications, and Webster refers to it as a "working model" (1998, p. 221).

Background and development

The research findings of Forster and Webster (2001) establish the existence and relevance of the two factors in this model. Forster and Webster found that recovered stutterers performed similarly to nonstutterers on tasks that claimed to involve SMA, but similarly to persistent stutterers on tasks that claimed to tax stability of hemispheric activation. The differences in performance of the persistent stutterers and the recovered stutterers on the two types of tasks provide support for the independence of the two factors in the model.

The influence of the Orton-Travis theory (see Chapter 4) in the development of the model is widely acknowledged; indeed, at least three of the publications describing the model contain figures showing the similarities and differences between the two theoretical positions. In contrast to the Orton-Travis theory, however, a premise of the Interhemispheric Interference model is that people who stutter have normal lateralization for speech production. While the left hemisphere is dominant for speech in people who stutter, the SMA in stutterers is fragile and susceptible to other ongoing neural activity. This inefficiency of the SMA is kinaesthetically based (Forster & Webster, 2001). The fragile SMA is susceptible particularly to overactivation of the right hemisphere, which is due, at least in part, to the negative emotions experienced as a result of stuttering.

People who stutter "do not demonstrate a left hemisphere activation bias but are similar to fluent left-handers by showing a distribution of hemispheric activation that is more equal and more labile" (Webster, 1997, pp. 128–129); in other words there is a "greater lability or flexibility of hemispheric activation" (p. 225) in people who stutter. There may also be a "lack of normal gating of information flow between hemispheres" (p. 223), although "the SMA may be susceptible to interference from any concurrent neural activity, not just that in the right hemisphere" (Webster, 1998, p. 225).

The model, then, involves an interaction between neurology and psychology. According to Webster (1997, p. 131):

> The anomalous brain mechanisms of the left hemisphere lead to speech dysfluency, and this dysfluency in turn leads to and reinforces negative emotional reactions to speech. These reactions in turn evoke greater right hemisphere activity which, in turn, interferes more with the fragile left hemisphere mechanisms, resulting in dysfluency, and so on.

According to the model, two factors are necessary to explain stuttering because the first factor – inefficiency of the SMA – does not explain variations in stuttering severity. A "dynamic process rather than a static structural defect or anomaly" (Webster, 1998, p. 222) is required to explain this variability. According to Webster (1998), it is unlikely that people who stutter have a lesion in the brain, but it is more likely that they have aberrant processing of information in various parts of the brain.

Webster (1993) maintains that the model is based on three assumptions. The first is that there is a biological basis to stuttering. This assumption is supported by the fact that stuttering is universal, being found in all cultures and languages, and that the concordance rate for stuttering is greater in monozygotic than dizygotic twins. The second assumption is that this biological basis is neurological in nature. In particular, it is a deficit of the neural processing related to speech motor control. The model assumes that any concomitant psychological disturbances are a result rather than a cause of stuttering. Nonetheless, the model states that the psychological sequelae of stuttering also impact on the neural processing underlying stuttering and so influence, for example, severity of the stuttering. The third assumption is that understanding of the neural mechanisms underlying stuttering can be gained through the study of the control of other motor activities, in particular the control of hand movement. The SMA is of particular relevance here because it is involved in the "initiation and control of both speech and nonspeech sequential activities" Webster (1988, p. 239). Interhemispheric connections between motor areas pass through the SMA, and it is involved in bimanual coordination.

In addition, the SMA has extensive connections with many areas of the brain and is considered "a central and key part of the motor control system" (Webster, 1993, p. 92). The SMA is crucial for the "planning of self-initiated and internally guided movements rather than ones that are externally signalled and externally guided" (Webster, 1998, p. 224) and is involved in the planning and initiation of new movements, rather than well-learned movement sequences. This makes the SMA of particular interest in stuttering.

Indeed, this third assumption – that stuttering can be understood through the study of other motor functions, particularly bimanual activities – has been the driving force in the development of the Interhemispheric Interference model. The model first appeared, albeit it in a primitive form, in 1985 (Webster, 1985) in response to findings of comparisons of stuttering and control subjects on finger-tapping tasks. Since that time Webster has continued to develop the model through a research programme that has adhered to the scientific principles of theory development. The studies that comprise this research programme have been conducted with the systematic development of hypotheses and the subsequent testing of these hypotheses. Interestingly, all these studies have been of sequential finger and hand movements, and the influence of other activities on those movements (Forster & Webster, 1991, 2001; Webster, 1986a, 1986b, 1987, 1988, 1989a, 1989b, 1990a, 1990b,

1991). This has involved the comparison of stuttering subjects and controls. The studies have typically had substantial numbers of subjects, with at least 16 subjects in each group in each study and as many as 24 (see Forster & Webster, 2001).

A variety of tasks has been used to explore the concept of interhemispheric interference that is the cornerstone of the model, such as index finger tapping, sequential finger tapping, bimanual writing, key pressing, knob turning, pedal pressing, and crank handle turning. Webster (1998) described the use of concomitant tasks as analogous to the "old parlour game of rubbing one's stomach and patting one's head at the same time" (p. 223). Interestingly, none of the studies conducted so far by Webster and colleague Forster has involved speaking (see Webster, 1993) and none has been conducted with children.

Excellent overviews of the research programme and the implications of the findings for the model are given in Webster (1993) and Webster (1998). In summary, these studies have yielded the following conclusions:

- There are no differences between stuttering and control subjects on finger-tapping tasks.
- However, stutterers perform more poorly on right-handed manual tasks when performing competing tasks with the left hand.
- Stutterers are slower to initiate responses and make more errors when tasks involve the learning of new sequences.
- The bimanual coordination deficit in stutterers is kinaesthetically based.
- The poorer performance of stutterers on manual tasks is not due to time pressure.
- Recovered stutterers perform similarly to nonstutterers in terms of motor control.

Testability

The model has internal logic. The two factors proposed in the model are together necessary and sufficient for stuttering to occur but neither is sufficient for stuttering to occur. This means that stuttering should always occur when both factors are present but should not occur when neither or only one of the factors is present.

However, testing the model at the empirical level is not so straightforward, as operational definitions of the two factors are not provided. For example, it is not apparent how it can be determined that the SMA is fragile and susceptible to interference, other than by the presence of stuttering. Of course, with developments in technology some marker of inefficiency of SMA function may emerge in the future.

It would seem, however, that the second factor – labile hemispheric activation – may be operationally defined by way of neural imaging. For example, Webster has cited numerous research findings indicating that stutterers do not have the normal clear tendency for left-sided activation. However, since patterns of activation tend to normalize under conditions where stutterers are not stuttering, such as after successful treatment and when reading in chorus, it is not clear if this aberrant activation is a cause or a result of stuttering. Webster has acknowledged this conundrum (see below).

The programme of research conducted by Webster and colleague Forster has provided extensive support for the model. In this programme of research, predictions arising from the model have been identified, and hypotheses arising from these predictions have been proposed and then tested. In this regard, it could be considered an exemplar of how theory can drive research.

However, identifying a way to falsify the model remains problematic. To falsify the model it is necessary to determine that (1) stuttering is present in the absence of one or both of the factors, or (2) stuttering is absent in the presence of both factors. It is not apparent how that might be done, even with a thought experiment.

Explanatory power

Topography

The model provides a general explanation of why people stutter. According to the model, stuttering is the behavioural manifestation of a deficit or inefficiency in initiating movement sequences. This difficulty in initiating the movements for speech is inferred from the poorer performance on manual tasks observed in stutterers. As stated by Webster (1993), "The difficulties encountered by people who stutter on various kinds of manual performance tasks parallel those they encounter in speech" (p. 93). Further, the problem stutterers have with finger-tapping tasks is, "the planning, organization, and initiation of new response sequences, not the execution of well practiced ones" (p. 116).

However, the model does not explain why stuttering takes the form of repeated movements and fixed postures of the speech mechanism. According to Webster (1998), it remains to be explained "how the hypothesized interference susceptibility of the SMA become(s) translated into the speech repetitions, hesitations, and blockages and the sense of impending loss of speech control [Perkins, 1985] that characterize stuttering" (p. 224). The model does not explain, for example, why this difficulty in initiation does not simply result in slower initiation times, as was observed in the manual tasks of the research subjects. There were no reports in the studies, for example, of repeated movements or fixed postures of the hands or fingers on the tasks argued to parallel speech.

Natural recovery

The model attributes natural recovery from stuttering to changes in the first factor in the model; that is, recovery from stuttering is due to maturation of the speech motor control system, particularly the SMA. This hypothesis was addressed by Forster and Webster (2001). In this study, nonstutterers and recovered stutterers performed similarly, and better than stutterers, on bimanual tasks. The two groups (persistent and recovered) performed equally poorly, however, on visual half-field tasks, suggesting that the recovered stutterers still had aberrant hemispheric activation.

Variability

The model explains natural variability in stuttering severity in terms of the amount of interference from the nondominant to the dominant hemisphere. According to Webster (1993), "The degree of baseline dysfluency in an individual reflects the nature of the structural weakness of the SMA. By contrast, the variability that rides on top of that baseline dysfluency reflects the operation of factors that affect right hemisphere activation" (pp. 99–100).

Parsimony

The model is parsimonious, in that it proposes two factors only that are together necessary and sufficient for stuttering to occur. Further, the explanatory power of the model is accounted for by these two factors.

Heuristic value

Webster highlights the heuristic value of the model in promoting understanding of why behavioural treatments that incorporate fluency-shaping procedures work (see Webster, 1997). These treatments typically incorporate a technique such as prolonged speech for controlling stuttering, along with procedures for reducing negative emotions. According to the model, these two components of treatment address – broadly speaking – the two factors of the model. Webster suggests that the fluency techniques simplify speech production, "bringing it within the capability of the inefficient speech motor control system" (Webster, 1998, p. 227). The emphasis on speech motor control that is a consequence of adopting a novel speech pattern also focuses attention on the activity of the fragile SMA, rendering it less susceptible to disruption from competing neural activity. According to Webster (1993), "Successful treatment in adults has its effects by compensating for the fragility, not by reversing or correcting the underlying problem" (p. 101). Consequently, the control over stuttering afforded by the fluency techniques will be lost when the techniques are no longer applied.

The main objective of the second component of these behavioural treatments is to help people "modify their self-talk" (Webster, 1998, p. 227) in order to reduce speech-related anxiety. The aim of reducing anxiety and avoidance behaviours is "to reduce right hemisphere activation and hence reduce and/or control a source of interference with the speech motor control system" (Webster, 1998, p. 227).

The model, then, explains the findings of recent imaging research showing aberrant patterns of activation in the brains of people who stutter, in particular overactivation of the SMA and lack of hemispheric asymmetry (see Webster, 1998), and consequently the normalizing effects on brain activity of fluency-shaping treatments, as reported for example by Boberg, Yeudall, Schopflocker, and Bo-Lassen (1983). However, there is a dilemma in trying to interpret these changes in brain activity:

> Does a particular change in brain activation reflect a direct effect of treatment on the brain which in turn results in greater fluency, or does it reflect a consequence on the brain of improved fluency and reduced struggle and apprehension?
>
> (Webster, 1998, p. 227)

Webster (1998) goes some way to explaining this dilemma: "not only is brain activity the origin of behavior, thought, and feelings, but behavior, thought, and feelings are themselves in part the origin of brain activity" (p. 227).

The heuristic value of the model for people who stutter is also highlighted by Webster (1998). Although there is a strong possibility of a neurological basis in stuttering, the model – when explained in the context of therapy – suggests that stuttering is not immutable. It also helps therapy participants to understand how to deal with relapse, as it provides a rationale for focusing attention on the procedures necessary to restore fluency. The following suggests a perspective on the interplay between treatment and the aberrant brain activity in stuttering, from a person who stutters: "when we control our brains, we are bringing an appropriate balance to the interhemispheric relations within them, a balance that enhances fluency and facilitates communication" (Webster, 1997, p. 134).

The model has prompted little discussion in the stuttering literature. This is unexplainable, given the clarity with which the model is presented and the extraordinarily rigorous programme of research supporting it. However, the chapter published in 1993 (Webster, 1993) is a report of a conference presentation and it includes discussion among conference participants. There was considerable interest in the model and it was well accepted. The model can be considered fruitful, however, in that it has continued to support Webster's extensive programme of research.

Chapter 7

Theories of stuttering: Systems control modelling

This chapter reviews three theories in which stuttering is modelled, to a greater or lesser extent, on systems control theory.

SENSORY-MOTOR MODELLING THEORY

This theory was developed by Megan Neilson and colleagues (Andrews et al., 1983; Neilson & Neilson, 1985, 1987, 2000; Neilson, Neilson, & O'Dwyer, 1992). We refer to it as the sensory-motor modelling theory because the author and colleagues have called it that (see Andrews et al., 1983). However, at other times it has been referred to it as a "theoretical position" (Andrews et al., 1983), a "hypothesis" (Andrews et al., 1983; Neilson & Neilson, 1987), and a "framework" (Neilson & Neilson, 2000; Neilson, et al., 1992).

The theory states, "Stutterers are deficient in the neuronal processing resources responsible for determining and adaptively maintaining the auditory-motor relationships which subserve speech production" (Neilson & Neilson, 1987, p. 332). The theory, then, proposes a constitutional condition that explains, in general terms, why people stutter. This deficit in neural processing is necessary for stuttering to occur. However, it is not sufficient for stuttering to occur, as it is postulated that some children who have the deficit will never stutter because they have sufficient resources, such as high intelligence, to compensate for it. Whether one becomes a stutterer depends on one's "neurological capacity for [these] sensory-to-motor and motor-to-sensory transformations and the demand posed by the speech act" (Andrews et al., 1983, p. 239).

The following summarizes this theory:

> Due to inadequate central capacity, stutterers have a diminished ability to evaluate the relationship between efferent activity and the associated reafferent activity produced during speech. As a consequence, the

stutterer must either spend longer in evaluating this relationship or must utilise additional capacity at the expense of other functions.

(Neilson & Neilson, 1985, p. 76)

Reducing the argument to a lower physiological level, Andrews et al. (1983) suggest that this underlying deficit in capacity may be due to an inherited pattern of cerebral organization, such as increased involvement of the right hemisphere during speech production. The model is unifactorial, in that it posits a single factor as the cause of stuttering. However, Neilson and colleagues note throughout their writings that other factors impact on stuttering severity.

Background and development

The theory emerged from Neilson's interest in cybernetic approaches to speech. This approach was developed primarily by Fairbanks (Fairbanks, 1954) and this model of speech production emphasized the contribution of auditory, tactile, and proprioceptive feedback to accurate speech production. The application of this idea to stuttering emerged with an interest in delayed auditory feedback (DAF) and the hypothesis that stuttering is an oscillation in the auditory feedback loop. It was later argued, however, that the disruptions to fluency that occur in normally fluent speakers when speaking with DAF do not imply that stutterers have disturbed auditory feedback during speech (Lane & Tranel, 1971).

Thus, Neilson and colleagues' research programme in this area began "at a time when stuttering was widely held to be the manifestation of an instability in a servomechanism system hypothesized to control speech production" (Neilson & Neilson, 1985, p. 70). The driving force in this research programme was what Marx described as true modelling (see Chapter 2), in that Neilson and colleagues applied a systems analysis approach as a model for understanding speech motor control, and then offered an explanation from this modelling as to how a breakdown in speech motor control might cause stuttering.

Neilson's programme of research involved a variety of tracking tasks, comparing groups of adults who stutter with groups of normally fluent control subjects. Input (independent) variables included pitch and intensity of a tone, and a visual stimulus, and output modes involved jaw and hand tracking. In explaining their use of tracking tasks, Neilson and Neilson (1985) give the example of how visual-motor tracking tasks had been used to establish the control capabilities of airline pilots. The equivalent of that for the control of speech is the auditory-motor tracking task.

The findings of the research programme are described in the various publications in which the theory is presented. For example, Neilson and Neilson (1985, 1987) reported that the stutterers performed comparably to the control subjects on visual tracking tasks but not as well as the controls on the auditory tracking tasks. According to Neilson and Neilson (1985), "Stutterers track a changing auditory stimulus with significant greater time delay than nonstutterers" (p. 74). Stutterers were also reported to demonstrate increased incoherent response power, or "noise" (Neilson & Neilson, 1987, p. 331). Consequently, it is hypothesized that stutterers have diminished ability "to evaluate adequately the relationship between the changes heard in the response tone and the motor activity which generated those changes" (Neilson & Neilson, 1985, p. 76). These findings and those of other studies related to motor control in general, then, led to the development of the sensory-motor modelling theory.

Neilson and Neilson (1987) argue that speech production is simply a special case of skilled sensory-motor performance and is under hybrid adaptive control, or adaptive feedback control. In this sense, feedback:

> is used intermittently to check that the characteristics of the controlled system are unchanged. If this is not the case, the feedback will be used to compute the new characteristics of the controlled system. An inverse model of those characteristics can then be employed to transform a required output signal into the appropriate input signal (p. 326).

The central nervous system monitors outgoing commands and compares them with their resulting sensory consequences. This is the adaptive internal model of sensory-motor relationships. Any discrepancy leads to automatic recalibration of the inverse internal model. The computational theory of this neuronal processing is known as adaptive model theory (see Neilson et al., 1992).

Drawing on this, Neilson and colleagues argue that speech motor activity is mapped in terms of its sensory consequences, and draw a parallel between auditory-motor tracking as investigated in the experiments and auditory control of speech, i.e., the integration of auditory and kinaesthetic signals. According to Neilson et al. (1992, p. 538):

> The task of speech requires the modelling of the relationship between the respiratory, laryngeal, and supralaryngeal activity and the concomitant auditory feedback of the speech signal produced by that activity.

The inverse internal model transforms desired acoustic speech output into appropriate motor commands and activates speech muscles, which then generate a motor response that will match the desired acoustic signal.

Testability

The theory is logical, and has internal consistency. It is falsifiable, at least at the logical level, because stuttering should not be present in individuals who do not have the deficit in neural processing. The theory would be proven false if stuttering were found to be present in such an individual. However, it is not falsifiable at the empirical level, at least not directly, because the postulates are constructs, not entities that can be operationalized and explored experimentally. One could not, for example, manipulate "inverse sensory-motor models" or "inadequate central capacity" or "the auditory-motor relationships which subserve speech" in order to determine whether they are causally related to stuttering. However, further data may emerge in the future to support the theory.

Explanatory power

Neilson and colleagues discuss at length how the theory can explain the various phenomena of stuttering.

Topography

The topography of stuttering is not explained in detail but it is suggested that inappropriate internal models might be used in sensory-to-motor transformations, or vice versa, and this may explain the actual behaviours of stuttering. It is suggested that other characteristics (presumably the equivalent of fixed postures and superfluous behaviours) are probably acquired through instrumental learning.

Onset and development

The timing of the onset of stuttering – that is, in early childhood after a period of apparently normal speech development – is explained as due to the fact that at this stage of development an "explosive growth in language ability outstrips a still immature speech motor apparatus" (Andrews et al., 1983, p. 239).

Natural recovery

It is proposed in this theory that some children recover naturally from stuttering because higher intelligence might well allow some predisposed children to compensate for the deficit in neural capacity; in which case they may either "never stutter or recover quickly" (Andrews et al., 1983, p. 239).

Genetics

According to this theory, the sex ratio in stuttering may be accounted for by stuttering being inherited with "sex limitations" (Andrews et al., 1983, p. 239), and also because females process linguistic material in both hemispheres.

Variability

According to Andrews et al. (1983) variation in severity of stuttering across individuals is difficult to explain because it is "independent of family history, therefore not associated with the postulated deficit in central capacity for efferent–reafferent modelling" (p. 239). Frequent stuttering, however, may be self-perpetuating because the sensory-motor model is constantly being updated in light of the prevailing sensory feedback (Andrews et al., 1983).

The natural variability of stuttering within individuals is explained as a function of linguistic demands or the competition of other tasks "for relevant resources" (Neilson & Neilson, 1987, p. 331). Stuttering increases in conditions "in which the speech motor control task is more difficult, for example the first word in a sentence" (Andrews et al., 1983, p. 239). It has been suggested that a feedback theory such as this cannot account for stuttering at the start of an utterance, prior to the occurrence of feedback. However, Neilson and Neilson (1985) argued that this may be accounted for by a delay in updating the sensory-motor model. There is an implication that stuttering may get worse under stress because stress impairs performance on tracking tasks generally, due to reduction in the "central capacity allocated to the task" (Neilson & Neilson, 1985, p. 75).

According to the theory, stuttering reduces in the fluency-inducing conditions because they all involve simplifying and/or slowing the speech process. It is suggested that slowing down allows more time for "the update of the underlying sensory-motor model" (Andrews et al., 1983, p. 239). The adaptation effect, in which stuttering reduces over repeated readings, is said to be attributable to simplification of the control task, which in turn is due to the reduced need for modification of the internal model. Response-contingent stimulation reduces stuttering because it encourages the speaker to "devote more resources to speech production" (Neilson & Neilson, 1985, p. 76). Auditory masking (an altered feedback condition) is thought to reduce stuttering because sensory-motor integration processes have "less than normal load because no auditory feedback is available to be processed" (p. 76), and whispering and lipped speech simplify speech production because there is no voicing. In overviewing the amelioration of stuttering that occurs under these conditions, Neilson and Neilson (1987) state: "Fluency will be possible only when the demands on limited resources do not exceed the supply" (p. 331).

Parsimony

The theory is parsimonious, because it has one construct and considerable explanatory power (see above).

Heuristic value

This is a particularly interesting theory as it is relies on the classic application of modelling to gain insights into stuttering. The application of systems control theory brings about new understanding of speech motor control and how that control might break down in stuttering (see Neilson et al., 1992). However, as stated above, it is not apparent how the theory can be tested. Thus, while modelling stuttering on systems control theory is an interesting idea, it appears that it is not possible to determine the appropriateness of the analogy.

Two reports of the model (Andrews et al., 1983; Neilson & Neilson, 1985) were followed by invited discussion. Two of the commentaries on the 1983 report (Kent, 1983; Wingate, 1983) were somewhat critical of the theory, suggesting that it was not elaborated sufficiently, that terms such as "additional cortical capacity" and "general mathematical operator" are not definitive, that the explicanda are only loosely related to the theory and can be accounted for just as satisfactorily with other theoretical positions, and that fluency-enhancing conditions and treatments that invoke speech pattern changes do not necessarily decrease the complexity of the speaking task. However, the theory is still current (see Neilson & Neilson, 2000).

As far as we are aware, the theory has not been fruitful in terms of generating new lines of research. This is probably because, as stated, the theory is not couched in operational terms. Interestingly, the sensory-motor modelling theory is sometimes referred to (for example see Adams, 1990) as the progenitor of the demands and capacities model, which is discussed in a later chapter. The opposite has also been suggested; namely, that the development of the theory was influenced by the demands and capacities model (see Curlee, 2000). However, the use of similar terminology (both refer to demands and capacities) and the fact that both contain the concept that certain factors place demands on the speech system is where the similarity ends. The sensory-motor modelling theory specifies quite clearly that stutterers have a deficit in capacity, while the demands and capacities model states quite clearly that this is not a necessary condition for stuttering to occur.

The theory proposes that environmental influences have a role in stuttering when an imbalance occurs with "especially fast-talking or slow-talking parents" (Andrews et al., 1983, p. 239). The theory also proposes that:

> Slower voice onset times, poorer performance on tests of central auditory function, delayed speech development, prevalence of articulation errors, and slower auditory response times for discrete and continuous stimuli could all be expressions of this deficit in central processing capacity.
>
> (Andrews et al., 1983, p. 239).

The theory provides some insights into the effectiveness of treatments that rely on speech retraining; namely, those that induce fluency with a novel speech pattern. It is suggested that they may be effective because the speech task is simplified. Treatment allows extensive practice in controlling speech "in terms of its sensory consequences . . . with a progressively normalized sensory-motor model".

(Andrews et al., 1983, p. 240)

THE NEUROSCIENCE MODEL

The neuroscience model (Nudelman, Herbrich, Hess, Hoyt, & Rosenfield, 1992; Nudelman, Herbrich, Hoyt, & Rosenfield, 1989; Rosenfield & Nudelman, 1987; Rosenfield, Viswanath, Callis-Landrum, DiDanato, & Nudelman, 1991) proposes that stuttering is caused by instability in speech motor control. Specifically,

a stuttered event is viewed as consisting of two components: (1) a momentary instability (in the control theory sense) in the speech motor control system and (2) the system's response (including its corrections) to this instability.

(Nudelman et al., 1992, p. 1883)

According to the neuroscience model, the instability of the speech control system that leads to stuttering depends on the interaction of two nested functional loops:

an outer cognitive loop that provides the reasoning behind and choice of the words being said and an inner production loop that programs and monitors the sounds being made.

(Nudelman et al., 1992, p. 1883)

According to the neuroscience model, the function of the outer "cognitive" loop relevant to stuttering is not concerned with ideation and lexical retrieval, but rather it "decides and monitors which sounds are to be produced" (Nudelman et al., 1992, p. 1887). The speech system becomes unstable when the phase lag of the outer loop equals the phase margin of the inner loop.

According to the neuroscience model there are two possible reasons why the speech systems of people who stutter are more likely to become unstable than those of normally fluent speakers: more processing time may be needed by the outer loop, and/or phase margins in the inner loop may be smaller. The phase margin is, in effect, the margin of error.

In lay terms, then, the neuroscience model says that stuttering occurs when there is a mismatch between the selection and programming of speech sounds and the production of these sounds. It is a causal theory in that it states the necessary and sufficient conditions for stuttering to occur. It proposes one constitutional factor as causing stuttering.

Background and development

The model draws on a reductionist or "top-down" (Nudelman et al., 1989, p. 401) model of motor control, which is described in terms of "functional control loops" (Nudelman et al., 1989, p. 402). Functional loops, as opposed to anatomical loops, perform various functions critical to stages underpinning observed behaviour. As far as speech motor control is concerned, functional loops underpin the four stages of speech production: ideation, linguistic programming, motor programming, and motor output. They presumably involve the "temporally overlapping, parallel execution of the stages with feedback" (Nudelman et al., 1989, p. 403). Functional control loops perform functions that hypothetically must be accomplished before the desired motor behaviour occurs. These loops are not observable, and they cannot be defined uniquely. Nudelman et al. (1989) stress that it is not known precisely how the components of the various loops contribute to behaviour. Loops should be lumped together, according to the behaviour under observation (Nudelman et al., 1989).

The neuroscience model has developed from research involving a series of vocal tracking tasks (see Nudelman et al., 1989, 1992). This has involved adults who stutter and control subjects tracking computer-generated frequency-modulated sound waves by humming. The stutterers responded as quickly as the control subjects to changes in frequency, but needed more time for processing the change in tracking frequency (see Nudelman et al., 1992). The stutterers were more variable in terms of phase shift and so, it was concluded, were more likely to develop momentary instabilities (Nudelman et al., 1989)

Testability

The model has logical consistency, in that it states the necessary and sufficient conditions for stuttering to occur. However, the terms of the model are not operational. As stated by the authors, functional loops are constructs, and so are not definable. Thus, as the model is presently stated, the presence of a momentary instability in the speech motor system can only be inferred from the occurrence of stuttering. This means that the model is not falsifiable. Of course, if the neuroscience model is viewed from the classical modelling perspective it can be argued that the analogy of functional loops simply provides a useful way of understanding stuttering and a guide for research, and so it is not necessary to disprove the model. Observation and research will ultimately indicate whether modelling stuttering on systems control theory in this way is sufficiently useful to yield further explanatory power.

Explanatory power

The explanatory power of the model is not discussed extensively.

Topography

The neuroscience model explicitly explains the occurrence of each stuttering event. It states that stuttering occurs when there is mistiming in the inter-action of the outer and inner loops underpinning speech production. How-ever, while the stuttering event is said to be the individual's response to a momentary instability in the speech motor system, topography *per se* is not explained.

Variability

According to the neuroscience model, the parameters of these functional loops fluctuate widely and continuously; consequently mistiming occurs intermittently. This explains the natural variability of stuttering within individuals; namely, why people do not stutter on every word or syllable, and why stuttering varies over time. Factors that may influence processing time in the outer loop may be psychological, linguistic, or sociologic (Nudelman et al., 1989). Factors in the inner loop that can increase the risk of breakdown are a function of "motor context" (1989, p. 411), namely the position and tension of articulators and the complexity of articulatory movements.

The neuroscience model also addresses certain aspects of induced fluency. According to Nudelman and colleagues, the model predicts that fluency can be enhanced in two ways. First, fluency will be enhanced by increasing the phase margin in the outer loop. This can be done directly by "making a therapeutic strategy automatic" (Nudelman et al., 1989, p. 425), and indirectly by the person adopting a speech pattern that "slows, rounds, or smoothly shapes the movements" (Nudelman et al., 1989, p. 435). Second, fluency will be enhanced by decreasing the amount of processing time required by the inner loop, for example by practice (Nudelman et al., 1989). According to Nudelman et al. (1989), these are the sorts of strategies used by speech-language pathologists in fluency-shaping treatments.

Parsimony

The model is parsimonious, in that it offers one explanation for the phenomena of stuttering.

Heuristic value

Like the sensory-motor modelling theory, stuttering in the neuroscience model is modelled according to system control theory. This brings a new perspective to stuttering, suggesting a mechanism that might underlie it. However, the heuristic value of the neuroscience model is limited somewhat by the fact that much of the writing about it uses control theory terminology. Nonetheless, the authors have attempted to explain why treatment works in terms of the model (see above). As far as we know, the model has not been fruitful in terms of generating research, although it has been referred to in the recent literature. Foundas et al. (2001) suggested that their findings of structural abnormalities in the brains of adults who stutter lend support to the neuroscience model. They suggested that the anomalies they identified, which were in the perisylvian speech-language areas, could cause stuttering by reducing the efficiency of neural processing in the outer loop referred to in the neuroscience model. This suggestion is endorsed by one of the authors of the model (see Rosenfield, 2001).

THE VARIABILITY MODEL (VMODEL)

The variability model (Vmodel) (Packman et al., 2000b; Packman et al., 1996) states that stuttering results from the task demands of oral language on an unstable speech motor system. The nature of this instability is not stated. Rather, the Vmodel assumes that there is some impairment or inefficiency in the speech motor systems of people who stutter that renders the systems unstable and so more prone to perturbation. The linguistic task demands referred to in the model are the motoric variability that is required to convey the linguistic features of spoken language. In particular, these demands arise from variation in syllabic stress (changes in emphasis from syllable to syllable). The Vmodel is a causal model. An unstable speech system is sufficient for the onset of stuttering and is necessary and sufficient for persistent stuttering.

It needs to be said that variable linguistic stress is not, in itself, a necessary or even a sufficient condition for stuttering to occur. It is a feature of normal spoken language and most people do not stutter when using it. Variable stress may be seen, then, as a trigger for stuttering in those who have an unstable speech system. It is an INUS condition (see Chapter 1) for individual moments of stuttering: An insufficient but necessary condition in an unnecessary but sufficient scenario for a stuttering moment to occur.

The Vmodel does not draw on systems control modelling to the same extent as the other two models in this chapter. Nonetheless, it is included here because stuttering is conceptualized as the response of an unstable speech system to perturbing influences. It is also a model rather than a theory or a hypothesis, in that it aims to simplify the relationships between critical variables and is depicted in publications with boxes and arrows, as described in Chapter 2.

Background and development

The Vmodel developed from attempts to explain findings in children and adults with persistent stuttering of reductions in variation in vowel duration associated with prolonged speech. Prolonged speech is a slow drawling way of speaking that is known to reduce or even eliminate stuttering. This speech pattern, or variants of it, is used to instate fluent speech in many current speech-restructuring treatments for stuttering (see Packman et al., 2000b). The slow drawling pattern is then shaped to the most natural-sounding speech that participants can achieve.

A study by Onslow, van Doorn, and Newman (1992) had shown a reduction in variation in vowel duration in school-age children after they had participated in a prolonged-speech treatment programme. Acoustic analysis indicated that the distribution of vowel duration was decreased after treatment in these children. Using single-subject laboratory experiments, Packman, Onslow, and van Doorn (1994) had three subjects imitate a very slow and exaggerated form of prolonged speech and then instructed them to try to stop stuttering by using whatever features of the speech pattern they needed. This design eliminated the need for the programmed instruction that is used to shape the slow exaggerated form of prolonged speech in treatment programmes. Programmed instruction may in itself instate a reduction in variability and force the speaker to use all features of prolonged speech, regardless of whether they contribute to stuttering reduction. Thus, it was argued, with this methodology the subjects in the Packman et al. (1994) study were more likely to only use those features of prolonged speech that they needed to control their stuttering.

All subjects virtually eliminated stuttering in this prolonged-speech condition, using quite natural-sounding speech. Acoustic analysis indicated a concomitant reduction in variation of vowel duration, similar to that found by Onslow et al. (1992). This reduction was apparent in the distribution of vowel duration, which was contracted compared to the distribution in the control condition.

It was inferred from this that there was a causal relationship in these two studies between reduction in variation in vowel duration and reduction in stuttering. To attempt to explain the findings, Packman et al. (1996) formulated the Vmodel, taking into consideration the known association between vowel duration and linguistic stress. In other words, it was argued that the reductions in variability of vowel duration detected in the acoustic speech signal reflected reductions in variation in stress at the linguistic level. Making syllables more evenly stressed reduces stuttering by reducing motoric demands on the speech system. In other words, making syllables more evenly stressed reduces the variation in effort from syllable to syllable that normal stress demands – at least, in adult patterns of speech.

A prediction of the Vmodel (see Packman et al., 1996) was that rhythmic speech, which is another novel speech pattern that reduces and eliminates stuttering and which has also been used, historically, in the treatment of stuttering (see Packman et al., 2000b), also invokes reduced linguistic stress. This prediction was supported in a subsequent study (Packman et al., 1997) of syllable-timed speech (a form of rhythmic speech). Packman et al. (1997) showed that stuttering was eliminated or almost eliminated when 10 subjects used syllable-timed speech, and that this reduction was accompanied by a reduction in variation of vowel duration. This reduction in variation occurred independent of speaking more slowly, which is an inherent part of the prolonged-speech pattern. The fact that variation of vowel duration also reduced in the 10 control subjects when they spoke in syllable-timed speech suggested that it was indeed a feature of the rhythmic speech pattern. If the effect had occurred only in the stuttering subjects, it could be seen as the result of the reduction in stuttering rather than a possible critical component in the speech pattern.

According to the Vmodel, then, stuttering reduces in both prolonged speech and rhythmic speech because these speech patterns require less motoric variability, and so reduce the demands on the speech motor system. In other words, the reduction in stress contrasts at the linguistic level translates, downstream, to reduced task demands at the motoric level. The fact that this reduction in task demands reduces stuttering assumes that stutterers already have some impairment or inefficiency in speech/language processing that renders the speech motor system unstable, and so prone to destabilization.

Of course, the findings from these experiments on prolonged speech and rhythmic speech do not confirm the Vmodel. The reductions in variations in stress and in stuttering in both speech patterns could in fact be due to the influence of some other variable. However, the findings were considered supportive.

In developing the Vmodel, then, Packman et al. (1996) reasoned that if reducing variation in syllabic stress reduces stuttering, then this variation might in fact induce stuttering in the first place. According to the model, children with a compromised speech motor system will start to stutter when they reach that stage in language development where they start to use varying linguistic stress.

Testability

The arguments of the model are logical and at least one of the terms in the model can be defined operationally. Variable syllabic stress can be measured and operationalized. However, defining the necessary condition is not straightforward. The unstable speech system that is hypothesized to be the necessary condition for stuttering to occur cannot be operationalized, at least at the present time. There are many research findings to suggest that there is some deficit or inefficiency of the speech motor system, but the nature of this deficit or inefficiency has yet to be identified. Nonetheless, the model is falsifiable. It would be shown to be false if stuttering did not reduce when the variability of syllabic stress reduced. Packman et al. (1996) say that it is not yet clear whether there is a linear relationship between variability and stuttering. It may be the case, they argue, that variability must reduce below a certain threshold before stuttering severity is affected. Nonetheless, the statement on falsifiability holds. If variability were to reduce to the extent, say, that it reduces in rhythmic speech (see above), and stuttering did not reduce, then the model would be falsified.

Explanatory power

Topography

The model explains the topography of stuttering and why children stutter under the disrupting influence of the development of variable syllabic stress. The syllable repetitions that are the typical signs of stuttering at onset are attempts by the child to restore stability to the speech system. The repeating of a syllable actually reduces variability of stress. Speech production during these repeated syllables, then, is similar to utterances at an earlier stage of speech development, before the onset of stuttering, when syllables were more evenly stressed (see below). After a few repetitions, the speech system is sufficiently stable to allow the child to continue speaking. It is proposed that children develop fixed postures and struggle behaviour in an attempt *not* to repeat syllables. According to the Vmodel, stuttering tends to occur at moments of high variability and the repetitions reflect the difficulty the child is having in moving from a stressed syllable to an unstressed syllable or vice versa.

Onset and development

The Vmodel has much to say about onset and development. In particular the model explains why stuttering starts after a period of apparently normal speech development. According to the model, stuttering first appears in small children at that stage in language development when the child starts to produce syllabic stress contrasts: "Children do not stutter when they babble, they do not stutter on single words, but they do start to stutter at around the time they start to use variable syllabic stress" (Packman et al., 1996, p. 245). Packman et al. (1996) describe how learning to stress syllables differentially involves learning to de-stress, which occurs at around 18 months to 2 years.

Packman et al. (1996) drew on various findings to argue that this developmental stage is difficult for many children, and that this may also explain the preponderance of so-called normal disfluencies in children at around this stage and the considerable perceptual overlap between stuttering and normal disfluency. They concluded (1996, p. 245):

> We suggest that the ability to produce syllabic stress contrasts is like a milestone. In time, the speech systems of "normal" children accommodate the requirements of adult stress patterns. These children pass the milestone and go on to develop normal fluency. The speech systems of stuttering children, however, continue to be disrupted by the production of stress contrasts. Without intervention, these children may never learn to cope with the demands of adult prosody.

This suggests that children with normally developing speech motor systems may also stutter, albeit transiently, at this stage of linguistic development.

The Vmodel, then, links the onset of stuttering to a stage of language development rather than to age. While language development is critical to the onset of stuttering, it is not necessary for the child to have any deficit in linguistic capacity or performance. This explains why a considerable amount of research has failed to find that children who stutter differ from normally fluent children in terms of language development. According to Packman et al. (1996, p. 250):

> The Vmodel does not suggest that there are any *differences* in this regard between stuttering and non-stuttering children; it proposes only that the speech systems of children predisposed to stutter are unusually *disrupted* at a certain stage of linguistic development. [italics are in the original]

And:

> In susceptible children, stuttering will emerge at a critical stage of language development, regardless of whether the child's development is normal, advanced, or delayed.

Natural recovery

The Vmodel offers a possible explanation for natural recovery in young children. As stated above, many children may display speech disruptions that are identified as stuttering as they reach the stage of adjusting speech motor control to cope with the demands of varying stress. However, these disappear as the children pass this milestone in speech development. Packman et al.

(1996), however, state that natural recovery may be influenced by other factors.

Genetics

The authors of the Vmodel do not address the genetics of stuttering.

Variability

The Vmodel addresses natural variability of stuttering only briefly. Packman et al. (1996) suggest that increased physiological arousal, such as may occur at times of excitement or anxiety, may decrease the threshold at which the speech system becomes perturbed. Thus, stuttering is more likely to occur at such times. They conclude (p. 241):

> Stuttering is triggered by the variability inherent in the production of syllabic stress, but in everyday speaking situations the threshold for that triggering is likely to be influenced by emotional and cognitive factors.

The Vmodel, however, has more to say on induced variability; namely on the reductions in stuttering that occur in certain speaking conditions. Indeed, the model was developed primarily to attempt to explain the ameliorative effects on stuttering of prolonged speech. A detailed exposition of this is given by Packman et al. (2000b) who discuss at length the use of these speech patterns in behavioural treatments for stuttering. They point out that rhythmic speech appears to be the most powerful of the fluency-enhancing conditions, and that it is associated with a substantial decrease in variation in vowel duration. In other words, these two fluency-enhancing conditions reduce stuttering because they reduce the demands on the motor system of variable stress.

Packman et al. (1996) suggest that the Vmodel also explains the lower incidence of stuttering in the hearing-impaired population. They say this is due to the well-known fact that the hearing-impaired are less likely, especially in severe cases, to develop adult patterns of variable linguistic stress.

Parsimony

The model is parsimonious in that it provides an overarching explanation for the phenomena of stuttering. Only two factors are proposed for stuttering to occur: an unstable speech system and adequate development and use of oral language; that is, the use of variable linguistic stress.

Heuristic value

The Vmodel has heuristic value. This depends, mainly, on its considerable explanatory power. Apart from this, it also provides a new way of looking at stuttering. As Packman et al. (1996) say, the model places stuttering at the linguistic–motor interface. It explains stuttering as the result of the impact of the normal features of spoken language on speech motor control. The authors acknowledge that they have relied on and incorporated the work of many others in developing the model but suggest that the model "incorporates that work into a parsimonious explanation for much of what is known about stuttering" (p. 257). The proposal in the model that stutterers have an unstable speech system is also quite consistent with many other theories of stuttering. In other words, the unstable speech system could be due to one of a number of the deficits or inefficiencies in the speech system proposed in other theories, including a number of those reviewed in this text.

Packman et al. (1996) discussed a number of new areas for research opened up by the Vmodel. Packman et al. (1997) indeed confirmed a prediction of the model that rhythmic speech invokes reduced variability, just as prolonged speech does.

Also, Max and Caruso (1998) discussed their findings in relation to the Vmodel. In their study, eight adults who stuttered showed the adaptation effect; namely, reduction in stuttering over six oral readings of the same material. No significant change in variability of vowel duration was found over the readings, and Max and Caruso concluded that this did not support the Vmodel as an explanation of the adaptation effect. However, this conclusion is incorrect. As discussed earlier, variable syllabic stress is neither necessary nor sufficient for stuttering to occur, but is an INUS condition; that is, a triggering condition. It triggers stuttering under typical speaking conditions. Thus, one cannot predict from the Vmodel that every reduction in stuttering will be accompanied by a reduction in variation in syllabic stress. What can be predicted from the Vmodel is that a reduction in variable syllabic stress will lead to a reduction in stuttering. However, variation in syllabic stress was not an independent variable in the Max and Caruso study.

Apart from this, however, the model has not been particularly fruitful in terms of prompting further research or discussion in the literature. The greatest heuristic value of the Vmodel probably lies in its explanations of and suggestions for treatment for stuttering, in both children and adults. The model developed, as discussed above, as an attempt to explain those behavioural treatments for adults that are based on novel speech patterns. Further, the Vmodel suggests that intervention for stuttering should be direct, and should be implemented soon after onset, before the repetitions of early stuttering become entrenched as a maladaptive response (see Packman et al., 1996). Packman et al. suggested that operant treatments for children are probably effective because of the inherent message to the children that they need to find some way of coping with impaired speech motor control that does not involve stuttering. Operant methods do not impose the complex speech restructuring of prolonged speech, which is probably unnecessary at this young age.

Chapter 8

Theories of stuttering: Cognitive and linguistic processing

This chapter reviews three theories that explain stuttering primarily, although not solely, in terms of cognitive processing.

THE NEUROPSYCHOLINGUISTIC THEORY

According to the neuropsycholinguistic (NPL) theory, stuttering is caused when sounds are not inserted in a timely fashion into syllables during speech production (Perkins, Kent, & Curlee, 1991). Stuttering occurs when articulatory rate "exceeds the rate at which segments can be integrated synchronously into their syllable frames" (p. 748). This condition is attributed to dyssynchrony of the two neural systems that are responsible for this insertion process, namely the symbol system and the signal system. The symbol system is concerned with linguistic processing, while the signal system is responsible for providing syllable frames. For the dyssynchrony between the two systems to cause stuttering it must be due to a delay in the arrival of the syllable frames, which contain the slots into which speech segments are to be inserted. Thus, only one type of dyssynchrony is a necessary condition for stuttering to occur.

There appear to be various possible reasons for this dyssynchrony. According to Perkins et al., 1991, p. 735):

> Because stutterers, for the most part, speak normally most of the time, we do not assume that a pathological condition is required to explain stuttering when it occurs. Conversely, a theory must be capable of explaining a predisposition to stutter as a consequence of heredity or pathology.

Going back even further in the causal chain set up in the theory, this delay in processing in the signal system is said to be due to "self-expressive uncertainty or inefficient neural resources" (Perkins et al., 1991, p. 739). The first of these, self-expressive uncertainty, is said to be due to conflict between striving for dominance and tending towards timidity, where "the urgency to speak out is pitted against not feeling privileged to speak out" (p. 749). According to the NPL theory, "These two opposed inherent tendencies are suspected of being predominant causes of signal-system conflict in stuttering" (p. 738). This is because "signal-system processing . . . is especially vulnerable to cognitive conflicts over dominance as expressed automatically in tone of voice about communicative intentions" (p. 739). As far as the second variable is concerned, according to Perkins et al., "neural resources may be limited by genetic constraints, brain injury, or competition for processing capacity". These are, however, "predisposing, not direct, causes of stuttering" (p. 739) and are not in themselves necessary or sufficient for stuttering to occur, as they can occur "singly or in combination" (p. 742).

In attempting to understand this theory any further, it is necessary at this point to look at how the authors define stuttering. As discussed in Chapter 5, Perkins' definition of stuttering differs radically from traditional definitions, and this is reflected in the NPL theory. According to Perkins et al., "stuttering is disruption of speech experienced by the speaker as loss of control" (1991, p. 734). This experience of loss of control "categorically differentiates stuttered from nonstuttered disfluency, irrespective of how normal or abnormal it sounds" (p. 750). This means that the identification of stuttering can only be made by the speaker. According to Perkins et al., the speaker experiences this lack of control because he or she does not know the cause of the disruption – and the cause of the disruption is unknown because it originates in the signal system, the activities of which are not at a conscious level. Thus, a speech disruption, even if it sounds abnormal, will only be considered to be a stutter if the speaker does not know the cause of the disruption (p. 734). To complicate the definition of stuttering even further, the authors say that stuttering can be described as covert when it involves "anticipation of stuttering that does not result in stuttered disfluency" (p. 734), and stuttering can also occur "irrespective of whether the speaker is considered to be a stutterer or 'normal' " (p. 735). Thus, only those dyssynchronies (as described above) that result in a disfluency that meets the criteria of stuttering can be said to cause it.

Moving forward in the causal chain from the dyssynchronous neural processing, the NPL theory states that "two variables, speech disruption and time pressure, are necessary and together are sufficient to account for stuttered speech" (Perkins et al., 1991, p. 735). According to the authors, time pressure refers to a situation where the person is aware of the speech disruption and attempts to continue speaking, despite feeling out of control (p. 735). In this circumstance, it is known as abnormal time pressure (p. 735). According to Perkins et al. if speakers "press to continue a dyssynchrony-disrupted utterance of unknown cause, the disfluency will be stuttered. If they press to continue disruptions of known cause, the disfluency will be nonstuttered" (p. 739). Thus, the terms "necessary" and "sufficient" as they are used here would appear to refer to the proximal cause of stuttering; namely the necessary and sufficient conditions adjacent to the moment of stuttering. However, in this case time pressure seems to refer simply to a situation where the person attempts to continue talking in the face of stuttering. This seems to be stating the self-evident, as stuttering could not occur if the person did not continue talking. Thus, abnormal time pressure (in the face of a speech disruption) is not a cause of stuttering but is simply a background condition for stuttering to occur. Stuttering cannot occur if the person stops speaking.

We have referred to the dyssynchrony in neural processing as the cause of stuttering in this theory, because it appears to be necessary and sufficient for stuttering to occur, given a particular causal field, or background variables.

In attempting to clarify the arguments of this theory, we have so far described the variables involved in absolute terms. However, that is not an accurate portrayal of the theory. First, the theory states that the dys-synchrony that causes stuttering is due to a delay in signal-system processing. However, this is not always the case, as according to the theory the other neural system, namely the symbol system, may at times also be involved. As stated by Perkins et al., stuttering is due to the combination of abnormal time pressure "and either signal-system disfluency or symbol-system disfluency, or both" (1991, p. 742). The authors refer to stuttering resulting from a delay in linguistic processing (mediated by the symbol system) as "linguistic stutter-ing" (p. 743). This delay can be the result of "segmental processing ineffi-ciency" (p. 743), which, in turn, can result from "interference mechanisms, slowed processing, or ineffective activation of the components that contrib-ute to the final act of speaking" (p. 743). According to the authors, however, disfluencies resulting from delays in the symbol system can only be regarded as stuttering if they are "unrelated to the utterance (and occur) during filled pauses" (p. 744).

The second exception to the theory as stated above refers to the speaker's awareness of the cause of the speech disruption. It was stated above that a disruption is not considered to be stuttered if the speaker knows its cause. However, Perkins et al. also say that stuttering can occur when "some vague awareness of the cause of the disruption is available" (p. 747). As may be apparent to the reader, it is frequently very difficult to identify – and so summarize here – the arguments in this theory.

Background and development

Perkins et al. (1991) provide considerable background information in support of their theory. First, they refer to studies of the identification of stuttering carried out by Perkins and colleagues in support of their contention that the definition of stuttering must include the experience of loss of control by the speaker (for example, see Moore & Perkins, 1990; Perkins, 1990).

Second, Perkins et al. (1991) include lengthy reviews of literature and ideas in five areas they consider relevant to the development of the theory. In *Speech-Language Pathology Background*, they develop their definition of stuttering as incorporating the experience of loss of control. In *Psycholinguistic Background*, they discuss how the cause of stuttering in their theory, namely failure of speech segments to be inserted in syllable frames in a timely manner, developed from a model of speech production proposed by Shattuck-Hufnagel (1979, 1983). In *Evolutionary Background*, they develop their arguments for the presence of two neural systems – the signal system and the symbol system – and for why the signal system is prone to interference from dominance conflict. They develop the evolutionary-based idea that males especially "show signs of struggling for dominance" (p. 738). In *Cognitive Science Background*, they explain their argument that the speaker will be aware of the cause of symbol-system delays but not of signal-system delays. In *Neuroscience Background*, they discuss the idea that speech involves multiple processes in various brain systems and that the various conditions that they propose contribute to the cause of stuttering involve competition for neural resources. The supportive arguments in at least two of these areas attracted criticism after the publication of the theory, and are addressed briefly later, in the Heuristic value section.

Testability

The theory is not amenable to falsification for at least two reasons. The first of these relates to the definition of stuttering adopted in this theory. As discussed previously, regardless of how abnormal a speech disruption sounds, it is only deemed to be a stutter if the speaker reports that it was accompanied by the experience of loss of control. This is a mentalistic construct and so is not amenable to disproof. It is not possible to know if people in fact experience loss of control when they report that they do, or whether there are times when they experience loss of control but do not report it.

Second, even if stuttering were identified objectively, it cannot be separated from the necessary and sufficient conditions that are proposed to cause it. The necessary and sufficient conditions are (1) a dyssynchrony in the two neural systems – and the subsequent speech disruption – and (2) abnormal time pressure. Abnormal time pressure is defined as "the pressure to begin, continue, or accelerate a disrupted utterance *when experiencing loss of control*" (Perkins et al., 1991, p. 735) (our italics). However, experience of loss of control constitutes part of the definition of stuttering. For a causal theory to be testable, the cause must be identified separately from the effect (van Hooft et al., 1995).

On logical grounds, then, the NPL theory would be shown to be false if a stutter occurred in the absence of one of these causal factors. However, it is logically impossible for a stutter to occur in the absence of the experience of loss of control, because if there were no experience of loss of control then the speech disruption of interest could not logically be identified as a stutter. Further, the idea in the NPL theory that stuttering is caused by a dys-synchrony of the signal and symbol systems rests on the integrity of yet another theoretical model, namely the frame/content model of organization of speech production proposed by Shattuck-Hufnagel and developed by others. This model is not falsifiable because the terms in it are not operational.

Perkins et al. (1991) provide 30 hypotheses, which they say arise from and explicate the theory. While Perkins et al. claim that the theory would be weakened if these hypotheses are disproved, there is also an implication that they are not amenable to scientific testing. According to Perkins et al. the hypotheses assume,"the factor under consideration is operating independently without influence of any other factor" (p. 742). Thus,

> The test of each hypothesis is not whether the predicted effect of a par-ticular factor occurs in most instances; the probability is that most instances involve multiple factors that would contaminate the predicted effect. The test is when the improbable instance occurs in which the predicted effect is without contamination (p. 742).

To clarify the nature of the 30 hypotheses provided by Perkins et al., selected examples are presented in Table 8.1. For brevity, the first hypothesis only in each of the six categories of hypotheses is provided. As can be seen, the hypotheses amount to little more than restatements of the postulates of the theory.

Explanatory power

Perkins et al. list a number of features of stuttering that need to be explained by a theory (see *Constraints* (1991, p. 740). However, they do not address all of these in detail.

Topography

The theory does not explain precisely why people stutter. Thus, it does not explain why people repeat syllables or parts of syllables, or why their speech mechanisms adopt fixed postures, in response to the neural dyssynchrony that is said to be the cause of stuttering. Perkins et al. state that stuttering arising from signal-system disfluency only occurs on "syllables or phones within the syllable" (1991, p. 745). The fact that stuttering can consist of the repetition of a multi-syllable or even multi-word unit, while the theory states that stut-tering is caused by a delay in inserting speech segments *within the syllable*, is not explained.

Table 8.1 Selected examples of the hypotheses that Perkins et al. (1991) derive from their NPL theory

Category	Hypothesis
I. General characteristics of disfluency	When articulatory rate exceeds Language, Segmental, Paralinguistic, or Integrator processing rates, integration of these components becomes dyssynchronous, thereby resulting in dysfluency (p. 742).
II. Symbol-system disfluency	The linguistic cause of disfluency that can result in stuttering (depending on time pressure) begins when Language or Segmental System processing delays arrival of segmental content for integration with appropriate slots in available syllable frames (p. 743).
III. Signal-system disfluency	The PP system cause of disfluency begins when integration of suprasegmental input with self-expressive requirements of the vocal signal system delays arrival of syllable frames into which available phonetic segments can be integrated (p. 744).
IV. Time pressure	Acceleration of articulatory rate is a function of time pressure (p. 746).
V. Nonstuttered disfluency	Nonstuttered disfluency occurs when time pressure is normal and the cause of disfluency is relatively available to awareness (p. 747).
VI. Stuttered disfluency	Stuttering occurs when time pressure is abnormal and the speaker is relatively unaware of the cause of the disruption (p. 747).

Onset and development

The theory suggests that the onset of stuttering occurs after a period of apparently normal speech development because a genetic neural processing inefficiency "begins with development of connected-speech discourse" (p. 744) and because social dominance conflict only begins to appear several years after the development of connected speech.

Genetics

According to Perkins et al., stuttering is more common in males because dominance conflict is more common in males.

Variability

The theory offers explanations for natural variability in stuttering. For example, variation in severity across individuals as a function of dominance conflict, which is different in each person; variation in severity within individuals is a function of abnormal time pressure. Low time pressure will be associated with very brief covert disruptions in fluency (see Perkins et al.,

1991, p. 747), which become perceptible stuttering as time pressure and articulation rate, and consequently degree of dyssynchrony, increase. Perkins et al. state that as time pressure increases "easy repetitions will give way to faster repetitions followed by prolongations and hesitations" (p. 747). However, there is no empirical evidence to support this claim.

The theory also states that the rate at which a syllable is repeated (reflecting severity to some degree) is a function of articulation rate. Rate of stuttering is also proposed to be function of the frequency at which "general temporal capabilities are exceeded by the speech-formulation/execution rate under abnormal time pressure" (p. 748). This is purported to be compatible with the demands and capacities model (see Chapter 9).

Stuttering does not occur when speaking alone as there is no dominance conflict in such a situation.

According to the theory, the fluency-inducing effects of various speaking conditions are a function of speaking more slowly because stuttering reduces as speech rate reduces.

Parsimony

The theory is parsimonious in so far as it proposes only one cause of stuttering, namely dyssynchrony in the neural systems that are responsible for the successful and timely insertion of speech segments into their syllable frames. However, parsimony is lost when Perkins et al. (1991) move back the causal chain to suggest reasons for the dyssynchrony. They propose a wide range of factors, drawn from psychology, genetics, and neurosciences, and suggest that these may occur singly or in combination. In some cases these are referred to as predisposing factors and, indeed, none can be considered a distal cause because they are neither necessary nor sufficient for stuttering to occur, and are not removed from the dyssynchrony by necessary steps.

Heuristic value

The idea that stuttering is caused by a dyssynchrony of neural systems is new, and the fact that it draws on an established linguistic processing model gives the theory plausibility. However, we suggest that the NPL theory has little heuristic value, primarily because it is extraordinarily difficult to follow the logic underpinning the theory, at least as it is expressed in the Perkins et al. (1991) article. The article is overly wordy and the reader is frequently left not understanding what has just been read. The fact that so many reasons for the lack of dyssynchrony are proposed also lessens the heuristic value of the theory.

To our knowledge, the NPL theory has not been fruitful in terms of generating research. However, it has prompted discussion in the literature. Two reports have challenged many of the claims and assumptions in the

NPL theory (see Christensen, 1992; Smith, 1992). Smith (1992, p. 808) was particularly critical of the theory, concluding:

> In the final analysis, the neuropsycholinguistic theory of Perkins, Kent, and Curlee is built largely on beliefs and speculations about stuttering and speech production, and thus it cannot serve as a secure foundation for research and clinical practice in the area of stuttering.

On a more positive note, Postma and Kolk (1993) highlighted some similarities between the NPL theory and their own hypothesis – to which we now turn.

THE COVERT REPAIR HYPOTHESIS

Although referred to as a hypothesis by its authors, the covert repair hypothesis (CRH) has many of the elements and characteristics found in fully developed theories. The CRH (Kolk & Postma, 1997; Postma & Kolk, 1993) proposes that stuttering is a response to an excessive number of errors or flaws in the speaker's phonetic plan. The response to these errors or flaws takes the form of covert attempts to correct them. It is not that stutterers have impaired self-monitoring or error-detection abilities, or that the errors they make are different in kind from the phonetic planning errors that normal speakers make. Rather, people who stutter make more errors than nonstutterers do and, consequently, stutterers have more need to make corrections. Thus the sound and syllable repetitions of stuttering are seen as attempts to repair or correct the errors. The repetitions are a response to the detection of an error wherein the sound or syllable is restarted. Restarting supposedly reduces the chances of making further encoding errors. Within this framework, repetitions or restarts are seen as a strategy to repair or reduce encoding errors. As Kolk and Postma (1997) state, "We see stuttering as a 'normal' repair reaction to an abnormal phonetic plan" (p. 193). Kolk and Postma (1997) propose that the repairs stutterers make are phonologic rather than motoric in nature.

According to the CRH, what distinguishes individuals who stutter from those who do not is to be found in the underlying phonological skills of the two groups. Kolk and Postma (1997) hypothesize that phonologic development and phonologic encoding are slower in stutterers than in normal speakers. These phonologic deviations from normal account for the greater number of errors in the stutterer's phonetic plan.

Background and development

This hypothesis of stuttering is based on a psycholinguistic explanation of speech and language production developed by Levelt. Because Levelt's views are too complex to be treated in any detail here, only an outline of those that the authors of the CRH consider significant to the CRH is given.

Levelt (1989) (as cited in Kolk & Postma, 1997) placed emphasis on the internal monitoring of speech, and the consequent detection of errors and the speaker's attempt to correct or repair those errors. In the normal course of speaking, errors are bound to occur and are followed by attempts to repair them. At the moment an error is detected, speech is interrupted; the speaker pauses and typically uses such fillers as "uh" or "um" which Levelt called "editing terms" (Kolk & Postma, 1997), and repair begins after the pause. These self-repairs can be either overt or covert; the covert repairs are of interest here. In order to execute a covert repair, there must be a mechanism available to enable the speaker to detect the error before it is realized in speech production. Indeed, Kolk and Postma (1997) describe the process of "pre-articulatory editing" (p. 183) that allows the speaker to repair the error before it is produced.

Both Postma and Kolk (1993) and Kolk and Postma (1997) present considerable empirical support for the CRH. Kolk and Postma (1997) report research into slow phonologic encoding and into self-repair, done by investigators other than themselves. In one study, adult stutterers learned a short list of word pairs and were then presented with the first word of a pair and asked to say the second word in the pair as quickly as possible. This was, therefore, a reaction time study. The results indicated that subjects were able to produce the second word of a pair more quickly if it had some homogeneous phonologic relationship to the first word in the pair – the same initial consonant, for example. A follow-up reaction time study used two lists of word pairs with stutterers and normal controls. Word pairs in one list had the same initial consonant (C) and pairs in the other list had the same initial consonant and vowel combination (CV). Stutterers performed much better in the CV condition than they did in the C condition; their performance was "negligible" in the C condition (Kolk & Postma, 1997, p. 196). Normal controls did well in the C condition and even better in the CV condition. Kolk and Postma offer the findings of these two studies as support for their belief that stutterers are slower in phonologic encoding, and as evidence of how phonologic encoding can be primed to assist both normal speakers and stutterers.

Kolk and Postma (1997) also report research evidence for the mechanism of self-repair and its relationship to stuttering. Kolk and Postma (1997) state that the results of studies into the effects of accuracy demands on speech repairs, self-repairs, and disfluencies support the prediction of the CRH that disfluencies "behave like self-repairs rather than speech errors" (p. 196). Speech errors were reduced under a condition that provided normal subjects with feedback on their performance as they rapidly repeated tongue twisters over a series of trials, but overt self-repairs remained unchanged. Kolk and Postma (1997) claim that accuracy instructions (information that is fed back to the subjects concerning the accuracy and speed of their performance) "focused speakers' attention on the process of speech programming, causing the number of programming errors to decrease" (p. 197), which would be followed by a decrease in overt errors. In addition, speakers were led "to monitor their speech plan and their output more thoroughly to optimise their performance" (p. 197). In turn, this increases error detection and repair. Since both effects are of about the same strength, the net effect amounts to zero (Kolk & Postma, 1997). Because disfluencies are the result of a repair process (see above), they should, according to Kolk and Postma (1997), behave like self-repairs and should not be affected by accuracy instructions. That very finding was obtained in studies on the disfluencies of normal speakers and of stutterers. However, since the adjustments that speakers actually make in response to accuracy instruction are internal and not directly observable, there is no telling what actually takes place when speakers are said to make adjustments. That is, there is no clear way to operationalize the effects of, or responses to, instruction (see also the discussion on the suprasegmental sentence plan alignment model later in this chapter). The same is true for knowing what is taking place when speakers focus their attention or monitor themselves.

Testability

The argument in the CRH is logical, in that it states that the necessary and sufficient condition for stuttering to occur is the covert repairing of excessively frequent errors in the phonetic plan. Distally, this is due to an impairment of phonological encoding. Thus, the hypothesis would be falsified if stuttering occurred in the absence of these conditions. However, it is not apparent how, empirically, such a test could be conducted, due to the lack of operational definitions of the constructs. First, as discussed above, the degree to which the frequency of covert repairs is greater in stutterers than in normally fluent speakers is not clear. Second, the existence of a priming mechanism and of slow phonologic encoding (see above) is also inferred. Because phonologic encoding and priming are internal mechanisms and are not directly observable, evidence of their existence depends on the assertion that they do exist and that they would, if they do in fact exist, behave in predicted ways when probed or tested. Doing so borders on reification or "to regard (something abstract) as a material or concrete thing" (Mish, 1993, p. 96). A third study into phonologic priming reported by Kolk and Postma (1997) suffers from the same problem. Pointing to the use of such inferential thinking and of reification is not meant to suggest that phonologic encoding and priming are not real. The scientific literature contains many instances of the eventual confirmation of the existence of phenomena after a period of observation and experimentation based on inference and on tests of phenomena in their hypothesized states. We mean to suggest that caution be exercised in accepting the reality of phonologic encoding and priming mechanisms and the ways in which their operations have been described.

Explanatory power

Topography

Kolk and Postma (1997) maintain that the CRH explains why people stutter: As a result of slower-developing phonologic abilities and slower than normal phonologic encoding, the phonetic plans of stutterers contain more flaws or phonologic encoding errors than are normal. As a result, there are more instances of error correction and repair than there are for normal speakers. In an attempt to eliminate the phonologic encoding errors, the stutterer repeats or restarts the speech element (sound, syllable, word) on which the error occurred (Kolk & Postma, 1997). These repetitions or restarts are the stutterings. "Phonologic encoding is the process that uses a syntactic representation to derive a phonetic plan that is specific enough to serve as a set of instructions for the articulators" (Kolk & Postma, 1997, p. 186). Thus phonologic encoding is a prearticulatory stage of speech production.

However, the CRH does not indicate how one can distinguish, operationally, between normal disfluency and stuttering. The CRH is based on models that attempt to explain why errors occur in the speech of normal speakers, and how those errors are detected and repaired. Kolk and Postma (1997) apply those models to an explanation of stuttering without explaining why the disfluencies that result from detection and repair in nonstutterers are normal and why the disfluencies that result from detection and repair in stutterers are stutterings. In the absence of a clear distinction, the answer borders on a tautology – the disfluencies are stutterings when children who are considered to be stutterers produce them. The only explicit difference offered by Kolk and Postma (1997) is that the frequency of detection, repair, and resulting disfluency is greater in stutterers than in normal speakers because stutterers have phonologic encoding problems. If that is the case, then it logically follows that the only criterion for considering someone to be a stutterer is the greater number of disfluencies in his or her speech. While it is true that *frequency of disfluency* is one measure used to distinguish stutterers from nonstutterers, it is neither necessary nor sufficient.

The CRH does, however, have a great deal to say about the topography of stuttering, which Kolk and Postma (1997) explain by the application of Levelt's Main Interrupt Rule and the restart hypothesis (see above). Levelt (as cited in Kolk & Postma, 1997) contended that speakers interrupt their speech as soon as they detect errors; the interruption is immediate. Kolk and Postma (1997) suggest that the preponderance of within-word interruptions in stuttering is a result of the Main Interrupt Rule. Upon the detection of an error, speech is interrupted and because the interruption is immediate, the stuttering occurs within the word rather than at its end. This reasoning explains why the unit stuttered upon is smaller than the word or phrase, but it does not explain why normal speakers, when they employ the Main Interrupt Rule, are not considered to be stuttering.

Detection of an error is followed by the attempt to repair it, and it is here that Kolk and Postma (1997) use the restart hypothesis to explain the type of stutter observed. The type of stutter produced is dependent on when the errors occur and on the word's structure. Kolk and Postma (1997) describe what the stutters would be like when the occurrence of error detection is early, intermediate, and late (the descriptions of topography are those of the authors). A phonologic error that occurs at the beginning of word onset is said to be early-occurring. Detection takes place before any audible sound is emitted and articulatory preforming or positioning has not yet taken place; consequently stuttering will be in the form of a silent pause if a restart takes place immediately after detection. If the error occurs later (but still considered to be early-occurring or located on an early segment of the word), articulatory preforming or positioning has occurred. When the restart takes place, the result will be repetitions of the positioning but with no sound being produced. Muscle tension builds and the stutter takes the form of tense pausing. Thus early-occurring errors and their detection and repair result in silent pauses, tense pauses, and blocking.

An error that occurs early in the word or syllable segment but beyond the initial position is said to be an intermediate occurrence. "It could occur later in word onset, for example, in the second consonant of 'place,' or it could be located in the vocalic nucleus, as in the vowel of 'lips' " (Kolk & Postma, 1997, p. 194). The detection and repair (restart) of intermediately occurring errors results in sound repetitions such as "p- p- p- place" (p. 194) or prolongation of a sound. Kolk and Postma (1997) see prolongation as ". . . a smooth consecutive repetition of the same phoneme" (p. 194).

Late-occurring errors are those that are located ". . . in the syllable coda, for instance in the final consonant of 'cup' or in the final consonant cluster of 'lips' " (p. 194). Detection and repair result in part-word repetitions ("cu- cu- cu- cup") (p. 194). A modified form of the restart hypothesis explains the prolongation of a non-initial sound ("cuuuup") and broken words ("cu -p") (p. 194). These last two types of stuttering may be the result of "a restart from the beginning of the word, but part of the word's onset would not be articulated" (p. 194). Alternatively, non-initial sound prolongations and broken words may result from the employment of a "postponement strategy" (p. 194) where by the speaker delays articulating part of the word to allow "the stutterer's activation process more time to be completed and increases the chance of selecting the intended unit" (p. 194).

The foregoing examples of topography help to clarify the concept of restart as a repair strategy. According to the CRH, the stutterings themselves are not the loci of the repair, and the units that are stuttered are not what are being repaired. The stutterings represent the restart strategy employed to reduce or eliminate future occurrences of error in phonologic encoding.

Onset

The CRH proposes that stuttering develops in those children who do not develop phonologic skills quickly enough to keep up with emergent communicative needs and pressures, although the fact that the onset of stuttering typically occurs after a period of normal fluency is not specifically addressed. Kolk and Postma (1997) state specifically that the CRH does not explain how childhood stuttering develops into adult manifestations of the disorder or how superfluous behaviours develop.

Natural recovery

Kolk and Postma (1997) acknowledge that natural recovery is not explained by the CRH.

Genetics

The CRH does not incorporate the role that genetics might play in stuttering. Kolk and Postma (1997) leave considerations of why certain children have slow-developing phonologic encoding skills to future research into the model.

Variability

Natural variability is not directly addressed by the CRH. However, conditions that induce fluency are explained. The reduction of stuttering that results for many stutterers when they speak more slowly is made possible because slowing down provides more time for the reliable selection of phonologic segments, thereby reducing the possibility of error. The adaptation effect, where stuttering is reduced over repeated reading of the same passage, is said to be the result of an increase in the activation rate of correct phoneme selection as a function of practice. Choral reading and shadowing, two other fluency-enhancing conditions, reduce or eliminate stuttering by priming; that is, by increasing "the activation level of the internal representation" of a phoneme or word that is heard or seen by a speaker (Kolk & Postma, 1997, p. 195). Priming, in other words, increases phonological encoding speed. Words that are to be spoken are presented auditorily (shadowing and choral reading) and visually (choral reading). In that way, priming occurs and facilitates future processing of those phonemes and words (Kolk & Postma, 1997).

Parsimony

Despite the fact that the CRH is based on a complex and multifaceted model, it is parsimonious because it posits one factor having two facets as necessary and sufficient for stuttering to occur. It is parsimonious as well, because it accounts for a number stuttering phenomena with one unifying explanation.

Heuristic value

The CRH has considerable heuristic value. An aspect of the CRH that recommends its use in the search to understand stuttering is that it is rich with questions that can serve to stimulate continued research. With refinement and more specificity, it has the potential to make significant contributions to the research on relationships between stuttering and language/phonology.

There are some features of stuttering, pointed to by the authors themselves, that the CRH does not explain. The CRH is not able to explain why some children have slower than normal phonologic development and slower than normal phonologic encoding skills, or why some children continue to have phonologic difficulties and others (the vast majority) do not. The CRH is likewise not able to explain the adult form of the disorder, including the use of accessory behaviours. Perhaps the most significant shortcoming of the CRH in its present formulation is the absence of any distinction between the topography of normal disfluency and the topography of stuttering at onset.

However, the heuristic value of the CRH is enhanced by Postma and Kolk's (1993) comparison of the hypothesis with other theories of stuttering. The CRH has also been fruitful in prompting discussion and generating research. Kolk and Postma's (1997) report led to an exchange about the hypothesis with Wingate (Postma & Kolk, 1994; Wingate, 1994), and Nippold (2002) reviewed three studies that sought to investigate the application of the CRH to stuttering. These studies are somewhat more empirically based than those presented by Kolk and Postma (1997) described above. Two of the studies reviewed by Nippold (2002) used children who were diagnosed as stutterers. Over the three studies, children were further categorized into two subgroups: stuttering children with normal phonology and stuttering children with diagnosed phonologic disorders. Predictions based on the CRH were that children who stutter and have phonologic disorders will stutter more frequently than children who stutter but do not have phonologic disorders; that "the frequency of and duration of speech disfluencies should increase during the production of words with greater syllabic complexity" (Nippold, 2002, p. 102); and that children who stutter and have phonologic disorders ". . . would produce a greater number of phonological process errors during stuttered compared to non-stuttered utterances, particularly when the utterances were long and grammatically complex" (p. 103). None of the hypotheses or predictions based on the CRH was upheld in any of the studies; however, it must be said that this is one of the few theories reviewed in this text that have prompted research by others.

THE SUPRASEGMENTAL SENTENCE PLAN ALIGNMENT MODEL

This model was developed by Karniol (1995) and proposes that stuttering is caused by two factors: (1) on-line changes in sentence formulation, which are underpinned by a deficiency in language processing, and (2) a deficiency in the capacity to modulate voice fundamental frequency in response to those changes. Individual instances of stuttering occur at "points of suprasegmental plan alignment" (Karniol, 1995, p. 104). According to Karniol (1995), "The difficulty stutterers have in modulating voice fundamental frequency and their concomitantly deficient language skills jointly underlie the stuttering syndrome" (p. 116).

Each of the two factors in this model, then, is necessary but not sufficient for stuttering to occur, and together they are the necessary and sufficient conditions for stuttering to occur. In other words, an on-line change in sentence formulation and an accompanying difficulty in modulating voice fundamental frequency are together necessary and sufficient for an individual moment of stuttering to occur, and therefore no moment of stuttering will occur without them.

The author does not say why this theoretical explanation of stuttering should be called a model rather than a theory. Modelling in its traditional usage is not employed here, in that a model from another field is not used to try to enhance understanding of why people stutter. Nonetheless, the suprasegmental sentence plan alignment (SPA) model does simplify the action of the variables proposed to be critical in causing stuttering, which is a feature of conventional models (see Chapter 2).

Background and development

This model of stuttering developed from models of speech production and from the study of speech errors in normal speakers. According to Karniol (1995), speakers often change their speech plans on-line. These on-line changes involve both lexical and syntactic planning, and are referred to as "frame changes" (Karniol, 1995, p. 113). They may occur during an utterance (sentence) or even before the utterance begins. The result of these frame changes is that the suprasegmental features (stress, intonation, timing) of the utterance that were planned prior to its initiation also need to be changed because they are no longer appropriate. In other words "the suprasegmental features of the planned utterance and the suprasegmental features of the revised utterance need to be aligned" (Karniol, 1995, p. 114) and

"muscle activity that has been initiated in preparation for upcoming segments and features must be stopped" (Karniol, 1995, p. 113). Based on this
understanding of normal speech production, "the need to adjust voice fundamental frequency to accommodate on-line processes and revisions as
spontaneous speech unfolds accounts for chronic stuttering" (Karniol, 1995,
p. 116).

Karniol puts forward a number of empirically based arguments in support of the model. These include, first of all, the premise that stuttering is a
sentence-level rather than a word-level phenomenon. This is supported by
the fact that the onset of stuttering occurs at the time children are starting
to combine words, rather than at the one-word level of linguistic development. Karniol (1995) draws here on a published study of the development
of stuttering in a bilingual child (Karniol, 1992). In this case study, a
child was reported to start stuttering in both English and Hebrew at age
26 months and "stuttering onset paralleled the emergence of productive use
of syntactic rules in both languages" (Karniol, 1995, p. 105). It is also argued
that stuttering occurs more frequently on tasks that require sentence formulation. One example given is that people stutter more during spontaneous
speech than when reading aloud. Also, the observations that stuttering
tends to occur at the beginning of sentences and is related to syntactic complexity are used to support the premise that stuttering is a sentence-level
phenomenon.

Second, considerable evidence is put forward to support the two factors
said to be responsible for stuttering. Regarding the first factor, a number
of studies are cited which Karniol claims show that people who stutter
have reduced linguistic capacity. According to Karniol (1995) "one correl-
ate of such a language deficiency is that stutterers require more time for
planning their utterances, and the need for more time is manifest both at
the point of utterance initiation and during utterance production" (p. 115).
Karniol also argues that treatment programmes for children incorporate
the teaching of language skills, and suggests that this supports the idea
that children who stutter have a deficit in language processing. Karniol
acknowledges, however, that the efficacy of such programmes is not
known.

Concerning the second factor – stutterers have reduced capacity to modulate pitch – Karniol argues that although stutterers do not have a chronic
dysfunction in speech motor control, they show greater variability in speech-
related movements. More specifically, Karniol argues "chronic stutterers evidence difficulties in modulating voice fundamental frequency" (1995, p. 115).
Karniol refers to evidence from Nudelman et al. (1989) (see Chapter 7) that
stutterers performed more poorly than controls when tracking the pitch of a
tone by humming. She also refers to the findings of Borden, Bayer, and
Kenney (1985) that "moments of stuttering often occur with abnormally high
voice fundamental frequency" (Karniol, 1995, p. 114).

Testability

As far as the first feature of testability is concerned, the SPA model has internal consistency. Two factors are deemed to be necessary and sufficient for stuttering to occur: (1) a frame change, and (2) impaired modulation of voice fundamental frequency at the time of the frame change. In other words, the logic of the model is sound. The model could be falsified by showing that stuttering occurs in the absence of one of these factors.

In terms of the second feature of testability, namely operationism, it is not clear how the first factor – a frame shift – can be operationalized, particularly when this shift constitutes a frame discard. A frame discard refers to a situation where the speaker changes the sentence plan before the utterance is initiated. Karniol (1995) does address this issue, and states that previous research has substantiated the presence of frame discards with anecdotal evidence and with work on spoonerisms. Of course, it is common sense that people may change what they are going to say prior to speaking. However, for the purposes of testing the SPA model it must be possible to establish empirically that a frame change occurs each time a stutter occurs, and this is particularly problematic when such a change is purported to occur before the onset of the utterance. Karniol does not say how this might be done, nor is it apparent from any other source how a frame change is to be identified. While it is possible to ask an adult if they changed what they were going to say immediately prior to a stutter, this is not feasible for a young child. Nor is it possible to establish the reliability of such a self-report. In other words, it does not seem possible to operationalize frame changes.

There is also a problem in operationalizing the second factor, which is a deficiency in the ability to modulate voice fundamental frequency. Karniol (1995) relies on the results of Nudelman et al.'s (1989) study that people who stutter performed less well on pitch-tracking tasks than control subjects. However, the generalizability of these findings has not been established. More importantly, if this impairment is to be considered a causal factor in stuttering, it must be possible to show that a person has difficulty modulating voice fundamental frequency *immediately prior to each moment of stuttering*.

In summary, then, while the SPA model is logically falsifiable, it is not testable at the empirical level because it is not apparent how one can determine – immediately prior to each moment of stuttering – that a frame shift has occurred and that there was a deficiency of modulation of voice fundamental frequency.

Explanatory power

Topography

According to Karniol (1995) "part-word repetitions occur to adjust the fundamental frequency with which voicing was initiated" (p. 114). No explanation is given for other topographical features of stuttering.

Onset

According to the model, the onset of stuttering occurs after a period of apparently normal speech development because the problem with stuttering "seems to be the transition to sentence-level prosody and the coordination of suprasegmental features with lexical and syntactic variation in sentences" (Karniol, 1995, p. 115). Karniol cites studies that show that at this stage of linguistic development children are developing adult stress patterns.

Natural recovery

Natural recovery is accounted for by the "greater proficiency children acquire with sentence production as they mature" (Karniol, 1995, p. 115). Thus, stuttering "becomes chronic in those children who are less proficient in their language skills, having either lexical access problems or difficulties with syntactic forms" (p. 115). Since Karniol argues that chronicity is also underpinned by a deficit in the capacity to modulate fundamental frequency, this implies that this lack of capacity must also continue to be present in children who fail to recover naturally.

Variability

According to the model, the adaptation effect occurs because "with repeated readings the individual acquires facility with the realization of those suprasegmental features that must be assigned within the passage to be read" (Karniol, 1995, p. 116).

Other fluency-enhancing conditions are also explained. Stuttering is reduced during whispering because there is no voicing, and hence no modulation of fundamental frequency is required. The effects of DAF are also explained. Normally fluent speakers become disfluent under DAF because it disrupts the suprasegmental sentence plan, and DAF and white noise masking reduce stuttering because they both lead to changes in voice fundamental frequency. In addition, an auditory feedback delay of 400 ms reduces stuttering because:

> stutterers are slower at all stages of sentence production, (and) this delay allows them to catch up during DAF onset: when their speech is fed back

to them, they can better superimpose the suprasegmental plan on the remaining part of the sentence.

(Karniol, 1995, p. 117)

Further, according to Karniol, the delay in receiving auditory feedback at the onset of an utterance gives the person time to realign voice fundamental frequency. According to the SPA model, rhythmic speech reduces stuttering because it "apparently reduces the need for coarticulation and changes the fundamental frequency contour of utterances" (Karniol, 1995, p. 118). In summary, according to Karniol (1995), "any technique that alters the rate of speech production and reduces the likelihood that SPA will be required should reduce stuttering" (p. 118). It can be inferred from this that fluency-enhancing conditions ameliorate stuttering by reducing the influence of one or other of the two factors that contribute to stuttering in this model: That is, they either allow more time for language formulation or they alter fundamental voice frequency.

The model accounts for a number of other research findings in stuttering. Karniol states that stuttering is associated with linguistic complexity because "the more complex the utterance the more difficult it is to impose a fundamental frequency contour on it" (Karniol, 1995, p. 116). Karniol also states that bilingual speakers tend to stutter more in their less proficient language because "the need for SPA is more likely to occur in the less proficient language" and because "the more proficient language may dominate at the point of sentence planning, before morpholexical insertion takes place" (Karniol, 1995, p. 116).

The model accounts for the tendency for stuttering to occur at the start of utterances. First, according to the model the fundamental frequency contour of an utterance is determined prior to utterance initiation and, second, "people are most likely to engage in on-line processing at sentence-initial positions rather than in sentence final positions" (Karniol, 1995, p. 116).

Parsimony

The SPA model proposes two factors as being necessary and sufficient for stuttering to occur. It is parsimonious because it offers one overarching explanation for stuttering and this explanation accounts for a range of stuttering phenomena.

Heuristic value

Karniol devotes considerable space to discussing the limitations of other current models and theories of stuttering. By so doing, she makes a good case for claiming the superior explanatory value of the SPA model. In summarizing, Karniol asserts that each of the models reviewed "accounts for some aspects of stuttering but not others" (1995, p. 111). In particular, according to Karniol the models and theories reviewed failed to account for the age of onset of stuttering and natural recovery.

One intuitively appealing feature of the SPA model is that – according to Karniol – it provides a rationale for stuttering treatments. Karniol states that various approaches address both factors in the SPA model. First, "therapy programs for young children who stutter explicitly incorporate some training in language skills" (Karniol, 1995, p. 108) and "any degree of success of programs whose focus is on language skills is hard to reconcile with models of stuttering in which chronic malfunctions of the articulatory system are posited" (p. 108). By this, Karniol is suggesting that an effective therapy for young children must address the linguistic deficit underlying the first factor in the SPA model. However, this may not be the case for all treatments for children who stutter. Studies published around the time of publication of the Karniol model (e.g., Lincoln, Onslow, Lewis, & Wilson, 1996; Onslow, Andrews, & Lincoln, 1994) indicate that simple operant procedures can effectively decrease or eliminate childhood stuttering without apparently invoking changes to linguistic functioning (Bonelli, Dixon, Bernstein Ratner, & Onslow, 2000).

According to Karniol, some stuttering treatments also address the second factor in the SPA model. Techniques that involve varying the habitual patterns of speech production "either slow down the rhythm (thereby slowing rate of output and reducing the need to coarticulate) or reduce the likelihood that a need for SPA will arise" (Karniol, 1995, p. 118).

There are some features of stuttering, however, with which the SPA model appears to be inconsistent. First, a prediction of the SPA model would be that people should not stutter at all when reading aloud, as changes in SPA are presumably not required during oral reading. Second, stuttering does not only occur on words at the onset of utterances. For example, some people stutter on 20–30% of syllables. According to the SPA model, then, these people must be changing SPA every third or or fourth syllable, which does not seem particularly plausible. Third, it has never been shown that all people who stutter have a deficit of linguistic processing (for example see Guitar, 1998; Nippold, 1990; Shapiro, 1999). Karniol's claims that stutterers have "lexical access problems or difficulties with syntactic forms" and are "slower at all stages of sentence production" are not supported empirically.

To our knowledge, the SPA model has not been fruitful in terms of generating research.

Chapter 9

Theories of stuttering: Multifactorial models

This chapter reviews two theories that their authors identify as multifactorial. We conclude the chapter with a brief commentary on confusion in terminology in these models. We have chosen to comment here because of the considerable prominence of these models in the current stuttering literature.

THE DEMANDS AND CAPACITIES MODEL

The demands and capacities (DC) model proposes that stuttering occurs when demands for fluency are greater than the child's capacity to produce it. Neither the child's capacity for fluency nor the demands placed on it are, in terms of the DC model, necessarily abnormal, deviant, or disordered for stuttering to occur. The DC model is described by the author Starkweather, and others, in a number of publications (Adams, 1990; Gottwald & Starkweather, 1995; Starkweather, 1987, 1997; Starkweather & Givens-Ackerman, 1997; Starkweather & Gottwald, 1990, 2000; Starkweather, Gottwald, & Halfond, 1990).

The DC model proposes four developmental factors or capacities related to fluency: speech motor control, language development, social and emotional functioning, and cognitive development. The demands on, or challenges to, those capacities may be within the child, in the external environment, or both, and they include time pressure, innate and environmental pressure to use more complex language, high levels of excitement and anxiety, and parental demands for increased cognitive functioning. According to the DC model, capacities are either inherent or acquired and contribute to the development of fluent speech (Starkweather & Givens-Ackerman, 1997). The environmental demands delineated by Starkweather have been garnered from research studies that have identified factors that affect fluency. The delineation of capacities, on the other hand, comes from studies that show stutterers to be inferior to nonstutterers in terms of the particular capacity studied (Starkweather & Givens-Ackerman, 1997).

The central points of the model, then, may be summarized as follows:

Capacities (motor, linguistic, socioemotional, cognitive) increase as children grow and develop. Simultaneously, demands from the communicative environment (motoric, linguistic, socioemotional, cognitive) increase because individuals in the children's environment and the children themselves come to demand or expect more mature behaviour. When capacities surpass demands, the child is able to speak fluently, but when demands surpass capacities, the child may stutter (Starkweather, 1987). Demands and capacities do not necessarily develop at the same rate. Starkweather and Givens-Ackerman (1997, p. 67) state:

> As long as the child's capacities for producing fluent speech are ahead of the demands for fluency that the child's environment presents, the child will speak fluently; however, when the demands become too great or the capacities have not developed fast enough, he or she will not be able to speak fluently. Because demands vary according to a number of factors, such as the speech situation, the listener, and even certain words and sentences, the child's ability to speak fluently will also vary. As the capacities for fluent speech improve with maturity, the child may well reach a point where dysfluent speech is no longer a problem because all speaking circumstances present demands that are within the child's ability.

Starkweather and colleagues have not explicitly proposed the DC model as a causal model but rather suggest that it is a guide to understanding stuttering. It is also used as a basis for treatment. However, the explanation of stuttering it offers is regarded by others as either one that is on "the edges" of causal (Manning, 2000, p. 318) or in fact causal (Guitar, 1998). We believe that Starkweather and Gottwald's (2000) recent statement that ". . . there is a continuing dynamic interaction between genetics and environment, and this is the kind of interactive process that the demands and capacities model expresses with regard to stuttering development" (p. 369) places the model squarely within the causal camp. This is confirmed by Starkweather and Givens-Ackerman (1997) when discussing the unique combination of factors proposed by the DC model for each case of stuttering: "there is no single etiology, but as many etiologies as there are stories of stuttering development" (p. 24). This means, then, that there are no conditions that are necessary, or sufficient, or both, for stuttering to occur, other than the construct that demands exceed capacity.

Background and development

The DC model is included within that category of models that are said to be interactional or multifactorial. Indeed, Starkweather and colleagues developed the model to synthesize the research on the multiple factors that are implicated in stuttering, with the suggestion that stuttering is best viewed as a complex disorder that results from the interaction of multiple factors rather than one that results from a simple or single factor.

One interpretation of Starkweather and Gottwald would lead to a rejection of explanations of stuttering that are based on a linear, cause–effect model, often referred to as the medical model because of that model's frequent use in medicine as an explanation of the aetiology and treatment of diseases. We suggest that such an interpretation and its consequent rejection of linear cause–effect is mistaken. We propose that the DC model is a linear cause–effect model that is best described as a complex version of a unidirectional linear cause–effect model (see Attanasio, 2003) (see also Chapter 2 for discussions of causal models in the human sciences).

A distinction has to be drawn between the model's use in the synthesis of research in stuttering and its explanation of the cause of stuttering. As a synthesis of research, the DC model does serve to remind us of the complexity of stuttering, but that synthesis does not uncover the possible causal significance of the factors that contribute to the complexity of stuttering. As we have written elsewhere (Attanasio, 1999; Attanasio et al., 1998), multifactorial does not mean multicausal. That stuttering is a multifactorial disorder would not be questioned by most researchers and clinicians; certainly, we do not question its complexity. That stuttering is caused by the *interaction* of multiple factors, as Starkweather and Gottwald (2000) suggest when they write of dynamic interactions between genetics and the environment, remains open to question. Our position, expanded upon in the paragraphs that follow, is that when applied to the question of cause, the DC model is a complex version of the linear cause–effect model rather than an interactional model.

To illustrate this, Figures 9.1 and 9.2 are examples of *simple* linear

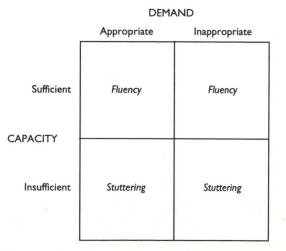

Figure 9.1 A simple linear cause–effect model that emphasizes constitutional factors (adapted from Hubbell, 1981).

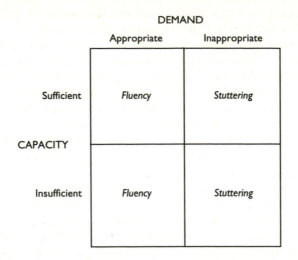

Figure 9.2 A simple linear cause–effect model that emphasizes environmental factors (adapted from Hubbell, 1981).

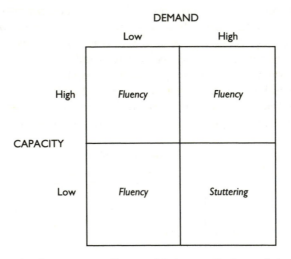

Figure 9.3 A complex linear cause–effect model that emphasizes relationships between capacity and demand (adapted from Hubbell, 1981).

cause–effect models, with one emphasizing the environment and the other emphasizing the child's constitution. We present these figures and use the terminology (demand and capacity) derived from the DC model so that it can then be seen in Figure 9.3 that the DC model is a *complex* version of a linear cause–effect model.

It can be seen in Figure 9.1 that stuttering will occur when the child's capacity is insufficient, irrespective of the level of demand. We define capacities as "insufficient" when they are at levels that could make it difficult for a given child to meet the demands placed on him or her, and as "sufficient" when they are at levels that would not reduce a given child's abilities to meet those demands. In other terms, insufficient capacities may be seen as constitutional factors that are compromised. We define demands as "appropriate" whenever they are at levels that present no difficulty to children as they develop, and as "inappropriate" whenever they are at levels that could be somehow taxing for children as they develop. In other terms, inappropriate demands may be seen as environmental factors that are not supportive of the development of speech and language skills.

In the simple linear cause–effect model that emphasizes constitutional factors only, stuttering occurs no matter what demands are made by the environment. That is, the causal factors of stuttering are within the child.

Using the illustration of the *simple* linear cause–effect model again, Figure 9.2 shows that stuttering will occur when demand is inappropriate, irrespective of the child's constitution. Thus, in the simple linear cause–effect model that emphasizes environment only, the child will stutter whenever demands are inappropriate; capacity or constitution is irrelevant or of no consequence. That is, the causal factors of stuttering are within the environment.

We emphasize here that the terms *appropriate, inappropriate, sufficient,* and *insufficient* are not used by the authors of the DC model. We have used them in Figures 9.1 and 9.2 to indicate when stuttering would occur if constitutional and environmental factors were viewed as causal factors independent of one another.

As an example of what we refer to in Chapter 2 as the *complex* linear cause–effect model, the DC model simply catalogues those constitutional factors on the one hand and those environmental factors on the other that have been implicated in stuttering. It suggests that a child stutters as a result of a capacity for fluency that is not up to the demands placed on it or, conversely, a child stutters because the demands overtax the child's capacity for fluency. The absolute levels of that capacity or of the demands of that environment are not at issue, and the demands and capacities are not necessarily abnormal. Instead, it is the mismatch between the two that is the culprit. The results of that mismatch on fluency are diagrammed in Figure 9.3. It can be seen, therefore, that stuttering will occur only when the demand for fluent speech is at a level higher than what the child's capacity for fluent speech can tolerate (of course, the converse is equally the case). Treatment based on the model, then, is directed at increasing capacity in the face of an unchanged environment, or decreasing environmental demands in the face of an unchanged capacity, or both increasing capacity *and* decreasing demands.

However, such an explanation for stuttering is a tautology because it comes down to saying that a child stutters because he cannot be fluent within his communicative environment. Furthermore, the causative agent or agents catalogued by the model act linearly and unidirectionally: Increased capacity or decreased demand (or both) result in reduced stuttering. Although the DC model states that stuttering does not result from a single cause – children stutter not only because of constitutional factors but also because of the nature of the environment in which they communicate – the causative factors are static. That is, a given level of capacity and a given level of demand for a particular child will result in stuttering. Similarly, the DC model does not suggest that the demand and capacity factors actually interact with one another to either cause stuttering or to eliminate it. In order for the DC model to be truly interactional, it would have to describe a dynamic and reciprocal relationship between capacity and demand, not simply that capacity is causatively related to stuttering in the presence of certain levels of demand, or that demand is causally related to stuttering in the presence of certain levels of capacity.

Testability

The model is not falsifiable (for more discussion on this see Packman et al., 2004). First, on logical grounds, the argument in the proposal that a child will stutter (be dysfluent) when capacity for fluency is insufficient to meet demands for fluency does not separate cause and effect. As alluded to above, lack of fluency can be defined by saying that capacity for fluency is insufficient to meet demands for fluency. Second, the terminology used in the argument is inconsistent. As we have discussed elsewhere (Packman et al., 2004) stuttering is not in fact the obverse of fluency (for discussion of confusion in terminology in stuttering, see Chapter 5). Many factors contribute to fluent speech, not just lack of stuttering. Thus, insufficient capacity for fluent speech does not necessarily imply stuttering. This is consistent with the third problem with the reasoning of the model, which is that the terms are not defined operationally. The only way we can assume that demands are excessive or capacities are insufficient – in relation to each other – is if the child stutters. They cannot be identified independently, despite Starkweather and Gottwald's (2000) suggestions as to how one can assess demands and test capacities. Since there are no required or defined levels that demands or capacities must reach in order for stuttering to occur, one can only reason backwards from the occurrence of stuttering to conclude that demands were too great for the capacities to withstand. The statement by Starkweather and Givens-Ackerman (1997) that the cause of stuttering is different in each child also renders the DC model untestable.

In short, the DC model is tautological in suggesting that an individual stutters because demands for fluency exceed capacities for fluency. This is the same as suggesting that an individual stutters because he or she cannot be fluent (see Ingham & Cordes, 1997). The tautology makes the model a closed system that is impervious to falsification through testing. Simply cataloguing demands and capacities, as the DC model does, does not provide a theoretical construct that leads to meaningful hypotheses about the nature or cause of stuttering beyond stating the obvious – that there are factors that contribute to the onset and development of stuttering. Further, the application of the DC model does not require that there be any identifiable difference between demands or capacities in a child who stutters and demands or capacities in a nonstuttering child. One need not measure demands or capacities because the stuttering itself is confirmation that capacities are not up to demands or that demands are too excessive. The model, in a sense, asks and answers its own questions without the need for scientific testing.

Explanatory power

Topography

Although it appears to do so, the DC model does not explain why children stutter. Thus, it does not explain the repeated movements and fixed postures of the speech mechanism that constitute stuttering.

Natural recovery

According to Starkweather and Givens-Ackerman (1997), children may stop stuttering naturally as capacity increases with maturity.

Variability

According to the model, stuttering varies naturally within the individual according to variations in demand.

Parsimony

The DC model is not parsimonious because it proposes that stuttering is caused by many permutations that can result in potentially unlimited combinations of demands and capacities, which could themselves have innumerable levels of magnitude. In other words, there is a different causal explanation for every child. Starkweather et al. (1990) state their belief that stuttering is caused by unique combinations of factors in each child: "it [the DC model] creates opportunities to construct explanatory theories about the etiology of stuttering in particular children" (p. 22) and "We believe strongly that every child's history of stuttering development is unique to the family in which the child lives . . ." (p. 24).

Heuristic value

The DC model has not been fruitful in terms of research, presumably because it is not logically possible to predict from it. However, the model has prompted much discussion in the literature. A forum on the DC model appeared in the 2000 edition of *Journal of Fluency Disorders*. The forum was prompted by Siegel (2000), who voiced concerns about the logic of the model. Almost all the forum participants were also concerned to some extent about the internal logic of the model, but some also felt that the model has heuristic value as a way of organizing various research findings. The authors of this text and a colleague have also written a critique of the model (Packman et al., 2004).

While it has prompted discussion, the DC model does not break new ground by introducing previously unrecognized conceptualizations of stuttering or new ways of thinking about the disorder. Siegel (2000), for example, suggested that the formulations of Johnson and of Bluemel can be seen in the DC model, and Yaruss (2000, pp. 347–348) stated, "The DCM has its roots in the Newcastle upon Tyne project, in which Andrews and Harris (1964) suggested that 'general lack of capacity to "think, talk, and behave" may be an important element in the initial development of stuttering' (p. 117), at least for some children who stutter."

Furthermore, the model incorporates new data in an ad hoc manner. Starkweather and Gottwald (2000) confirm the model's ad hoc approach when they write, "When there was evidence that a particular capacity was diminished in stutterers, we incorporated it, with other similar findings, as part of the model" (p. 370). Arguably, the authors would continue to add information on an ad hoc basis should that information become available. The ad hoc nature of the DC model, and the fact that it does not help us to conceptualize, stuttering in ways that differ from past or current thinking, significantly reduce its heuristic value. The lack of explanatory power (see above) also diminishes the heuristic value of the model.

Perhaps the most serious threat to heuristic value, however, is the suggestion that stuttering is caused by a unique combination of factors in each child. This appears, at first glance, to be a new and interesting insight into the nature of stuttering. However, at a time when the biomedical sciences are seeking to uncover universals from what may appear to be particular instances, this proposal is troubling. Uniqueness is not necessarily a reflection of deeper understanding; rather, the evocation of unique or idiosyncratic explanations of cause may instead reflect incomplete understanding of the phenomenon under study. Perhaps the heuristic value of the DC model indeed lies in what its authors described it to be at its inception: a descriptive catalogue of factors that have been implicated in one way or another with stuttering or stutterers.

Starkweather and colleagues have developed a treatment programme for young children, based on the DC model, called the Multiprocess Approach (see Gottwald & Starkweather, 1999). This treatment aims to reduce for each child the demand factors (as proposed by the model) that the clinician hypothesizes are excessive (relative to capacity), and/or to increase the capacity factors (as proposed by the model) that the clinician hypothesizes are insufficient (relative to demands). In accordance with the postulate of the model, then, treatment is different for each child, and so is not replicable.

THE DYNAMIC MULTIFACTORIAL MODEL

The underlying principles of the dynamic multifactorial (DM) model of stuttering (Smith, 1999; Smith & Kelly, 1997) were described earlier in Chapter 4 and are supplemented and expanded upon here.

The DM model is identified by its authors as multifactorial and interactional, with nonlinear, dynamic relationships between and among the factors. Stuttering is seen as emerging from dynamically interacting factors rather than being the result of a single factor. As we understand the explanation of stuttering provided by the model, environmental factors dynamically interact with factors intrinsic to the individual; these intrinsic factors are genetic, organismic, emotional, cognitive, and linguistic. The intrinsic factors themselves interact with one another while they may also be interacting with environmental factors. For example, there can be interactions between and among the emotional, cognitive, and linguistic factors, which in turn interact with the speech motor system. It appears from the DM model that stuttering results when the interacting factors affect the operations of the speech motor system. The speech motor system can also affect the emotional, cognitive, and linguistic factors – that is, the effects can be reciprocal.

There is infrequent reference to cause in reports of the model. Indeed, according to Smith (1999), the model moves us "beyond traditional notions of causality" (p. 35). However, there are statements to indicate that the model is indeed causal. For example, Smith and Kelly (1997, p. 209), state that:

> The essence of our model, then, is that stuttering emerges from the complex, nonlinear interaction of many factors. No single factor can be identified as "the cause" of stuttering.

Further, Smith (1999) states that the model "implicates cognitive, linguistic, emotional and motor factors in the etiology of stuttering" (p. 32).

Also, the DM model is clearly causal when it proposes why some people are identified as stuttering and others are not. According to Figure 10.2 in Smith and Kelly's (1997) chapter, the factors that are hypothesized to "underpin" (p. 209) stuttering in people diagnosed as stutterers are also present in a person who has not been diagnosed as stuttering. According to this illustration of the model, then, no condition (factor or combination of factors) is necessary or sufficient for stuttering to occur. According to Smith and Kelly, it is the weighting of factors that determines whether an individual is in the "diagnostic space" of stuttering (p. 209). According to Smith (1999), "the relative weighting of the factors producing stuttering in each individual varies" (p. 34). Yet Smith and Kelly's figure is confusing. It graphically portrays five factors as underpinning stuttering, yet the legend implies that these are only some of the "many contributing factors" (Smith & Kelly, 1997, p. 209). While it is acknowledged that the figure is an attempt to show how the model simplifies relationships between variables, we are left with the proposition that many unidentified factors, not all of which are present in each person who stutters and which, when they are present, vary in weight, interact in unique ways to cause stuttering.

The model clearly states that stuttering is not necessarily caused by any pathological condition, setting itself apart from other models and theories of stuttering that propose such a condition. Smith (1999) states that stuttering may be due to "interactions of component neural systems that are essentially normal" (p. 37) and "there is no core factor, a brain lesion, a DNA sequence, a type of disfluency, a phonological buffer problem, that generates all the phenomena associated with stuttering" (p. 38).

Background and development

As discussed in Chapter 4, and as stated by the authors, this model is strongly influenced by nonlinear dynamics, and chaos and complexity theories. Support for the model comes from two recent studies by Smith and Kleinow (Kleinow & Smith, 2000; Smith & Kleinow, 2000). However, we suggest here that the authors are attempting to support their multifactorial model with unifactorial methodology. In the Smith and Kleinow (2000) study, the articulatory kinematics of a group of adult stutterers and a matched group of normally fluent adults were assessed ". . . to determine if adults who stutter are generally poorer at speech movement pattern generation and if changing speech rate affects their stability in the same way that it affects normally fluent controls" (p. 521). Three speaking conditions were used in the experiment: All subjects were instructed to utter a phrase (Buy Bobby a puppy) at their normal, habitual speech rate and at rates slower and faster than their normal, habitual rates. Because the speaking task across conditions involved a "simple utterance" (p. 531), the authors state that processing demands were thereby reduced and consequently it would be reasonable to ". . . assume that emotional, cognitive, and linguistic factors would have had minimal effects on motor performance" (p. 531), leaving "time pressure" as ". . . the only variable manipulated that would increase or decrease processing demands" (p. 531). The findings of the study – that the kinematic parameters in the fluent speech of stutterers reveal a ". . . susceptibility to speech motor breakdown when performance demands increase" (p. 521) – while interesting, are not relevant to the point being made here. Rather, the point – actually the question – has to do with why the authors rely on a unifactorial approach when considering a multifactorial model's validity, by controlling for the emotional, cognitive, and linguistic factors that are said to interact with one another and with the speech motor system.

In a companion study, Kleinow and Smith (2000) studied the effects of utterance length and syntactic complexity on the speech motor stability of adult stutterers as measured by the spatiotemporal index (STI), a measure also used in the Smith and Kleinow (2000) study described above. Although the results of this study are also interesting (STI values of stutterers were larger during conditions that used utterances of greater length/syntactic complexity than the utterance used in the baseline condition), Kleinow and Smith (2000) do not present statistical or methodological justification for their conclusion that the study's results support a multifactorial, dynamic, nonlinear model of stuttering. The methodology used in the study is unifactorial, with STI values as the dependent variable and length/syntactic complexity as the independent variable. That is, utterance length/syntactic complexity is the only factor of interest to emerge from the study, and although four length/syntactic complexity utterances (conditions) were used, the four utterances are essentially identical to one another in terms of length and syntactic complexity.

Furthermore, the statistical procedures used in the study (ANOVAs), are tests of differences between and among means, and are not designed to describe relationships, or the nature of relationships, between or among variables. At the very least, the analysis of scatterplots would be required to describe relationships between or among variables and to establish whether those relationships are linear or nonlinear. To demonstrate, for example, that STI values and length/syntactic complexity are nonlinearly related, a scatterplot would have to show deviations from linearity – for example, that small increases in one variable (in the present case, length/syntactic complexity) produce marked or large increases in the other variable (in the present case, STI values). To do so would require a methodology that enables the manipulation of length/syntactic complexity, in order to see what the effects of the manipulation are on STI values and then to plot the nature of the relationship, if any. What Kleinow and Smith (2000) found was that adult stutterers had higher STI values than adult nonstutterers in two conditions that required the production of utterances that were of increased length/syntactic complexity when compared to a baseline utterance. The authors did not present utterances of varying length/syntactic complexity in order to plot the relationship between STI values and length/syntactic complexity. It is true, however, that when length of utterance alone was considered, no differences from the baseline utterance were found, but when length and complexity were considered together, differences from baseline were found in two of four conditions (the authors report separately in the study that there were no differences in STI values between high and low complexity conditions for either group of subjects). That finding may reflect an interaction between length and complexity as a factor that affects STI, but that is quite different from saying that length/syntactic complexity itself is dynamically and non-linearly related to STI values and, by extrapolation, to stuttering.

It is our view, then, that the methodologies and levels of analysis used in Smith and Kleinow (2000) and Kleinow and Smith (2000) are not adequate approaches to support the model, and that separately investigating the effects of single independent variables (e.g., speech rate; length/syntactic complexity) does not probe what is said to be a dynamic, nonlinear, emergent disorder (stuttering). It is important to point out, however, that the two studies did not set out to test the DM model. Their purpose was to investigate the impact on the motor system of certain variables thought to influence stuttering. The point here is that the claims made in the articles about the implications of the findings for the DM model may be unwarranted.

There is a curious aspect to the studies reported by Smith and Kleinow (2000) and Kleinow and Smith (2000). Although the studies used subjects who stutter, and although the studies were designed to investigate factors that are said to be implicated in stuttering, measures were taken from productions during which there were no overt signs of stuttering or fluency breakdown. According to Folkins (1991), "if one wishes to understand how the motor system is involved in stuttering, one should study the motor system during stuttering" (p. 567).

Testability

It seems that the model is unfalsifiable. At the logical level, no condition (factor or group of factors) is necessary and/or sufficient for stuttering to occur. Further, it is not possible to deduce from the model what constitutes stuttering. Thus, in the argument

A causes B,

neither A nor B can be defined operationally.

Smith (1999) states that dynamic nonlinear models are testable. Smith's (1999) proposition is that ". . . all individuals who stutter experience break-downs in speech motor processes" (p. 33) and that there are a number of factors that can have a negative impact on speech motor processing. From this proposition, Smith (1999, p. 33) recommends experiments in which each of these factors becomes an independent variable and speech motor output becomes the dependent variable:

> The experimental approach generated by this model is to specify variables that are hypothetically linked to speech motor breakdown: as shown, examples include memory load, syntactic complexity, or speaker anxiety. Experiments can be designed to directly test whether variables impact the stability and/or perceived fluency of the individual's speech motor output.

We say again that it is not made clear how such methodology can test nonlinear, dynamic interactions. Further, while such experiments may – and do – provide valuable insights into speech motor control, they do not test hypotheses about stuttering. Stuttering cannot be studied empirically under this model, in any case, as it cannot be identified operationally. Further, while memory load, syntactic complexity, and speaker anxiety may affect stuttering severity, they are clearly not necessary or sufficient for stuttering to occur.

Explanatory power

Topography

The model's treatment of the definition and topography of stuttering may be its most provocative and problematic aspect. The authors of the model state many times that stuttering does not consist of behavioural events. According to Smith and Kelly (1997), "Units of stuttering are a convenient fiction that have no biological reality. They are fictive in time and space" (p. 206). Also, according to Smith (1999), "stuttering 'events' do not exist; there is not a millisecond or a nanosecond that can be identified as the onset or offset of a disfluency . . ." (p. 30).

According to the model, then, there are no definable boundaries between stuttered and nonstuttered speech. Stuttering events or moments of stuttering are said not to exist, and the traditional descriptors of stutters (repetitions, prolongations, blocks, etc.) are said to be misleading if they are used as the sole basis upon which to define stuttering. The judgements of repetitions, prolongations, and so forth that listeners make are dismissed as the tendency of the human brain to organize perceptions into categories.

The model's authors go to great lengths to state what stuttering is not. One is left wondering, then, how they define stuttering. What, in operational terms, is the model explaining? The answer to this is elusive. The best description of what the authors regard stuttering to be is, "Stuttering is a continuous disorder; it is present even when we do not perceive disfluencies" (Smith, 1999, p. 29). In other words, according to the model stuttering is a dynamic process that is in operation before, during, and after any putative stuttering event.

Since stuttering cannot be satisfactorily identified perceptually, then, one assumes from the model that there are certain physiological markers of stuttering. According to Smith (1999, p. 27):

> Stuttering is not a series of "stutter events." Stuttering is a dynamic disorder, and the many processes related to stuttering can be observed at multiple levels, within time frames that range from milliseconds to lifespans, and with many different types of tools.

However, also according to Smith, "There is not a necessary relationship between physiological data and the traditional classifications of fluency" (1999, p. 30). Clearly, then, the authors of the model do not have an operational definition of stuttering, at either a perceptual or a physiological level, and the reader cannot know what it is that the model is attempting to explain.

Onset

The model explains the onset of stuttering as the interaction of "complex, multileveled, and dynamic processes" that "produce failures in fluency that the individuals and their culture judge to be aberrant" (Smith & Kelly, 1997, p. 210). Although we see no direct explanation of why onset typically occurs between the ages of 2 to 5 years after a period of normally developing speech, Smith and Kelly (1997) do suggest that sudden or gradual shifts in the behaviour of factors that support fluency or are implicated in fluency failure can take place, with the emergence of stuttering as the result. The factors are dynamic, change over time, and are present in different degrees in individuals who stutter (Smith & Kelly, 1997).

Natural recovery

The explanation of variability (see below) is used to account for natural recovery.

Genetics

The model incorporates genetic and organismic components into an explanation of stuttering, but its authors carefully point out that these are part of a complex, interacting system. Unless other factors interact with the genetic factor or factors in ways that produce fluency failure, stuttering will not emerge. The nature and pattern of the interaction, however, are not explicitly described or specified.

Variability

The dynamic and changing interactions of the factors (emotional, cognitive, and linguistic) with one another and with the speech motor system at any given time within the individual are said to explain the natural variability of stuttering and the observation that a given individual can move into and out of "the stuttering diagnostic space" (Smith & Kelly, 1997, p. 209). According to Smith (1999), there are "a limited number of factors that have been demonstrated to systematically impact speech motor performance or fluency" (p. 42), such as autonomic arousal (Smith, 1999). The authors do not address how the model might explain the artificial variability that results from fluency-inducing conditions

Parsimony

The DM model is not parsimonious because it postulates, like the DC model, that stuttering is due to a combination of various factors with varying weights that are different in each individual. Smith (1999) offers the heterogeneity of stuttering behaviours and their variability as reasons for viewing stuttering as a multifactorial disorder, and suggests that a multifactorial view accounts for investigating the "... range of variables, from linguistic to motor, to psychosocial ... that have been implicated in stuttering" (p. 32). Yet Smith admits that stuttering occurs "... in all cultures and all languages ..." (p. 32). However, Smith takes that admission of the universality of stuttering to support the idea that no single factor – in this case, a single factor in the gene pool or in the environment – can account for the universality of stuttering. The obvious question, "Why not?", is not answered because it is not asked. It is not explained why a universally present phenomenon cannot be ascribed to a universal origin, given that various constitutional and environmental variables may influence how it is expressed.

Rather than focusing on what might be superficial aspects of the heterogeneity of stuttering, it would perhaps be more parsimonious to focus on the homogeneous aspects of the disorder.

Heuristic value

Despite the fact that the authors describe the DM model as multifactorial and interactional, it appears that such a description is inaccurate for the same reasons we give in our discussion of the DC model. Specifically, for the DM model, it appears that the core mechanism for stuttering is to be found in the speech motor system. The other factors that the authors describe serve to affect the speech motor system's ability to generate fluent speech. Smith and Kleinow (2000, pp. 530–531), in describing the multifactorial model being discussed here, write:

> Our working model of stuttering ... has as its central tenet that speech motor processes interact with a range of factors often conceived as remote from the motor system, including cognitive, linguistic, and emotional processes. Further, speech motor processes may be positively or negatively affected by these factors.

We do not see how this central tenet explains stuttering. Why does the impact on the speech motor system of varying combinations of factors with varying weights cause some people to stutter but not others? It implies no more than that the mechanism that causes fluency failure does not do so in a vacuum. We have no argument with a view such as that; we do not believe, however, that the tenet convincingly makes the case that "No single factor can be identified as 'the cause' of stuttering" (Smith & Kelly, 1997, p. 209).

It may very well be that Smith and colleagues are using the terms "multi-factorial" and "nonlinear" in ways that are not common or typical. If by multifactorial they mean that there can be a number of factors that work to destabilize the speech motor system, then little is added to our theorizing on cause. We see in Travis's (1986, p. 118) comments on his cerebral dominance theory, for example, the idea that different factors can contribute to stuttering for different individuals who stutter:

> I think that stuttering is a truly psychosomatic disorder. The problem is not that one factor or the other, constitutional or environmental, is the culprit, but rather, how much of one or of the other.

Despite his belief that a number of factors can contribute to stuttering, Travis (1986) maintained, "Our presupposition is that the stutterer differs significantly from the normal speaker only in his neuro-anatomical organization for speaking" (p. 119). This statement by Travis is not too far removed from the DM model that appears to posit a problem in the stability of the stutterer's speech motor system as measured by the STI.

The DM model presents the same kind of tangled situation that we find in the DC model; namely, that there can apparently be as many causes of stuttering as there are people who stutter, or different factors can contribute to stuttering in different individuals in different ways. For example,

> If we understand that we are looking for multiple factors related to stuttering, rather than a "key factor" that explains all stuttering phenomena, we recognize that to play a role in stuttering, a factor need not be significant in all individuals diagnosed as stuttering. Just as all individuals at risk for cardiovascular disease are not overweight or smokers, all individuals at risk for developing stuttering do not exhibit significant deviations from the nonstuttering population on measures of motor, linguistic, phonological, emotional, familial, or other factors.
>
> (Smith & Kelly, 1997, p. 210)

If what Smith and Kelly write is true, then understanding and treating stuttering will continue to be more daunting than any of the other communication disorders we study and treat. Rather than accept and reinforce the state of affairs described in the passage quoted above, it might be more productive to hypothesize that what we see as multifactorial is actually a reflection of our current inability to understand the nature and cause of stuttering. From that premise, research could move ahead to clear the clutter.

According to Smith (1999), "Multifactorial accounts of stuttering are not retreats from scientific solutions: rather, they recognise the complexity of the disorder" (p. 33). As we have said previously, most people would have no problem with stuttering being multifactorial or complex. A caveat to that, however, is that such accounts must be testable.

Smith and colleagues may also use the term "nonlinearity" in an uncommon or untypical way. It appears that nonlinearity in their terms means that the same level of a given factor has different effects in different individuals. The STIs of stutterers, for example, are larger or show greater increase over a baseline condition than the STIs of nonstutterers when both are asked to perform the same task at the same level (e.g., the production of an utterance of a given length and complexity). Typically, however, nonlinear refers to a relationship in which predictions cannot be made in the manner in which they may be made when variables are linearly related – the result or outcome cannot be predicted by a straight-line path back to the original condition when there is a nonlinear relationship.

On the face of it, it can appear that Smith and colleagues satisfy the typical definition of nonlinearity when they demonstrate that the responses (STIs) of stutterers are different from the responses (STIs) of nonstutterers to the same stimulus; that is, the same condition leads to different outcomes. However, the problem is that the different outcomes reflect differences between groups of subjects and not the nature (linear or nonlinear) of the relationship between the initial or same conditions and the outcome.

The heuristic value of the DM model is compromised, we suggest, by the failure to define stuttering satisfactorily. Although no exception is taken to the view that there can be processes at work before and after the perceptually observable occurrence of stuttering, in the final analysis stuttering must be regarded as a behavioural phenomenon and cannot be defined with physiological measures (Cordes & Ingham, 1997; Folkins, 1991). According to Folkins, "atypical physiological processes are not necessarily a problem until they reach the level of transmitted behavior" (1991, p. 564). The model's dismissal of the relevance of stuttering topography introduces unnecessary complexity and has the potential to foster the unwarranted belief ". . . that it is difficult to define stuttering, and that the concept and identification of moments of stuttering are elusive" (Attanasio, 2000, p. 55).

It also seems that the analogies used in the reports of the model sometimes confuse rather than clarify what is being explained. For example, Smith (1999) likens attempting to understand volcanoes and their eruptions from static or non-dynamic descriptions of them to attempting to understanding stuttering from the (to her) mistaken belief that units of stuttering can be identified. Smith (1999) argued that it is unproductive to attempt to identify stuttering events, just as it is unproductive to merely count and classify volcanoes ". . . based on the shape of the landform [its topography] and the type and shape of eruptive materials" (Smith, 1999, p. 24) without recognizing the need to understand volcanoes on a deeper and more complex level. Smith argued that the nature of volcanoes was only truly understood when scientists understood more about the movement of tectonic plates.

In our view, quite the opposite point can be made; namely, that it is possible to identify perceptually when stuttering occurs, just as it is possible to identify perceptually when a volcano erupts. Both can be defined, at least operationally, by gaining consensus among experts. It is difficult to decide precisely when stutters and volcanic eruptions start and precisely when they stop, but that does not disqualify these phenomena as events. The issue of imprecision at the onset and offset of events is not an insurmountable problem at the empirical level.

Taking our illustration of the heuristic value of the analogy even further, both types of events are underpinned by mechanisms that are not identifiable perceptually but which can be identified by alternate means: The eruptions of volcanoes are underpinned by the dynamics of tectonic plate movements, and stuttering events are underpinned by aberrant movements of the speech motor system. Smith and colleagues are correct when they say that the study of the dynamics of the speech motor system and the factors that impact on it is valuable in attempting to understand stuttering. Indeed, that appears to be the greatest heuristic value of the model. However, as we see it, aberrant activity of the speech motor system is not stuttering, just as movements of tectonic plates are not volcanic eruptions.

It is clear from reports of the DM model that it is intended primarily as a reminder of the complexity of stuttering. To this end, then, it has considerable heuristic value. However, this reminder may be of little value to clinicians. According to Smith and Kelly (1997, p. 214):

> We predict that multileveled indices of stability, complexity, and nonlinearity, together with the more traditional measures of familial, linguistic, phonological, and motor factors, will be crucial to improved success in the early diagnosis and treatment of stuttering.

This suggests that clinicians – and more importantly the stutterers and families they serve – would benefit from these "multileveled indices". The heuristic value of the DM model would have been enhanced if Smith and Kelly had explained what those benefits might be.

COMMENTARY ON MULTIFACTORIAL MODELS

According to the criteria we set up in Chapter 3 for evaluating theories, these two multifactorial models do not appear to have particular heuristic value. We suggest that the models suffer somewhat because of confusion in terminology. This confusion occurs, in the first instance, in relation to type of model. The authors of both the DC model and DM model describe them as interactional models. As we pointed out previously, the term "interactional" means that various factors, or variables, change each other (see Chapter 2).

We have no problem with the proposal that this may be the case in stuttering. However, our review suggests that the DC model is not interactional but is in fact a complex linear cause–effect model. There is nothing in the way the model is described to indicate that factors interact to cause stuttering. Rather, the model proposes that varying factors, *in concert*, cause stuttering. We have no problem with this proposal, either; the point we are making is that the impression given by reports of the model that factors interact is misleading.

Nor is it clear from the descriptions of the DM model that it is inter-actional. For the model to explain stuttering, it needs to say which factors have an effect on others, in what way factors interact, and how this causes stuttering.

The second way in which terminology serves to confuse rather than clarify in these models has to do with the term "multifactorial". As we have stated earlier, no one would disagree that stuttering is influenced by multiple factors. The well-documented variability in stuttering severity across and within stut-terers is sufficient testimony to that. Confusion arises when multifactorial is taken to mean multicausal. We suggest that this confusion arises because these terms are from different epistemologies. "Factors" (which is inter-changeable with "variables") is an empirical term, whereas "cause" is – at least when discussing theory – a logical term.

In reasoning about cause (see Chapter 1), the cause (always singular) of an event consists of the conditions that are necessary and sufficient for the event to occur. In stuttering, then, we could say that the cause can – and is likely to – consist of a number of factors. However, the fact that a number of factors, or variables, are operating at a moment of stuttering does not negate the possibility that one variable may constitute the necessary condition – not only for that moment of stuttering but for all other moments of stuttering. This becomes clearer if we return to the idea of causal fields and INUS conditions discussed in Chapter 1. It is then possible to sustain the position that stutter-ing could be caused by (1) a necessary condition consisting of one factor (for example an inefficiency in neural processing for speech) in conjunction with (2) one or more INUS conditions (for example physiological arousal, variable linguistic stress, and so forth). In any one causal field (a moment of stutter-ing) INUS conditions will be operating at various strengths. The point here is that it is fallacious to argue that since stuttering is multifactorial no single factor can constitute the necessary condition.

We have used the term "cause" here in the logical sense of necessary and sufficient conditions. However, of course the term is used much more loosely in everyday parlance. When one asks what causes influenza one does not expect a lengthy explanation of necessary and sufficient conditions, causal fields, and INUS conditions. The answer would be, simply, a virus (the neces-sary condition). We are not suggesting here that stuttering can be modelled on influenza. We are simply suggesting that we need to be mindful that the term "cause" is used differently in different contexts.

According to the DC and the DM models there is no necessary condition in stuttering. We are not concerned here with the truth of this proposal, only the logic of it. The proposal may be true, but it would be impossible to show that it is true.

If we seem to focus on the DC and DM models more than on any of the other theories and models reviewed in this text, and to be especially critical of them, it is only because they represent the now widely, though not universally, accepted view that stuttering is a multifactorial disorder. Given the fact that clinicians in particular seem to have embraced multifactorial explanations of stuttering, we felt we had the obligation to analyse them in greater detail.

Chapter 10

Theories of stuttering: Anticipatory struggle

In this chapter we review a theory that does not fit comfortably into any of the previous chapters. We conclude with a brief discussion of the findings of our review of all nine theories

THE ANTICIPATORY STRUGGLE HYPOTHESIS

According to the anticipatory struggle (AS) hypothesis, stuttering is a type of cognitive disorder in that the child, for reasons to be described below, comes to believe that the act of speaking is difficult and, at the same time, valued (Bloodstein, 1995). According to Bloodstein (1997), stuttering is learned behaviour.

Whether to call this a theory or a hypothesis is somewhat problematic. For example, Guitar (1998) uses the term theory and Bloodstein (1997) refers to it as both theory and hypothesis in the same sentence: "The anticipatory struggle hypothesis is first and foremost a cognitive theory of stuttering" (p. 169). We will use the term hypothesis throughout this discussion only because that is the term most familiar to us in our reading on Bloodstein's ideas about stuttering.

Faced with the belief that speech is difficult, the child approaches the act of speaking with tension, and then fragments the motor output into segments in order to manage speech production. This idea of tension with the accompanying fragmentation of complex and serially ordered motor activity is central to Bloodstein's (1995, 1997) version of the anticipatory struggle hypothesis. Bloodstein (1997, p. 169) states:

> All of the surface features of stuttering, whether repetitions, prolongations, hard attack on sound, or stoppage, may be viewed as manifestations of underlying tension and fragmentation in the initiation of speech units.

The child's belief that speech is difficult, according to Bloodstein (2000a), is "baseless" (p. 87) as is the child's belief that speech "requires effort, caution, or elaborate preparation if it is to be said without stuttering" (p. 87). Thus, the child may be said to have a cognitive mind-set about speech, albeit unwarranted, that leads to the anticipation of difficulty, which in turn causes struggle, tension, and the fragmentation of speech motor activity; stuttering is the result of this sequence of events.

What are the sources of the child's belief that speech is difficult? Bloodstein (1997) suggests a number of possibilities, all of which point to communicative failure in the face of challenges to communicative performance: a history of delayed language development or articulation defects; the child's experiences in therapy for language and speech disorders; and pressure that may come from excessive praise by parents for early speech and language performance, from "parental perfectionism about speech", or from holding the child to high and perfectionistic standards for speech (Bloodstein, 1997, p. 175). The child's belief in the difficulty of speech that arises from these sources may be vague or undefined initially, and may take the form of a generalized self-concept of being a poor speaker, but eventually grows into the anticipation of difficulty on specific words or in specific situations (Bloodstein, 1997).

Until recently, as reported above, the AS hypothesis proposed one cause for stuttering, and that was an unfounded belief that speaking is difficult. However, in his 2001 publication, Bloodstein changed the postulates of the AS hypothesis by stating that there are two causes of stuttering, one for incipient stuttering, which refers to stuttering when it first appears, and another for more developed stuttering. This was presaged earlier, in his response (see Bloodstein, 2000b) to a challenge to the idea that children can have an unfounded belief that speaking is difficult. In his 2001 publication Bloodstein referred to incipient and developed stuttering as "two distinct disorders" (p. 67). It appears that this change to the hypothesis is ad hoc, and is a response to the growing and now incontestable evidence of a strong genetic influence in stuttering (see Chapter 5). Bloodstein also supports this modification to the AS hypothesis by arguing that early and developed stuttering have different topographies.

In short, then, Bloodstein (2001) proposed that stuttering when it first appears in young children is caused by genetic factors, and that stuttering in older children and adults (developed stuttering) is caused by the anticipation of difficulty and the subsequent tension and fragmentation that are the child's learned response to the initial genetically based stuttering. Not all children with incipient stuttering develop these learned responses and so stuttering in these children is transient. Bloodstein (2001) does not say precisely what the genetically based "biological predisposition" (p. 70) to stuttering is, but states, "When we know what the gene or genes involved in stuttering code for, the disorder may prove to have closer links to difficulties in language acquisition than to any problem of motor coordination" (p. 71).

Bloodstein (2001) also argues that this genetic predisposition "peters out like various other genetic influences – for example like the human gift for language acquisition itself" (p. 70). It is not clear what is meant by this, as it is not explained how a predisposition can diminish.

Bloodstein (2001) also does not make clear if genetic factors contribute to stuttering in every child with the disorder, or if every child who develops stuttering has a genetic predisposition to do so. He does, however, make statements that give a prominent role to genetic factors. For example, he states that ". . . it seems clear that a significant role in the etiology of stuttering is played by biologic heredity, with the implication that the disorder is in part a neurologic one" (Bloodstein, 2001, p. 67). We take Bloodstein's (2001) statements and the propositions in his most recent position as indications that he considers a genetic predisposition to stutter to be a necessary condition for the disorder to occur. Bloodstein's views on this matter are revisited in the section on genetics that follows below.

We point out that Bloodstein's recent ad hoc alteration to a theory that he has been writing about for 45 years poses considerable difficulties as we attempt to review it. While we acknowledge that theories may be modified to incorporate new findings, in this particular instance Bloodstein's 2001 publication presents us with what is in effect a new theory. While the idea of anticipatory struggle is still an important construct in the modified version, anticipatory struggle can no longer be said to be the *only* cause of stuttering. This is clearly different from the previous version of the AS hypothesis which stated that stuttering is "an anticipatory struggle reaction even in its earliest manifestations" (Bloodstein, 1997, p. 176). For clarity, we will refer to the 2001 version as the modified AS hypothesis.

Background and development

Despite the fact that Guitar (1998) credits Bloodstein as the developer of the original AS theory [*sic*], the idea that stuttering is the result of some form of anticipatory struggle has been extant for a good number of years and has been proposed by a number of theorists (Bloodstein, 1997). We believe, however, that it would not be gainsaid by the majority of researchers in stuttering that Bloodstein has been, and continues to be, the primary explicator and proponent of the anticipatory struggle hypothesis.

Testability

The arguments within both versions of the hypothesis are logical. In the original version, a baseless belief that speech is difficult is a necessary and, presumably, a sufficient condition for stuttering to occur. Thus, the hypothesis would be falsified if it were shown that stuttering occurred in the absence of such a belief.

However, the ability to test the hypothesis at the empirical level was challenged recently (Packman, Menzies, & Onslow, 2000a). They said that it is doubtful that an experiment can be structured to show that, when individuals stutter, they are not possessed of the belief that speech is difficult. We add here the doubt that an experiment can determine if, just prior to the moment of stuttering, stutterers *do* anticipate difficulty *and* that this anticipation is based on a false belief. Bloodstein (2000b, p. 358) rebutted Packman et al. (2000a) by stating, "the concept that stuttering blocks are precipitated by the anticipation of stuttering, or by a belief in the difficulty of speech, is not logically impossible to verify by experiment, it is only technically difficult to do so, like other hypotheses about the moment of stuttering".

We find Bloodstein's (2000b) rebuttal to be unsatisfactory, especially because he does not go on to suggest how the necessary experiment might be structured. It is telling that Bloodstein (2000b) does not point to extant experimental tests of the hypothesis but simply asks us to observe "the conditions under which stutterings happen" (p. 358) and the behaviours of stutterers when under those conditions. We acknowledge the importance of observation in science (Packman & Onslow, 2000), but such observations as Bloodstein reports are only the first steps towards the corroboration (or falsification) of a hypothesis.

As far as falsifying the modified version of the hypothesis is concerned, it would be necessary to show that stuttering occurred in the absence of a predisposition to do so. Since predisposition cannot be defined operationally, it can only be assumed to be present from the presence of stuttering. Family history of stuttering cannot be regarded as evidence of this predisposition, as many people who stutter do not have any family history. If, however, this predisposition is an inherited difficulty with language acquisition – as Bloodstein (2001) implies – then it would be possible to falsify the hypothesis by showing that children start to stutter in the absence of such a difficulty. To date, there is no evidence that children who stutter necessarily have difficulty with language acquisition.

Explanatory power

Since the earliest appearances of the AS hypothesis approximately 45 years ago (Bloodstein, 1958), Bloodstein has been steadfast in claiming that the hypothesis is able to explain all of what is known about stuttering (see for example, Bloodstein 1972, 1997, 2000a, 2000b, 2001). In his view, "the hypothesis is consistent with all of the many conditions and factors that are known to influence the occurrence of stuttering" (Bloodstein, 1997, p. 173).

Topography

Bloodstein's assertions, however, go beyond stating that the hypothesis is consistent with the phenomena of stuttering. The hypothesis proposes an explanation of why people stutter. According to the modified AS hypothesis, in incipient stuttering children repeat whole words at the start of utterances because they are having difficulty "in the execution of whole utterances and their constituent phrase structures" (Bloodstein, 2001, p. 67), whereas the topography of developed stuttering reflects "difficulty in the execution of words" (p. 67). That is, as a result of a belief that given words are difficult to produce, the individual anticipates difficulty, struggles, brings tension to the initiation of speech, and then fragments the motor activity of speaking.

In an exchange of viewpoints with Bloodstein (Packman & Onslow, 2000), one of us, with a colleague, took exception to Bloodstein's claim that the documented changes in the locus and typography of stuttering over time are the result of a diminution of genetic factors. It may very well be, according to Packman and Onslow (2000), that a more parsimonious explanation of the differences between the locus and typography of early stuttering and the form it eventually takes after some time has elapsed is that they "reflect changing responses to the *same* underlying problem, whatever that might be" (p. 360).

Onset

The explanation of onset in the original version of the hypothesis is based on observations, clinical interviews with parents of young stutterers, and research, which according to Bloodstein, identify conditions that are associated with onset (Bloodstein, 1958, 1997). These conditions contain, in one way or another, chronic experiences of communicative failure that may arise from deficits in speech and language ability; pressures on the child from overbearing, overanxious, perfectionistic parents for unrealistic levels of speech and language proficiency; and a family history of stuttering. In the original version Bloodstein allowed a place for heredity in family history, but placed at least equal emphasis on an environment created by parental behaviours, beliefs, and pressures in the cause of stuttering.

The modified version of the hypothesis, however, states that the onset of stuttering is due to an inherited difficulty in executing utterances, while stuttering in older children and adults develops through (presumably instrumental) learning.

Natural recovery

It is apparent that Bloodstein (2000b, p. 358) presages the subsequent modifications to the hypothesis:

It seems to me possible that genes may predispose a child in some way to being excessively disfluent, but that in its later forms stuttering is a learned reactive development that has persisted after the genetic influence has diminished or gone. If so, this would go far to explain the high rate of spontaneous recovery from stuttering.

As stated above, then, stuttering is transient when children do not develop learned responses to the incipient stuttering.

Genetics

In the original version of the AS hypothesis, Bloodstein (1997) stated that genetic or hereditary factors interact with the environmental factor of communicative pressure in the development of stuttering. He used the observation that stutterers are able to say words other than the stuttered word with perfect fluency to suggest that genetic factors alone are insufficient to account for the disorder. Bloodstein's (1997, 2000b) view on heredity's role in stuttering has a remarkable twist. He proposed that, although some children may be genetically predisposed to be excessively disfluent and this still unknown genetic factor may be implicated in the cause of stuttering, stuttering on a given word or on a given occasion may be entirely explained as anticipatory struggle. Bloodstein (1997) stated that "... little or nothing that stutterers have inherited seems to play an important part [in given moments of stuttering]. The hypothetical organic predisposition to stutter has disappeared or exists in such minimal amount that it can be ignored" (p. 177). In the original version, then, everything that is known about fully developed stuttering and the conditions under which stuttering occurs and why stuttering occurs on a given word or on a given occasion (the moment of stuttering) can be explained by the anticipatory struggle hypothesis without the need to bring genetics or heredity into the picture. This is not the case for the modified version, in which a genetically based predisposition is a necessary condition for stuttering to occur.

Variability

In the original AS hypothesis, Bloodstein (1997) has an explanation for variability between stutterers, or the observation that different stutterers stutter on different words or on different occasions: Different stutterers have come to find different words and different occasions difficult and therefore have different episodes of anticipation and struggle. Natural variability within individuals is also readily explained by the AS hypothesis (Bloodstein 1997, 2000b). When stutterers are fluent or not stuttering, they are so because they have forgotten that they are stutterers. Having forgotten that they are stutterers, they do not have the anticipation of difficulty and consequently do not stutter.

In 1972, Bloodstein published an account of the ways in which the original AS hypothesis explains a number of fluency-enhancing conditions. The metronome effect, or the reduction of stuttering when individuals time their speech to a rhythm established by a metronome, is attributed to simplification of speech motor planning which causes the stutterer to evaluate what is being spoken as easy, rather than holding to the more typical belief in the difficulty of speech. Speaking in time to the metronome may also distract the stutterer's attention away from stuttering because of the novel speech pattern that is induced. The adaptation effect, or the reduction in stuttering over repeated readings of the same passage (or the repetition of the same utterance over and over again), is attributed to the stutterer's rehearsal of the speech motor plan which results in the evaluation that speech is easy rather than difficult. The reduction of stuttering under white noise is the result of distraction. Thus, Bloodstein (1972) suggests that fluency-enhancing conditions operate either by altering the stutterer's evaluation of the difficulty of speech or by distracting the stutterer's attention from stuttering.

Bloodstein's (1972) conceptualization of distraction requires some clarification. Despite the fact that Bloodstein (1972) believes that a satisfactory operational definition of distraction has yet to be achieved, he nevertheless thinks it a useful concept for thinking about stuttering that can be defined in some manner. Bloodstein (1972, pp. 491–492) states:

> We may define distraction in terms of two broad observations. First, stuttering, like so many learned responses, may be inhibited temporarily by extraneous stimuli: the stronger or more unusual the stimuli, or the less adapted the stutterer is to them, the more likely the effect. Parallel observations of laboratory subjects have a long history in the experimental psychology of learning. Second, stuttering may be momentarily inhibited when another response is simultaneously evoked, even when the other response seems overtly compatible with stuttering. The more automatic or "habituated" the other response, the less the effect on stuttering.

Stuart (1999), however, argued forcefully that distraction cannot be defined operationally, and so is not a useful construct in attempting to explain stuttering.

Based on a review of studies that have investigated the distribution of stuttering events, Bloodstein (1997) concluded that stutterers have more difficulty on words that begin with consonants rather than with vowels, on longer rather than on shorter words, on content rather than on function words or pronouns, on words that begin sentences, on words that have a low frequency of occurrence in the language, on words that are difficult to guess from context, and on words that receive the most linguistic stress (p. 174). Stutterers have difficulty with such words as these because, according to

Bloodstein, their features make the words conspicuous and apparently difficult. Thus, stutterers tend to anticipate difficulty on these words and consequently stutter on them.

Parsimony

There can be no doubt that the AS hypothesis in its original form is parsimonious. Indeed, all that is required to explain stuttering – its onset, development, topography, and variability – is the faulty belief that speech is difficult. That faulty belief leads to the anticipation of difficulty and thence to the tension, struggle, and fragmentation that is stuttering.

However, parsimony is reduced in the modified version of the AS hypothesis because there is no longer an overarching explanation for stuttering. Rather, the hypothesis now has two postulates to explain early and developed stuttering, which Bloodstein (2001) now describes as two distinct disorders.

Heuristic value

Given that Bloodstein himself traced the origins of the AS hypothesis to 19th-century writers (Bloodstein, 2000a) and that elements of the hypothesis can be seen in the moribund diagnosogenic theory of Johnson, the original AS hypothesis does not prompt us into new ways of thinking about or conceptualizing stuttering. We are not suggesting that the AS hypothesis has little heuristic value simply because of its longevity. We suggest quite the opposite: A theory that has been as long-standing as this one ought to have been fruitful in terms of producing, over the many years of its existence, experimental or solid clinical evidence of its correctness. This has not occurred. We believe that satisfactory scientific evidence does not exist and concur with the view, "Presumably that longevity [of the anticipatory struggle hypothesis] can be accounted for, in part, by the resistance of this hypothesis to *experimental* [italics added] investigation" (Packman et al., 2000a, p. 88).

In its modified version, the AS hypothesis now resembles Bluemel's theory of primary and secondary stuttering from the 1930s (see Chapter 4). This is acknowledged by Bloodstein (2001). As with the original version, then, the modified version of the AS hypothesis appears to add little if anything to our understanding of stuttering.

Chapter 11

Theories and treatment

INTRODUCTION: DISCUSSION OF REVIEW OF THEORIES

In the preface we expressed the wish that the book's contents would be helpful to its readers. We wonder, now, if that wish has been granted. After all, we have presented an analytical review of an array of theories that, in a number of ways, are as different from one another as night is to day. We are certain, too, that it becomes clear after reading the text that the nine theories we have reviewed not only differ from one another, but contradict one another as well. At what point, then, have we arrived? What are we to make of these theories of stuttering?

While it is the case that one of the functions of a scientific theory is to generate research and that to some degree there is research into stuttering that is theory-driven, we can detect no organized or cohesive research agenda that would encourage us to think that the investigation of the nature and cause of stuttering is moving towards an accepted working framework shared by the majority of researchers or, at the very least, towards a consensus. We maintain, based on our review, that the nine theories examined in the text have not led to much research. We admit that we are not certain why that is so. If these theories of stuttering have not prompted much research, what, then, is their utility?

Perhaps their use lies in attempts to clarify beliefs about stuttering, to question views, to argue a position, to put forward a thesis and encourage responses to it; in short, to create what the ancient Greek philosophers called the dialectic (Kolenda, 1974). The dialectic is a form of "Philosophical argument and discovery" (Kolenda, 1974, p. 64). Kolenda (1974) writes, "If A says something, but B objects, a conversation or argument thus gets started" (p. 64). There is merit in dialectical argumentation. The value of the nine theories, therefore, may be that they have contributed to theory development, rather than to research, and that they sharpen our efforts to explain therapies. The nine theories compel us to continue the conversation on the nature, cause, and treatment of stuttering. We continue here with some aspects of this conversation.

One use of theory construction is to provide a means of arriving at the cause of phenomena or an understanding of their nature. In disciplines that are concerned with human diseases or disorders, the search for cause or for an understanding of the nature of phenomena, interesting and important in and of themselves, is inevitably linked to prevention and treatment.

In this chapter, we explore the links between theories of stuttering and the treatment of stuttering. The exploration is done within the context of such questions as: Do theories of stuttering generate treatment for the disorder? Are therapies, in fact, based on theories? Is a theory validated when treatment based on it is shown to be effective? Is theory necessary for effective treatment? Is it necessary to bring causal theories of stuttering into therapy? Do non-causal theories or models of stuttering have any relationship to therapy? What are the repercussions of basing therapy on false theories? Is it possible that therapy generates theory? The answers to these questions, as the reader will see below, are not always straightforward.

THERAPY BASED ON THEORY

It may seem obvious to anyone familiar with the literature of stuttering that the answer to the first two questions is patently "yes". Indeed, readers of this text may be puzzled by the questions having been asked at all. All that need be done is to give some examples to make the case. The treatment for young children called the multiprocess approach (see Gottwald & Starkweather, 1999) is based directly on the demands and capacities (DC) model. The treatment suggestions or rationale can be traced back directly to the central tenet of the DC model that stuttering is the result of levels of demands exceeding levels of capacities. According to Gottwald and Starkweather (1999, p. 66):

> This multiprocess intervention program is designed to (a) reduce demands on the child's current level of fluency, which may stem from the environment or from the child, and (b) enhance the child's capacities for producing fluent speech.

The anticipatory struggle (AS) hypothesis offers another example of the connection between theory and therapy. Given that the hypothesis states that stuttering is the result of the belief that speaking is difficult coupled with the anticipation of that difficulty, therapy takes the form of helping stutterers change their belief systems and reduce or eliminate the anticipations of difficulty in speaking. Another example to make the case is the covert repair

(CR) hypothesis. The CR hypothesis proposes that stuttering is a response to an excessive number of errors or flaws in the speaker's phonetic plan. A consequent implication for treatment given by the authors of the CR hypothesis (Kolk & Postma, 1997) is that changes in the rate and complexity of utterances might have a salutary effect on stuttering. Kolk and Postma (1997, p. 200) state:

> Clinicians often try to bring about slower speech in these children by (1) asking them directly to slow down; (2) asking them to wait a little longer before taking turns in conversation; (3) asking parents to speak more slowly when talking to their children. CRH provides a theoretical rationale for these treatment procedures.

It would be instructive for readers of this text to analyse the treatments based on these three theories or others to determine how the treatments are conducted and the extent to which the treatments match the theories.

Authors of theories are not alone in thinking that theories inform, guide, or influence treatment. To appreciate the link between theory and therapy in clinical practice, we need only recall, as one illustration, the considerable and long-lasting influence that Johnson's diagnosogenic theory (see Chapter 4) had on the treatment and management approaches that clinicians adopted in their work with individuals who stutter.

However, Siegel (1998), in commenting on a book that he and Curlee edited (Curlee & Siegel, 1997), writes that contemporary stuttering treatment does not seem to be anchored in theory. Instead, Siegel (1998) sees treatment, as reflected in the clinical chapters of Curlee and Siegel (1997), as being based on practical considerations and on clinical experience and intuition. There is little, if any, attempt to use theory to justify treatment.

How, then, can Siegel's (1998) analysis be reconciled with assertions, some made in this text, that theories can and do inform therapy? We would expect that, if you asked researchers and clinicians if they based their research and treatment on a particular theory of stuttering, many would answer in the affirmative. We would not know this for certain, of course, unless we took an adequate sample of opinion. Then there is always the possibility of dissonance between what is claimed and what is actually practised. What continues to be troubling is a comment that a friend and colleague made years ago. He said, on more than one occasion, that he had never observed in clinical practice a single instance of theory-based treatment for any communication disorder despite clinicians' sincere claims to the contrary.

The fact remains, however, that there *are* theories of stuttering that suggest treatment approaches. We draw attention to the fact, though, that current theories that do suggest treatment, as outlined above, do so only for stuttering in young children. We can think of no treatments for stuttering in adults that are theory-driven although, as we saw in our reviews of theories, many have been justified by theory. Thus, Siegel is partially correct in saying that treatment is not theory-driven. The problem may be that, even with children, there are so many theories that clinical practice is seen as theoretically unanchored.

EFFECTIVE THERAPY AS CONFIRMATION OF THEORY

When a therapy that is based on a theory has demonstrable success in the treatment of stuttering, is the theory thereby confirmed? Is the theory thereby shown to be true? Would that it were so straightforward. Imagine that treatment B, shown to be effective in the treatment of stuttering, is based on theory A. The argument that theory A is valid and true because treatment B has been shown to be effective would take the form: *If A is a valid and true theory, then B as a treatment based on it would be effective. Data indicate that treatment B is effective; therefore A is a valid and true theory*. Readers will recall from an earlier section of the text that the argument

If A, then B
B, therefore A

is known as *affirming the consequent* and that, on purely logical grounds, is a fallacy. It is a logical fallacy because it does not account for the possibility that B could be true for reasons other than A. Because the argument does not state that "the truth of A was a necessary prerequisite for the truth of B" (Sidman, 1960, p. 127), "the truth of B does not logically permit any inference concerning A" (Sidman, 1960, p.127). It can be seen then, that effective treatment B, despite the fact that it was derived from theory A, cannot be used to confirm that theory. It could very well be that treatment B is effective for a variety of reasons that are only partially accounted for by theory A. It is possible that reasons for treatment B's effectiveness have nothing to do with theory A. It is also possible that theory A could be wrong even though treatment B is effective. Sander (1975) addresses the problem, stating, "Therapy results add notoriously little to the resolution of competing theory, since they too are capable of diverse explanation" (p. 261).

The possibility that an effective treatment can be based on an incorrect theory – the treatment works but the theory is wrong – can very easily mislead us, unless the dangers and pitfalls of using the affirmation of the consequent as a method of theory validation are kept in mind.

Damer (1987) suggests that the fallacy of affirming the consequent can be put into sharp focus by using an absurd example. Adapting an example that he gives (p. 151), the following is offered: *If you read this book (A), you will be able to judge the merits of a theory of stuttering when you hear or read it (B)*.

You are able to judge the merits of a theory of stuttering (B). Hence, you must have read this book (A). As Damer (1987, p. 151) states:

> Although you may indeed have read this book, the fact that you are able to [judge the merits of a theory of stuttering] in no way entails or requires that you must have read this book.

On the other hand, Sidman (1960) stated that the scientist's view of affirming the consequent is different from the logician's view. Despite its dangers and shortcomings, Sidman (1960) feels that affirming the consequent "is very nearly the life blood of science" (p. 127) and that scientists use affirming the consequent as one way to replicate experimental data (see Sidman, 1960, for a review) but employ it most often in testing theories. As for using affirmation of the consequent to validate a theory, the following comment (Sidman, 1960, pp. 127–128) is relevant:

> [establishing] the truth of B does tell him [the scientist] something about A. For one thing, he has eliminated one of the conditions which could have proved A to be false. If B had turned out to be false, then the truth of A could not be upheld.

All is not lost when a theory fails to be confirmed by a crucial experiment. The theorist may be able to identify a fault in the experiment that could account for the negative result and continue to hold on to the theory and continue to test it. Obviously, if negative results continue to occur, the theory may be abandoned. Sidman (1960), however, cautions that the usefulness of affirming the consequent for theory testing is limited if theories lack specificity or if the basic theoretical statements are ambiguous. For Sidman (1960), it is not the technique of affirming the consequent that is the problem. The problem, rather, is the application of the technique to testing poorly constructed, ambiguous, and less-than-specific theories.

Returning to the question asked at the beginning of this discussion – is a theory shown to be true when a therapy based on it has demonstrable success? – we find that the question is not easily answered.

THE PROOF OF THE PUDDING IS IN THE EATING: THE PRIMACY OF EVIDENCE

Despite the fallacious reasoning inherent in using treatment success to support the theory from which it is derived, the validity of a theory would be questionable if its treatment were shown not to be successful. It is obvious that an unsuccessful treatment cannot be a candidate for theory-confirming status. It is appropriate, therefore, to ask if treatments for stuttering are supported by data-based evidence. That is, are there adequate data to support the claims of success made for treatments that are recommended to clinicians? It is not the intent of this discussion to answer that question for each of the currently published treatments for stuttering. Rather, the general status of data-based evidence for the support of treatment claims is explored.

A number of early workers of significance in the field of stuttering (Bluemel, Johnson, Travis, van Riper, for example) were the foundational thinkers on stuttering whose contributions to speech-language pathology are legendary, and clinicians turned to them for theories on stuttering and for the treatment approaches they recommended (see Bloodstein, 1993). These individuals were arguably unquestioned authorities, not pressed to support their views by data-based evidence. That they said what they said was enough. All that clinicians had to do to justify their approaches to stuttering was to state the names of the authorities they took as their guides. There was comfort in having recourse to authority. It seems, however, that influential authorities with the status of Bluemel, Johnson, van Riper, or Travis are no longer on the scene (Siegel, 1998). There may be many reasons for their absence; nevertheless, the days of arguing from authority without offering data-based evidence to support treatment claims are over. Or are they?

We take as the base for this discussion some of the papers presented at the Third Annual Leadership Conference held by the American Speech-Language-Hearing Association's Special Interest Division for Fluency and Fluency Disorders in 1996, and subsequently published in *Stuttering Research and Practice: Bridging the Gap* (Bernstein Ratner & Healey, 1999). The discussion on the relationships between research and treatment framed by the collected papers in Bernstein Ratner and Healey (1999) continues to be relevant.

At least one of the participants at the 1996 conference appeared to reject the use of data-based research to support claims of treatment effectiveness or to recommend treatment methods for clinical use (see Attanasio, 2000). Starkweather suggested that the scientific method might not be appropriate to research into treatment effectiveness (Attanasio, 2000; Starkweather, 1999). The comments of other participants have been interpreted as "the willingness to adopt treatment approaches that are based on an inadequate analysis of the validity of the research used to support those approaches" as well as a willingness to adopt "approaches that are based on impression or speculation" (Attanasio, 2000, p. 54). This is reflected in the suggestion of one participant that clinicians should adopt approaches to treatment that they are personally comfortable with (Manning, 1999). Based on this Manning concluded, "doing studies that compare one treatment with another seems a lot like discussing the relative merits of religions or political parties" (p. 127).

It is in the paper by Ingham and Cordes (1999) that the paucity of data-based evidence is illustrated and decried. At the same time, Ingham and Cordes (1999) are unyielding in their instance on relevant and extensive data-based evidence. In their review of the April 1995 issue of *Language, Speech, and Hearing Services in the Schools* (a special issue devoted to the treatment of stuttering in preschool, school-age, and adolescent children), Ingham and Cordes (1999) report that none of the seven articles in the issue "provided information documenting that the described therapy procedure had ever produced clinically meaningful benefits" (p. 213). Furthermore, Ingham and Cordes (1999) reported that a number of the articles recommended therapy approaches "that had previously been demonstrated to be ineffective" (p. 213). The articles also did not report therapy procedures that have been documented through clinical research as effective – a suggestion that data-based evidence for some treatments does exist. When the authors of the articles in the April 1995 issue of *LSHSS* reported success with their programmes, the figures given were typically the percentages of children who were successful rather than data to support the claims of success (Ingham & Cordes, 1999). Ingham and Cordes (1999) believe that what they found in the April 1995 issue of *LSHSS* would be found in other reports on stuttering treatments.

In his review of a 1998 textbook on stuttering, Onlsow (1999) made a similar complaint about the relative absence of science and evidence in the recommendations made for treatment. Onslow (1999, p. 328) stated:

> Treatments that are in the early stages of scientific development are over-looked . . . Treatments are presented as having the same value with no encouragement to consider evidence of effectiveness when evaluating them. Further, the author makes no mention of the fact that many children recover from stuttering without the professional interventions he describes, despite the implications of such scientific findings for the treatment of childhood stuttering . . .

Onslow (1999) also points out that the text recommends procedures of unknown scientific merit to change family interactive dynamics. An examination of a more recent textbook on stuttering (published in 2001) finds the situation a bit improved, but not sufficiently so to warrant the conclusion that the treatment approaches that are recommended are supported by scientifically valid data.

Without meaning to minimize the importance of clinical insight and artistry, we maintain that it is incumbent upon theorists and clinicians to conduct scientific research into the development or identification of treatment programmes that are as effective and efficient as possible and that are supported by data-based evidence, so that individuals who stutter are provided with appropriate treatment programmes. The profession of speech-language pathology has the responsibility to offer treatments that have demonstrated value. One hopeful sign that movement on this front is taking place is the recent interest in conducting randomized controlled trials (RCT) similar to those used in medical and drug research (Jones, Gebski, Onslow, & Packman, 2001). "RCT are controlled experiments that compare the effectiveness of different treatments, or compare a treatment to a placebo" (Jones et al., 2001, p. 264). Another positive sign is the increasing prominence in the treatment of stuttering, and in speech-language pathology in general, of the twin ideas of evidence-based practice and the scientist-practitioner (for example, see Bothe, 2003; Lum, 2002).

This section, then, ends on an optimistic note. Ryan and Ryan (2002) believe that there are "presently proven clinical treatments available to the clinician in the public schools" (p. 15) and they highlight their Monterey Fluency Program and the Lidcombe Program. The Ryans suggest that the two programmes "have a great deal of published efficacy (effectiveness and efficiency) data to support them" (p. 15). Perhaps soon the day will arrive when the present discussion on the need for data-based evidence will be part of the history of the treatment of stuttering rather than a description of the current state of affairs.

THE NECESSITY OF THEORY FOR TREATMENT

Applied helping professions such as speech-language pathology and medicine that strive to be scientific seek to base their treatment methods on clearly understood and articulated rationales. In turn, rationales for treatments may be based on theories of the causes of the disorders or diseases; in such cases as these, clinical thinking proceeds from what is seen as the cause of the disorder to the selection of approaches to the treatment of the disorder. Although the best of all possible worlds would be one in which the treatment of every disorder or disease is based on the clear understanding of its cause, we do not live in such a world. It is quite likely that many clinicians have successfully treated clients for whom the causes of their disorders were never fully or finally known. In such cases as these, treatment rationales may be based on principles other than those derived from guiding theories.

Perkins (1986) discussed some issues surrounding the relationships between theory and therapy and concluded that until the day comes when we have a valid theory of the nature and cause of any given communication disorder (he includes stuttering), clinicians would "be well-advised to proceed pragmatically, using clinical sessions experimentally to determine the effectiveness of our procedures irrespective of whether they fit a particular rationale" (p. 33). For Perkins (1986), in the absence of valid theory, it is the clinician's skills, experience, and intuition that provide the framework for effective treatment.

Siegel and Ingham (1987, p. 103) have taken Perkins' comments to mean that Perkins (1986) disdains the role of theory in therapy. They give a more prominent place for theory's role in therapy than does Perkins (1986):

. . . there are many examples where at least potential approaches to therapy emerged from a theory. It is the fate of theories to be disproved, as Perkins and others have observed, but it is also the fate of any therapy method to be changed or discarded, and theories can provide a rationale basis for considering and also for rejecting such methods.

Siegel and Ingham (1987) argue that theory can assist clinicians in assessing the merits of commercial programmes for the treatment of stuttering, and in judging the correctness of those who claim that the questions of how to treat stuttering have been answered. Furthermore, Siegel and Ingham (1987) suggest that an evaluation of the theoretical assumptions upon which a treatment approach is based can assist clinicians in deciding if the kind of pragmatic evaluation that Perkins (1986) suggests is worth doing.

Elsewhere, Siegel (1987) argues that the issue is not whether a therapy method works "but rather whether it makes sense" (p. 309). It is Siegel's (1987) belief that the therapies we choose to investigate or bring into our clinical practice ought to be those that are related to the knowledge base in communication disorders, a knowledge base that is created by research and theories.

Wingate (2002, p. 368) states the following concerning the basis for the management of stuttering:

Routinely, management of a disorder is based on knowledge of the disorder acquired from careful study, and typically with special reference to the relevant normal condition. Being knowledgeable about the nature of speech and the structure of stuttering is essential for dealing effectively with the disorder, for this knowledge supplies the rationale for the direct assistance undertaken and the counsel offered.

Wingate (2002) does not mention cause specifically but, without attempting to second-guess his view on the need to base treatment on theory, we take his position to be closer to Siegel's (1987) and Siegel and Ingham's positions (1987) than to Perkins' (1986). On the other hand, Wingate (2002) suggests that, in actual practice, treatments are pragmatically based. He states, "In spite of the various 'theories' of stuttering, therapies for the disorder are essentially pragmatic; that is, treatment methods are not derived from theories but, rather, are practically based efforts" (p. 375).

To treat a disorder without knowing its cause or without having a confirmed and valid theory of cause arguably is to treat the symptom. There was a time in speech-language pathology when symptomatic therapy was derided. A more forgiving, because a more realistic, attitude prevails today in part because of the lessons learned from clinical medicine. Speech-language pathologists have come to the realization that treatment often cannot wait for the cause of a disorder to be found and that intervention on the disorder itself can be effective. Perhaps Perkins (1986, p. 33) is correct when he expresses gratitude for learning theories and the behaviour modification approaches that are based on operant theory – theories that make no assumptions about cause:

> What operant and other learning theories do provide that is of special value to us are the conditions by which behavior can be changed, regardless of cause. We can be confident in deriving behavior-changed procedures from these theories because they have survived extensive experimental testing across a wide range of conditions.

In any event, the contribution of behaviour therapy to the treatment of stuttering has indeed been "plentiful" (Ingham, 1984, p. 433).

ATHEORETICAL TREATMENT: AN EXAMPLE

An example of a treatment approach to stuttering that is not based on a theory of cause is the Lidcombe Program (see Onslow et al., 2003). The Lidcombe Program (LP) is a behavioural treatment for young children who stutter that does not rest on a causal theory. In fact, the authors of the LP do not yet know why the programme is effective in reducing or eliminating early stuttering (Onslow, 2003). The Australian Stuttering Research Centre (ASRC), however, has an active research programme into finding out why the treatment works.

The LP is administered by parents (or care givers) in children's everyday environments. Parents visit the speech-language pathologist weekly to learn how to do the programme and to obtain feedback from the speech-language pathologist to ensure that the programme is being conducted appropriately. Daily parental ratings of stuttering severity in everyday situations and weekly measures of rate of stuttered syllables in the clinic guide the conduct of the programme. A complete description of the features of the LP can be accessed at the ASRC's website; therefore, only a brief description of the programme's primary technique is given here.

Treatment is direct and involves comments from the parent to the child about the child's speech. The parent acknowledges or praises intervals of non-stuttered speech and acknowledges or requests the child to correct instances of stuttering. Reinforcement (verbal contingencies for stutter-free speech) predominates and may take the form of the parent saying, "that was good talking, there were no bumpy words" or "that was smooth talking". Punishment (verbal contingencies for stuttering) occurs only occasionally and in a supportive and encouraging manner. This may take the form of the parent saying "I heard a bumpy word; say it again without the bumps". Whatever the particular comment given, the idea is to highlight non-stuttered speech and to gently call the child's attention to stutters along with a request to repeat the word without stuttering. Although the primary technique used in the LP may appear to be simple, the full description of the programme will show that the technique is imbedded in a carefully designed and administered programme that is far from simple.

Interestingly, this treatment met with considerable opposition in its early days (see Cook & Rustin, 1997; Hayhow, 1997; Onslow, O'Brian, & Harrison, 1997a, 1997b), precisely because it did not conform to the two prevailing theoretical positions on stuttering. The first of these is that drawing attention to stuttering or to speech generally, in young children, will cause stuttering and/or make it worse. This belief reflects the influence of Johnson's diagnosogenic theory (see Chapter 4), Bloodstein's AS hypothesis (see Chapter 10), and the DC model of Starkweather and colleagues (see Chapter 9). A treatment based on operant methodology such as the Lidcombe Program is the antithesis of the treatment approaches proposed by the authors of these theories (for a discussion of this see Packman et al., 2004). The second prevailing theoretical position is that stuttering is a multifactorial disorder (see Chapter 9). Critics of the Lidcombe Program argued that it is a simple treatment and so was inconsistent with:

> the view taken by the majority of accepted authorities in this field, who, supported by evidence from wide-ranging research, place it consistently within a multi-factorial framework incorporating physiological, linguistic, environmental, and psychological components.
>
> (Cook & Rustin, 1997, p. 251)

More than 10 years after the first publication of the treatment (Onslow, Costa, & Rue, 1990), the Lidcombe Program is now becoming accepted in the western world (see Onslow et al., 2003). This is despite the fact that the cause of stuttering is still unknown, and the programme remains free of any theoretical position on cause. Presumably, the programme is becoming accepted more widely because of the extensive empirical evidence of its effectiveness (for overviews see Onslow et al., 2003).

Other examples of treatment programmes that are not based on causal theories can be found in the treatment literature. The LP is offered as one example of how a structured programme can be developed, administered, and its effectiveness studied without recourse to a causal theory.

THEORIES AS POTENTIAL SOURCES OF ERROR IN THE SELECTION OF TREATMENT

The history of stuttering is replete with theories of the causes of the disorder and with therapies based on those causes. The interested reader may wish to consult *Stuttering: A Short History of a Curious Disorder* (Wingate, 1997) for an informative treatment of that history.

One of the lessons learned from reading the history of the study of stuttering is that harm can be done when treatment is based on an incorrect or unscientific theory. Some of these treatments, when judged on the basis of what we understand today, seem utterly barbaric or, at the very least, absurd. Fortunately, we no longer perform surgeries on the tongue (including the removal of a section of the tongue) to relieve hypothetical spasms of the tongue muscles, or fit oral devices to restrain tongue movement, or apply electrical current to the individual's body (Wingate, 1997). Obviously, those procedures resulted in physical harm or discomfort. The forced change of stutterers' handedness from left to right, a procedure that was used at times in the treatment of stuttering because it was thought this would rectify incomplete cerebral dominance for speech, was conceivably a source of emotional or psychological harm or discomfort.

Although these are perhaps extreme examples from a bygone era in stuttering's history, there are examples of the harm that erroneous theories can do that are more subtle in nature and more recent. Think, for example, of the number of parents who were made to feel unnecessarily guilty about their children's stuttering by the implications of the diagnosogenic theory, or the number of parents asked to make changes, often onerous, in the environments they structure for their children in the absence of any compelling research data to indicate the need for environmental manipulation or change.

Less drastic, but equally important, is the loss of time (and money) that results when ineffective treatment methods based on an incorrect theory are employed. It may be that we can never know the number of individuals for whom critical treatment time was lost because their clinicians persisted in the use of ineffective methods born of erroneous theories, or because their clinicians based their views on the timing of intervention on mistaken beliefs encouraged by those theories. It is only relatively recently, for example, that clinicians have come to see the wisdom of direct intervention for early stuttering for many children. The willingness to intervene directly is an outgrowth of at least two factors: the research that demonstrates the efficacy and effectiveness of early intervention, and the realization that data do not support those theories of stuttering that prompt the fear that the disorder would worsen with direct intervention (see Attanasio, 1999).

FROM TREATMENT TO THEORY

We saw from earlier discussions in this text that a theory may develop out of the accumulation of scientific observations and data that were originally made or gathered in a non-theoretical context. The regularity of the results of the observations and the consistency of the data compel the development of a theory that can organize our thinking, explain what has been observed and the data that have been gathered, and make connections among what can no longer be considered isolated or disparate findings. If theories may be born this way, might we be able to see that same birth process at work in stuttering? Can effective treatment approaches for stuttering that have no basis in theory give rise to a theory or model of stuttering?

The Vmodel, which was described earlier in this text, provides an affirmative answer to the question. Starting with the observation (data) that stuttering decreases when stutterers use rhythmic speech or prolonged speech, Packman and colleagues sought to investigate the effects of those two novel speech patterns on prosody. They found that both speech patterns reduced the variability of vowel duration and so, it was argued, the variability of syllabic stress. The Vmodel was developed to explain the role of variable syllabic stress in stuttering.

Of course, as we have seen, the Vmodel has been neither confirmed nor falsified. We mention it here only because it demonstrates another interesting aspect of the relationships between theory and therapy in stuttering: The development of a theory or model of stuttering does not necessarily lead to change in treatment approaches. It can also be the case that therapy – or more accurately, treatment research – generates theory, without the theory necessarily changing the therapy. The use of prolonged speech for the treatment of stuttering was not altered or abandoned as a result of the Vmodel's development. It is also the case that theory may serve to justify therapy. As discussed in Chapter 6, Webster goes to considerable lengths to explain how the inter-hemispheric interference model is consistent with current fluency-shaping treatments.

All this suggests the possibility that, even if a theory that best describes the nature and cause of stuttering is eventually discovered, treatment approaches for the disorder may not change. What may happen is that only those treatment approaches that fit the one theory accepted as the true and valid explanation of stuttering will remain in clinical practice (the assumption here is that those approaches are effective) and the treatment approaches that do not fit will be discarded. Such is the way of scientific change.

POSTSCRIPT

One theory accepted as the true and valid explanation of stuttering – legitimate goal or wishful thinking? To have a theory that provides a common context for scientific investigation, an agreed-upon vocabulary, a unified point-of-view, and a collective research programme – a Kuhnian paradigm, perhaps – is not wishful thinking but a legitimate goal of a mature science. The very fact, however, that there are many theories of stuttering, with a number of them suggesting treatment approaches, and the fact that more than one theory can provide a rationale for the same treatment approach, are indications that we have yet to agree on a single valid theory (Perkins, 1986). In short, we do not have a paradigm. If we had a single valid theory available to us, then perhaps we could derive "an optimally effective treatment of stuttering" (Perkins, 1986, p. 31). What of the reverse? Would the discovery of that optimally effective treatment of stuttering serve to confirm the theory from which it was derived?

The questions raised in this chapter will continue to occupy us for some time. Among other questions that deserve our attention are the following: Would it be that if we knew the cause of stuttering, we would try to find ways to treat the cause rather than treat the effect? Is it possible that there are causes of disorders, the cause of stuttering among them, that cannot be treated and that we will only be able to treat their effects? Is it possible that finding the cause of stuttering would not change the way we treat the disorder?

Chapter 12

Final comments

One of the major problems with the theories presented in this text is a weakness in, or lack of, heuristic value. Almost none of them have led to any systematic programme of research or contributed much to the development of treatment, particularly for the treatment of early stuttering. One exception to this last criticism is the demands and capacities (DC) model. This model has provided the basis for a comprehensive treatment for young children who stutter (see Chapter 9), although as yet there are no scientific data to indicate that it is effective (Packman et al., 2004). Of course, as discussed in the previous chapter, evidence of effectiveness would not confirm the model.

The theories presented in this text were selected on the basis of specific criteria described in earlier sections; they are not the only extant theories of stuttering. It is not necessary to enumerate all of the current theories of stuttering or those of the past, however, to conclude that the search for explanations of the nature and cause of the disorder occupies the attention of clinicians and researchers with considerable intensity; some might say that that intensity is disproportionate to the disorder's prevalence compared to that of other communication disorders. Nevertheless, stuttering can disrupt communication and have a seriously negative impact on the lives of stutterers, their families, and their associates. Those are reasons enough to continue the search for understanding. Then too, not knowing why one or one's child has a disorder, not knowing what the cause or causes might be, can add to the disorder's impact. It is often palliative to know why, even in those cases where that knowledge does not necessarily lead to treatment or cure. Conversely, it is often palliative to know what are the unlikely or unsupportable reasons for a disorder's occurrence – fear, blame, guilt, shame, misdirection, and confusion are reduced or eliminated. Obviously, there are other reasons to investigate the nature and cause of stuttering, one being the hope that that understanding will lead to the most effective treatment possible or to, dare we say, a cure. Research into the cause or causes of stuttering or research that eliminates incorrect beliefs about cause is greatly enhanced by scientific theories – theories that can be tested and that are open to being falsified.

It is certainly true, as it is with stuttering, that the treatment of a disorder can proceed without a theory that provides an explanation of the nature and cause of the disorder. Empirical evidence – data-based, treatment efficacy evidence – can be used to establish the validity of a treatment approach outside a theoretical or explanatory framework. However, knowing that a treatment works does not provide a full scientific understanding of the disorder or of the treatment. For many individuals, knowing that something is so, but not knowing *why* it is so, is not personally satisfying. Perhaps the desire to know the reasons for the phenomena we observe and to seek explanations is, as we suggested at the beginning of this text, a basic characteristic – perhaps a need (innate or acquired) – of human beings. Spend even brief amounts of time among children of a certain age and you will be simultaneously entertained, delighted, and annoyed by their insistence on knowing *why*. Without meaning to be disrespectful, it could be said that scientists, or others with a scientific frame of mind, have never outgrown the urgent need to know why.

The field of stuttering has had, and continues to have, many theories of stuttering. What the field does not seem to have had is the equivalent of a paradigm shift whereby the currently subscribed to theory is replaced by a new one. Theories come, but they do not go. The following comment by Ingham and Ingham (2002, p. 1) is apt:

> Professor Bill Perkins, a well-known American scholar of stuttering, once pointed out that a hallmark of the field of stuttering is that no theory ever dies – they all live on forever. This could serve as a commentary on the fact that many theories of the cause and nature of stuttering have not been testable using the scientific method and so have not been able to be disproved – thus they linger on.

We emphasize again the need to base our clinical practice on data-based evidence that comes from treatment efficacy research, rather than on speculation, personal preference and experience, or authoritative statements of a treatment's effectiveness in the absence of acceptably derived outcomes data. The latter is ideology or doctrine, not science. One component in the methodologies used to obtain such data is a falsifiable hypothesis (see discussions within the text), theoretically or clinically based, whose predictions can be tested and then observed to have occurred or not. In order to test a hypothesis, the terms used to describe what is being tested must be precise (e.g., how is stuttering being defined?; what are the criteria that, if met, signal effective treatment?), the conditions under which the testing is done must be carefully explained (e.g., have competing explanations for the potential or observed outcome been controlled or accounted for?), and the validity of the outcome must be demonstrated (e.g., have the results been repeated in subsequent research, especially research that used randomized controlled trials?). By taking the scientific approach just described to decide on the treatment programme to use, clinicians will have a better understanding of why they have selected a particular treatment for a specific client.

Having a theory of stuttering that is not falsifiable serves to clutter thinking on the nature and cause of stuttering. It is not by any means desirable to have so many theories from which to choose, especially when those theories do not meet the criterion of falsifiability. Ferris (2002, p. 20) quotes the physicist Steven Weinberg:

> One can imagine a category of experiments that *refute* [emphasis in the original] well-accepted theories, theories that have become part of the standard consensus of physics. *Under this category I can find no examples whatever in the past one hundred years* [emphasis in the original].

Weinberg is boasting here of the consensus among physicists about their major theories. Although speech-language pathology is not physics, the advent of the day when a similar statement about stuttering can be made would be welcomed indeed. That day would signify that researchers have reached consensus about the nature of stuttering and an agreed-upon context within which to conduct research, while remaining open to the refutation or falsification of hypotheses and theory.

While waiting for that day to arrive, clinicians and researchers need to be mindful of the fact that the cause of stuttering is as yet unknown, and it is our view that they need to honestly explain that ignorance of cause to parents of children who stutter and to older children and adults who stutter. At the same time, parents and those who stutter can be reassured that treatments are available that can eliminate stuttering or reduce its severity and interference with communication. Of course, where appropriate, treatments may also address the psychological, social, emotional, and vocational ramifications of stuttering. They can be told, too, that research into the nature and cause of stuttering is ongoing and that the methods of science can be used to assess current and any future theories of stuttering.

While we are committed to the scientific approach to the study and treatment of stuttering, we acknowledge the real possibility that answers may not reach the level of certainty found in the physical sciences. Evidence for or against a particular theory of stuttering or a treatment approach is unlikely to be decisive enough to bring about the level of consensus found in the physical sciences. Clinicians and researchers may hold on to the theories that guide their work in stuttering for many reasons. What is important, we think, is that clinicians and researchers approach their work and evaluate their beliefs within a scientific frame of mind. We have endeavoured in this text to provide ways by which theories may be assessed within that scientific frame of mind so that speech-language pathologists and others interested in stuttering will be in an informed position when deciding on the merits of theories of stuttering published in the professional literature. In a sense, it is our hope that we have offered ways by which individuals can be more informed consumers of the literature on stuttering.

References

Adams, M. R. (1990). The Demands and Capacities Model I: Theoretical elaborations. *Journal of Fluency Disorders, 15*, 135–141.

Ambrose, N., Cox, N., & Yairi, E. (1997). The genetic basis of persistence and recovery in stuttering. *Journal of Speech, Language, and Hearing Research, 40*, 567–580.

Anderson, J. (1962). *Studies in empirical philosophy*. Sydney, Australia: Angus & Robertson.

Andrews, G., Craig, A., Feyer, A., Hoddinott, S., Howie, P., & Neilson, M. (1983). Stuttering: A review of research findings and theories circa 1982. *Journal of Speech and Hearing Disorders, 48*, 226–245.

Andrews, G. J., & Harris, M. (1964). *The syndrome of stuttering*. London: Heinemann.

Attanasio, J. S. (1999). Treatment of early stuttering: Some reflections. In M. Onslow & A. Packman (Eds.), *The handbook of early stuttering intervention* (pp. 189–203). San Diego, CA: Singular Publishing Group.

Attanasio, J. S. (2000). Where is the gap? A diverse view of stuttering and stuttering research. *Contemporary Psychology APA Review of Books, 45*, 53–55.

Attanasio, J. S. (2003). Some observations and reflections. In M. Onslow, A. Packman, & E. Harrison (Eds.), *The Lidcombe Program of early stuttering intervention: A clinician's guide* (pp. 207–214). Austin, TX: Pro-Ed.

Attanasio, J., Onslow, M., & Packman, A. (1998). Representativeness reasoning and the search for the origins of stuttering: A return to basic observations. *Journal of Fluency Disorders, 23*, 265–277.

Baker, A. J. (1986). *Australian realism: The systematic philosophy of John Anderson*. Cambridge: Cambridge University Press.

Bernstein Ratner, N., & Healy, E. C. (Eds.). (1999). *Stuttering research and practice: Bridging the gap*. Mahwah, NJ: Lawrence Erlbaum Associates Inc.

Blalock, H. M. Jr. (1964). *Causal inferences in nonexperimental research*. Chapel Hill, NC: The University of North Carolina Press.

Bloodstein, O. (1958). Stuttering as an anticipatory struggle reaction. In J. Eisenson (Ed.), *Stuttering: A symposium* (pp. 1–69). New York: Harper & Row.

Bloodstein, O. (1972). The anticipatory struggle hypothesis: Implications of research on the variability of stuttering. *Journal of Speech and Hearing Research, 15*, 487–499.

Bloodstein, O. (1993). *Stuttering: The search for a cause and cure*. Boston, MA: Allyn & Bacon.

Bloodstein, O. (1995). *A handbook on stuttering* (5th Ed.). San Diego, CA: Singular Publishing Group.

Bloodstein, O. (1997). Stuttering as an anticipatory struggle reaction. In R. F. Curlee & G. M. Siegel (Eds.), *Nature and treatment of stuttering: New directions* (2nd Ed., pp. 169–181). Boston, MA: Allyn & Bacon.

Bloodstein, O. (2000a). Anxiety and stuttering: Some thoughts on reading Menzies, Onslow, and Packman (1999). *American Journal of Speech-Language Pathology*, *9*, 87.

Bloodstein, O. (2000b). Genes versus cognitions in stuttering: A needless dichotomy. *American Journal of Speech-Language Pathology*, *9*, 358–359.

Bloodstein, O. (2001). Incipient and developed stuttering as two distinct disorders: Resolving a dilemma. *Journal of Fluency Disorders*, *26*, 67–73.

Bluemel, C. (1932). Primary and secondary stammering. *Quarterly Journal of Speech*, *18*, 187–200.

Boberg, E., Yeudall, L. T., Schopflocker, D., & Bo-Lassen, P. (1983). The effect of an intensive behavioral program on the distribution of EEG alpha power in stutterers during the processing of verbal and visuospatial information. *Journal of Fluency Disorders*, *8*, 245–263.

Bonelli, P., Dixon, M., Bernstein Ratner, N., & Onslow, M. (2000). Child and parent speech and language and the Lidcombe Program of Early Stuttering Intervention. *Clinical Linguistics and Phonetics*, *14*, 427–446.

Borden, G. J., Bayer, T., & Kenney, M. K. (1985). Onset of voicing in stuttered and fluent utterances. *Journal of Speech & Hearing Research*, *28*, 363–372.

Borsodi, R. (1967). *The definition of definition*. Boston, MA: Porter Sargent.

Bothamley, J. (Ed.). (1993). *Dictionary of theories*. London: Gale Research International Ltd.

Bothe, A. K. (2003). Evidence-based treatment of stuttering: V. The art of clinical practice and the future of clinical research. *Journal of Fluency Disorders*, *28*, 247–258.

Briggs, J., & Peat, F. D. (1989). *Turbulent mirror*. New York: Harper & Row, Publishers.

Casti, J. L. (1989). *Paradigms lost: Images of man in the mirror of science*. New York: William Morrow & Company, Inc.

Chalmers, A. F. (1999). *What is this thing called science?* (3rd Ed.). St Lucia, Australia: Brisbane University Press.

Chapanis, A. (1963). Men, machines, and models. In M. H. Marx (Ed.), *Theories in contemporary psychology* (pp. 104–129). New York: Macmillan.

Christensen, J. M. (1992). Did primitive man really talk like an ape? *Journal of Speech and Hearing Research*, *35*, 805.

Cook, F., & Rustin, L. (1997). Commentary on the Lidcombe Programme of early stuttering intervention. *European Journal of Disorders of Communication*, *32*, 250–258.

Cooper, E. B. (1993). Red herrings, dead horses, straw men, and blind alleys: Escaping the stuttering conundrum. *Journal of Fluency Disorders*, *18*, 375–387.

Conture, E. (1990a). Childhood stuttering: What is it and who does it? In J. A. Cooper (Ed.), *Research needs in stuttering: Roadblocks and future directions. ASHA Reports*, *18*, 2–14.

Conture, E. (1990b). *Stuttering* (2nd Ed.). Englewood Cliffs, NJ: Prentice-Hall.

Cordes, A. K., & Ingham, R. J. (1994). The reliability of observational data: II. Issues in the identification and measurement of stuttering events. *Journal of Speech and Hearing Research, 37*, 279–294.

Cordes, A. K., & Ingham, R. J. (1995). Stuttering includes both within-word and between-word disfluencies. *Journal of Speech and Hearing Research, 38*, 382–386.

Cordes, A., & Ingham, R. J. (1997). The concept of subperceptual stuttering: Analysis and investigation. In W. Hulstijn, H. F. M. Peters, & P. H. H. M. van Lieshout (Eds.), *Speech production: Motor control, brain research and fluency disorders* (pp. 385–394). Amsterdam, The Netherlands: Elsevier Science.

Culatta, R. (1976). Fluency: The other side of the coin. *Asha, 18*, 795–799.

Culatta, R., & Goldberg, S. A. (1995). *Stuttering therapy: An integrated approach to theory and practice.* Needham Heights, NJ: Allyn & Bacon.

Culatta, R., & Leeper, L. (1988). Dysfluency isn't always stuttering. *Journal of Speech and Hearing Disorders, 53*, 486–487.

Curlee, R. F. (2000). Demands and capacities versus demands and performance. *Journal of Fluency Disorders, 25*, 329–336.

Curlee, R. F., & Siegel, G. M. (Eds.). (1997). *Nature and treatment of stuttering: New directions* (2nd Ed.). Boston: Allyn & Bacon.

Damer, T. E. (1987). *Attacking faulty reasoning* (2nd Ed.). Belmont, CA: Wadsworth Publishing Company.

Drayna, D. (1997). Genetic linkage studies of stuttering: Ready for prime time? *Journal of Fluency Disorders, 22*, 237–241.

Drayna, D. (2003). *Genetic research on stuttering* [On-line]. Available: http://www.stut-tersfa.org/Research/drayna.htm. 19 January 2003.

Dunbar, R. (1995). *The trouble with science.* Cambridge, MA: Harvard University Press.

Einhorn, H. J., & Hogarth, R. M. (1986). Judging probable cause. *Psychological Bulletin, 99*, 3–19.

Fairbanks, G. (1954). Systematic research in experimental phonetics: 1. A theory of the speech system as a servosystem. *Journal of Speech and Hearing Disorders, 19*, 133–139.

Felsenfeld, S. (1996). Progress and needs in the genetics of stuttering. *Journal of Fluency Disorders, 21*, 77–103.

Ferris, T. (2002). The whole shebang: How science produced the big bang model. *American Educator, 26*, 20–23; 43–45.

Finn, P. (1998). Recovery without treatment: A review of conceptual and method-ological considerations across disciplines. In A. K. Cordes & R. J. Ingham (Eds.), *Treatment efficacy for stuttering: A search for empirical bases.* San Diego, CA: Singular.

Finn, P., & Ingham, R. J. (1989). The selection of "fluent" samples in research on stuttering: Conceptual and methodological considerations. *Journal of Speech and Hearing Research, 32*, 401–418.

Folkins, J. W. (1991). Stuttering from a speech motor perspective. In H. Peters, W. Hulstijn, & C. W. Starkweather (Eds.), *Speech motor control and stuttering* (pp. 561–570). Amsterdam, The Netherlands: Elsevier Science.

Forster, D. C., & Webster, W. C. (1991). Concurrent task interferences in stutterers: Dissociating hemispheric specialization and activation. *The Canadian Journal of Psychology, 45*, 321–335.

Forster, D. C., & Webster, W. C. (2001). Speech-motor control and interhemispheric relations in recovered and persistent stuttering. *Developmental Neuropsychology*, *19*, 125–145.

Foundas, A., Bollich, A., Corey, D., Hurley, M., & Heilman, K. (2001). Anomalous anatomy of speech-language areas in adults with persistent developmental stuttering. *Neurology*, *57*, 207–215.

Fox, P. T., Ingham, R. J., Ingham, J. C., Hirsch, T. B., Downs, J. H., Martin, C. et al. (1996). A PET study of the neural systems of stuttering. *Nature*, *382*, 158–162.

Froeschels, E. (1915). Stuttering and nystagmus. *Monatschrift für Ohrenheilkunde*, *49*, 161–167.

Froeschels, E. (1933). *Speech therapy*. Boston, MA: Expression Co.

Glauber, I. P. (1958). The psychoanalysis of stuttering. In J. Eisenson (Ed.), *Stuttering: A symposium* (pp. 73–119). New York: Harper & Row.

Gleick, J. (1987). *Chaos: Making a new science*. New York: Viking.

Goodson, F. E., & Morgan, G. A. (1976). Evaluation of theory. In M. H. Marx & F. E. Goodson (Eds.), *Theories in contemporary psychology*. New York: Macmillan.

Gottwald, S. R., & Starkweather, C. W. (1995). Fluency intervention for preschoolers and their families in the public schools. *Language, Speech, and Hearing Services in Schools*, *26*, 117–126.

Gottwald, S. R., & Starkweather, C. W. (1999). Stuttering prevention and intervention: A multiprocess approach. In M. Onslow & A. Packman (Eds.), *The handbook of early stuttering intervention* (pp. 53–82). San Diego, CA: Singular Publishing Group.

Guitar, B. (1998). *Stuttering: An integrated approach to its nature and treatment* (2nd Ed.). Baltimore, MD: Williams & Wilkins.

Hamre, C. (1992). Stuttering prevention II: Progression. *Journal of Fluency Disorders*, *17*, 63–79.

Hayhow, R. (1997). Commentary on Onslow, O'Brian, & Harrison. *European Journal of Disorders of Communication*, *32*, 258–266.

Herbert, J. D., Lilienfeld, S. O., Lohr, J. M., Montgomery, R. W., O'Donohue, W. T., Rosen, G. M. et al. (2000). Science and pseudoscience in the development of eye movement desensitization and reprocessing: Implications for clinical psychology. *Clinical Psychology Review*, *20*, 945–971.

Horgan, J. (1996). *The end of science: Facing the limits of knowledge in the twilight of the scientific age*. New York: Addison-Wesley Publishing Company, Inc.

Hubbell, R. D. (1981). *Children's language disorders: An integrated approach*. Englewood Cliffs, NJ: Prentice-Hall, Inc.

Ingham, J. C., & Ingham, R. J. (2002). *The brains of adult stutterers: Are they different from nonstutterers?* Retrieved 7 October 2000 from the World Wide Web: http://www.mnsu.edu/comdis/isad5/papers/ingham.html

Ingham, R. J. (1984). *Stuttering and behavior therapy: Current status and experimental foundations*. San Diego, CA: College-Hill Press.

Ingham, R. J. (1998). Learning from speech-motor control research on stuttering. In A. K. Cordes & R. J. Ingham (Eds.), *Treatment efficacy for stuttering: A search for empirical bases* (pp. 67–101). San Diego, CA: Singular Publishing Group.

Ingham, R. J., & Bothe, A. K. (2001). Recovery from early stuttering: Additional issues within the Onslow & Packman-Yairi & Ambrose (1999) exchange. *Journal of Speech, Language, and Hearing Research*, *44*, 862–867.

Ingham, R. J., & Cordes, A. K. (1997). Self-measurement and evaluating stuttering treatment efficacy. In R. F. Curlee & G. M. Siegel (Eds.), *Nature and treatment of stuttering: New directions* (2nd Ed., pp. 414–437). Boston, MA: Allyn & Bacon.

Ingham, R. J., & Cordes, A. K. (1999). On watching a discipline shoot itself in the foot: some observations on current trends in stuttering treatment research. In N. Bernstein Ratner & E. C. Healey (Eds.), *Stuttering research and practice: Bridging the gap* (pp. 211–230). Mahwah, NJ: Lawrence Erlbaum Associates Inc.

James, W. (1981). *The principles of psychology.* In F. Burkhardt, & F. Bowers (Eds.), *The works of William James volume 2.* Cambridge, MA: Harvard University Press.

Johnson, W. (1956). Wendel Johnson. In E. F. Hahn (Ed.), *Stuttering, significant theories, and therapies, 2nd Edition* (pp. 59–70). Stanford, CA: Stanford University Press.

Johnson, W. (1957). Perceptual and evaluational factors in stuttering. In L. E. Travis (Ed.), *Handbook of speech pathology* (pp. 897–915). New York: Appleton-Century-Crofts, Inc.

Johnson, W. (1961). *Stuttering and what you can do about it.* Danville, IL: The Inter-state Printers & Publishers, Inc.

Jones, M., Gebski, V., Onslow, M., & Packman, A. (2001). Design of randomized controlled trials: The Lidcombe Program of early stuttering intervention. *Journal of Fluency Disorders, 26,* 247–267.

Karniol, R. (1992). Stuttering out of bilingualism. *First Language, 12,* 255–283.

Karniol, R. (1995). Stuttering, language, and cognition: A review and a model of stuttering as suprasegmental sentence plan alignment (SPA). *Psychological Bulletin, 117,* 104–124.

Kent, R. D. (1983). Facts about stuttering: Neuropsychologic perspectives. *Journal of Speech and Hearing Research, 48,* 249–255.

Kleinow, J., & Smith, A. (2000). Influences of length and syntactic complexity on the speech motor stability of the fluent speech of adults who stutter. *Journal of Speech, Language, and Hearing Research, 43,* 548–559.

Kloth, S., Kraaimaat, F., Janssen, P., & Brutten, G. (1999). Persistence and remission of incipient stuttering among high-risk children. *Journal of Fluency Disorders, 24,* 253–265.

Kolenda, K. (1974). *Philosophy's journey: A historical introduction.* Reading, MA: Addison-Wesley Publishing Company.

Kolk, H., & Postma, A. (1997). Stuttering as a covert repair hypothesis. In R. F. Curlee & G. M. Siegel (Eds.), *Nature and treatment of stuttering: New directions* (pp. 182–203). Boston, MA: Allyn & Bacon.

Kuhn, T. S. (1996). *The structure of scientific revolutions* (3rd Ed.). Chicago, IL: The University of Chicago Press.

Lane, J., & Tranel, B. (1971). The Lombard sign and the role of hearing in speech. *Journal of Speech and Hearing Research, 14,* 677–709.

Levelt, W. J. M. (1989). *Speaking: From intention to articulation.* Cambridge, MA: MIT Press.

Lieberman, P. (2000). *Human language and our reptilian brain: The subcortical bases of speech, syntax and thought.* Cambridge, MA: Harvard University Press.

Lincoln, M., Onslow, M., Lewis, C., & Wilson, L. (1996). A clinical trial of an operant treatment for school-age children who stutter. *American Journal of Speech-Language Pathology, 5,* 73–85.

Lum, C. (2002). *Scientific thinking in speech and language therapy*. Mahwah, NJ: Lawrence Erlbaum Associates Inc.

Lundin, R. W. (1972). *Theories and systems of psychology*. Lexington, KY: D. C. Heath & Co.

Luoko, L. J., Edwards, M. L., & Conture, E. G. (1990). Phonological characteristics of young stutterers and their normally fluent peers: Preliminary observations. *Journal of Fluency Disorders*, *15*, 191–210.

Mackie, J. L. (1974). *The cement of the universe: A study of causation*. Oxford: Clarendon Press.

Mackie, J. L. (1975). Causes and conditions. In E. Sosa (Ed.), *Causation and conditionals* (pp. 15–38). Oxford: Oxford University Press.

Manning, W. H. (1999). Progress under the surface and over time. In N. Bernstein Ratner & E. C. Healy (Eds.), *Stuttering research and practice: Bridging the gap* (pp. 123–129). Mahwah, NJ: Lawrence Erlbaum Associates Inc.

Manning, W. H. (2000). The demands and capacities model. *Journal of Fluency Disorders*, *25*, 317–319.

Månsson, H. (2000). Childhood stuttering: Incidence and development. *Journal of Fluency Disorders*, *25*, 47–57.

Martin, R., & Haroldson, S. (1986). Stuttering as involuntary loss of speech control: Barking up a new tree. *Journal of Speech and Hearing Disorders*, *51*, 187–191.

Martin, R. R., Kuhl, P., & Haroldson, S. (1972). An experimental treatment with two preschool stuttering children. *Journal of Speech and Hearing Research*, *15*, 743–752.

Marx, M. H. (1963). The general nature of theory construction. In M. H. Marx (Ed.), *Theories in contemporary psychology* (pp. 4–46). New York: The Macmillan Co.

Marx, M. H. (1976a). Formal theory. In M. H. Marx & F. E. Goodson (Eds.), *Theories in contemporary psychology* (2nd Ed., pp. 234–260). New York: Macmillan.

Marx, M. H. (1976b). Theorizing. In M. H. Marx & F. E. Goodson (Eds.), *Theories in contemporary psychology* (2nd Ed., pp. 261–286). New York: Macmillan.

Max, L., & Caruso, A. J. (1998). Adaptation of stuttering frequency during repeated readings: Associated changes in acoustic parameters of perceptually fluent speech. *Journal of Speech, Language and Hearing Research*, *41*, 1265–1281.

Menand, L. (2001). *The metaphysical club*. New York: Farrar, Straus & Giroux.

Mill, J. S. (1967). *A system of logic: Ratiocinative and inductive*. London: Longmans. [Original work published 1843.]

Mish, F. C. (Ed.). (1993). *Merriam Webster's collegiate dictionary* (10th Ed.). Springfield, IL: Merriam-Webster, Inc.

Moore, S. E., & Perkins, W. H. (1990). Validity and reliability of judgments of authentic and simulated stuttering. *Journal of Speech and Hearing Disorders*, *55*, 383–391.

Moore, W. H. (1993). Hemispheric processing research. Past, present, and future. In E. Boberg (Ed.), *Neuropsychology of stuttering* (pp. 39–72). Edmonton, Canada: The University of Alberta Press.

Neilson, M. D., & Neilson, P. D. (1985). Speech motor control and stuttering. In D. G. Russell & B. Abernathy (Eds.), *Motor memory and control* (pp. 68–80). Dunedin, New Zealand: Human Performance Associates.

Neilson, M. D., & Neilson, P. D. (1987). Speech motor control and stuttering: A computational model of adaptive sensory-motor processing. *Speech Communications*, *6*, 325–333.

Neilson, M. D., & Neilson, P. D. (2000). A computational theory of motor synergy development: Implications for stuttering. *Journal of Fluency Disorders*, *25*, 171. [Special edition Abstracts of the Third World Congress on Fluency Disorders, Nyborg, Denmark.]

Neilson, P., Neilson, M., & O'Dwyer, N. J. (1992). Adaptive model theory: Application to disorders of motor control. In J. J. Summers (Ed.), *Approaches to the study of motor control and learning* (pp. 495–548). Amsterdam: Elsevier Science.

Newton, R. G. (1997). *The truth of science: Physical theories and reality*. Cambridge, MA: Harvard University Press.

NIH Clinical Research Studies (1997). *Non-parametric and parametric linkage studies of stuttering* [On-line]. Available: http://clinicalstudies.info.nih.gov/detail/A_1997-DC-0057.html

Nippold, M. (1990). Concomitant speech and language disorders in stuttering children: A critique of the literature. *Journal of Speech and Hearing Disorders*, *55*, 51–60.

Nippold, M. (2002). Stuttering and phonology: Is there an interaction? *American Journal of Speech-Language Pathology*, *11*, 99–110.

Nudelman, H. B., Herbrich, K. E., Hess, K. R., Hoyt, B. D., & Rosenfield, D. B. (1992). A model of the phonatory response time of stutterers and fluent speakers to frequency-modulated tones. *Journal of the Acoustical Society of America*, *92*, 1882–1888.

Nudelman, H. B., Herbrich, K. E., Hoyt, B. D., & Rosenfield, D. B. (1989). A neuroscience model of stuttering. *Journal of Fluency Disorder*, *14*, 399–427.

O'Neil, W. M. (1962). *An introduction to method in psychology* (2nd Ed.). Melbourne, Australia: Melbourne University Press.

Onslow, M. (1996). *Behavioral management of stuttering*. San Diego, CA: Singular Publishing Group.

Onslow, M. (1999). [Review of *Stuttering: An integrated approach to its nature and treatment, 2nd Edn.*]. *Journal of Fluency Disorders*, *24*, 319–332.

Onslow, M. (2003). Overview of the Lidcombe Program. In M. Onslow, A. Packman, & E. Harrison (Eds.), *The Lidcombe Program of early stuttering intervention: A clinician's guide* (pp. 3–20). Austin, TX: Pro-Ed.

Onslow, M., Andrews, C., & Lincoln, M. (1994). A control/experimental trial of an operant treatment for early stuttering. *Journal of Speech and Hearing Research*, *37*, 1244–1259.

Onslow, M., Costa, L., & Rue, S. (1990). Direct early intervention with stuttering: Some preliminary data. *Journal of Speech and Hearing Disorders*, *55*, 405–416.

Onslow, M., O'Brian, S., & Harrison, E. (1997a). The Lidcombe Program of early stuttering intervention: Methods and issues. *European Journal of Disorders of Communication*, *32*, 231–250.

Onslow, M., O'Brian, S., & Harrison, E. (1997b). The Lidcombe Programme: Maverick or not? *European Journal of Disorders of Communication*, *32*, 261–266.

Onslow, M., Packman, A., & Harrison, E. (2003). *The Lidcombe Program of early stuttering intervention: A clinician's guide*. Austin, TX: Pro-Ed.

Onslow, M., van Doorn, J., & Newman, D. (1992). Variability of acoustic segment durations after prolonged-speech treatment for stuttering. *Journal of Speech and Hearing Research*, *35*, 529–536.

Osborne, R. (1992). *Philosophy for beginners*. New York: Writers & Readers Publishing, Inc.

Packman, A., Menzies, R. G., & Onslow, M. (2000a). Anxiety and the anticipatory struggle hypothesis. *American Journal of Speech-Language Pathology*, *9*, 88–89.

Packman, A., & Onslow, M. (1998). The behavioral data language of stuttering. In A. Cordes & R. J. Ingham (Eds.), *Treatment efficacy for stuttering: A search for empirical bases* (pp. 27–50). San Diego, CA: Singular Publishing Group.

Packman, A., & Onslow, M. (2000). Cause and effect in stuttering: An examination of the anticipatory struggle hypothesis. *American Journal of Speech-Language Pathology*, *9*, 359–360.

Packman, A., Onslow, M., & Attanasio, J. (2004). The demands and capacities model: Implications for evidence-based practice in the treatment of early stuttering. In A. K. Bothe (Ed.), *Evidence-based treatment of stuttering: Empirical issues and clinical implications* (pp. 65–79). Mahwah, NJ: Lawrence Erlbaum Associates Inc.

Packman, A., Onslow, M., & Menzies, R. G. (2000b). Novel speech patterns and the treatment of stuttering. *Disability and Rehabilitation*, *22*, 65–79.

Packman, A., Onslow, M., Richard, F., & van Doorn, J. (1996). Syllabic stress and variability: A model of stuttering. *Clinical Linguistics and Phonetics*, *10*, 235–263.

Packman, A., Onslow, M., & van Doorn, J. (1994). Prolonged-speech and modification of stuttering: Perceptual, acoustic and electroglottographic data. *Journal of Speech and Hearing Research*, *37*, 724–734.

Packman, A., Onslow, M., & van Doorn, J. (1997). Linguistic stress and the rhythm effect in stuttering. In W. Hulstijn, H. F. M. Peters, & P. H. H. M. van Lieshout (Eds.), *Speech production: Motor control, brain research and fluency disorders* (pp. 473–478). Amsterdam, The Netherlands: Elsevier Science.

Perkins, W. (1983). The problem of definition: Commentary on "Stuttering". *Journal of Speech and Hearing Disorders*, *48*, 246–249.

Perkins, W. (1984). Stuttering as a categorical event: Barking up the wrong tree – reply to Wingate. *Journal of Speech and Hearing Disorders*, *49*, 431–434.

Perkins, W. (1985). Horizons and beyond: Confessions of a carpenter. *Seminars in Speech and Language*, *6*, 233–245.

Perkins, W. H. (1986). Functions and malfunctions of theories in therapies. *ASHA, February*, 31–33.

Perkins, W. H. (1990). What is stuttering? *Journal of Speech and Hearing Disorders*, *55*, 370–382.

Perkins, W. H. (1996). *Stuttering and Science*. San Diego, CA: Singular Press.

Perkins, W. H., Kent, R. D., & Curlee, R. F. (1991). A theory of neuropsycholinguistic function in stuttering. *Journal of Speech and Hearing Research*, *34*, 734–752.

Peters, T. J., & Guitar, B. (1991). *Stuttering: An integrated approach to its nature and treatment*. Baltimore, MD: Williams & Wilkins.

Pinker, S. (1995). *The language instinct*. New York: HarperCollins.

Place, U. T. (1996). Linguistic behaviorism as a philosophy of empirical science. In W. O'Donogue & R. F. Kitchen (Eds.), *The philosophy of psychology* (pp. 126–148). London: Sage Publications.

Polanyi, M. (1958). *Personal knowledge: Towards a post-critical philosophy*. Chicago, IL: The University of Chicago Press.

Popper, K. R. (1959). *The logic of scientific discovery*. New York: Basic Books, Inc.

Popper, K. R. (1979). *Objective knowledge: An evolutionary approach* (Rev. Ed.). Oxford: Clarendon Press.

Popper, K. R. (1999). *Realism and the aim of science* (Rev. Ed.). New York: Routledge.

Postma, A., & Kolk, A. (1993). The covert repair hypothesis: Prearticulatory repair processes in normal and stuttered disfluencies. *Journal of Speech and Hearing Research, 36,* 472–487.

Postma, A., & Kolk, H. (1994). Stuttering and word planning processes: A reply to Wingate. *Journal of Speech and Hearing Research, 37,* 581–582.

Prins, D., & Hubbard, C. P. (1988). Response contingent stimuli and stuttering: Issues and implications. *Journal of Speech and Hearing Research, 31,* 696–709.

Rakover, S. S. (1990). *Metapsychology: Missing links in behavior, mind and science.* New York: Paragon House.

Robey, R. R., & Schultz, M. C. (1993). *Optimizing theories and experiments.* San Diego, CA: Singular Publishing Group.

Robinson, D. (1985). *Philosophy of psychology.* New York: Columbia University Press.

Rosenfield, D. (2001). Do stutterers have different brains? *Neurology, 57,* 171–172.

Rosenfield, D. B., & Nudelman, H. B. (1987). Neuropsychological models of speech dysfluency. In L. Rustin, H. Purser, & D. Rowley (Eds.), *Progress in the treatment of fluency disorders* (pp. 3–18). London: Taylor & Francis.

Rosenfield, D. B., Viswanath, N. S., Callis-Landrum, L., DiDanato, R., & Nudelman, H. (1991). Patients with acquired dysfluencies: What they tell us about developmental stuttering. In H. F. M. Peters, W. Hulstijn, & C. W. Starkweather (Eds.), *Speech motor control and stuttering* (pp. 277–284). Amsterdam, The Netherlands: Elsevier.

Rothbart, M. K., & Bates, J. E. (1998). Temperament. In N. Eisenberg (Ed.), *Handbook of child psychology: Vol. 3 Social, emotional and personality development* (5th Ed., pp. 105–176). New York: Wiley.

Rustin, L., Cook, F., Botterill, W., Hughes, C., & Kelman, E. (2001). *Stammering: A practical guide for teachers and other professionals.* London: David Fulton.

Ryan, B., & Ryan, B. (2002). Can effective treatment for stuttering be accomplished in the public schools? *Perspectives on Fluency and Fluency Disorders, 3,* 14–17.

Sander, E. K. (1975). Untangling stuttering: A tour through the theory thicket. *ASHA, 17,* 256–262.

Schultz, D. P., & Schultz, S. E. (2000). *A history of modern psychology* (7th Ed.). New York: Harcourt College Publishers.

Shapiro, D. A. (1999). *Stuttering intervention.* Austin, TX: Pro-Ed.

Shattuck-Hufnagel, S. (1979). Speech errors as evidence for a serial ordering mechanism in sentence production. In W. Cooper & E. Walker (Eds.), *Sentence processing: Psycholinguistic Studies* (pp. 295–342). Hillsdale, NJ: Lawrence Erlbaum Associates Inc.

Shattuck-Hufnagel, S. (1983). Sublexical units and suprasegmental structure in speech production planning. In P. MacNeilage (Ed.), *The production of speech* (pp. 109–139). New York: Springer-Verlag Inc.

Sheehan, J. G. (1970). *Stuttering: Research and therapy.* New York: Harper & Row.

Sidman, M. (1960). *Tactics of scientific research: Evaluating experimental data in psychology.* New York: Basic Books Inc.

Siegel, G. M. (1970). Punishment, stuttering, and disfluency. *Journal of Speech and Hearing Research, 13,* 677–714.

Siegel, G. M. (1987). The limits of science in communication disorders. *Journal of Speech and Hearing Disorders, 52,* 306–312.

Siegel, G. M. (1989). Exercises in behavioral explanation. *Journal of Speech-Language Pathology and Audiology, 13*, 3–6.

Siegel, G. M. (1998). Stuttering: Theory, research, and therapy. In A. K. Cordes & R. J. Ingham (Eds.), *Treatment efficacy for stuttering: A search for empirical bases* (pp. 103–114). San Diego, CA: Singular Publishing Group.

Siegel, G. M. (2000). Demands and capacities or demands and performance? *Journal of Fluency Disorders, 25*, 321–327.

Siegel, G. M., & Ingham, R. J. (1987). Theory and science in communication disorders. *Journal of Speech and Hearing Disorders, 52*, 99–104.

Smith, A. (1992). Commentary on "A theory of neuropsycholinguistic function in stuttering". *Journal of Speech and Hearing Research, 35*, 805–809.

Smith, A. (1999). Stuttering: A unified approach to a multifactorial, dynamic disorder. In N. Berstein Ratner & E. C. Healey (Eds.), *Stuttering research and practice: Bridging the gap* (pp. 27–44). Mahwah, NJ: Lawrence Erlbaum Associates Inc.

Smith, A., & Kelly, E. (1997). Stuttering: A dynamic, multifactorial model. In R. F. Curlee & G. M. Siegel (Eds.), *Nature and treatment of stuttering: New directions* (2nd Ed., pp. 204–217). Boston, MA: Allyn & Bacon.

Smith, A., & Kleinow, J. (2000). Kinematic correlates of speaking rate changes in stuttering and normally fluent adults. *Journal of Speech, Language, and Hearing Research, 43*, 521–536.

Smith, A., & Weber, C. (1988). The need for an integrated perspective on stuttering. *ASHA, 30*, 30–32.

Sommer, M., Koch, M. A., Paulus, W., Weiller, C., & Büchel, C. (2002). Disconnection of speech-relevant brain areas in persistent developmental stuttering. *Lancet, 360*, 380–383.

Starkweather, C. W. (1987). *Fluency and stuttering*. Englewood Cliffs, NJ: Prentice-Hall.

Starkweather, C. W. (1997). Therapy for younger children. In R. F. Curlee & G. M. Siegel (Eds.), *Nature and treatment of stuttering: New directions* (2nd Ed., pp. 257–279). Boston, MA: Allyn & Bacon.

Starkweather, C. W. (1999). The effectiveness of stuttering therapy: An issue for science? In N. Bernstein Ratner & E. C. Healey (Eds.), *Stuttering research and practice: Bridging the gap* (pp. 231–244). Mahwah, NJ: Lawrence Erlbaum Associates Inc.

Starkweather, C. W., & Givens-Ackerman, J. (1997). *Stuttering*. Austin, TX: Pro-Ed.

Starkweather, C. W., & Gottwald, S. R. (1990). The demands and capacities model II: Clinical applications. *Journal of Fluency Disorders, 15*, 143–157.

Starkweather, C. W., & Gottwald, S. R. (2000). The demands and capacities model: Response to Siegel. *Journal of Fluency Disorders, 25*, 369–375.

Starkweather, C. W., Gottwald, S. R., & Halfond, M. M. (1990). *Stuttering prevention: A clinical method*. Englewood Cliffs, NJ: Prentice-Hall.

Stewart, I. (1996). *From here to infinity*. Oxford: Oxford University Press.

Stuart, A. (1999). The distraction hypothesis and the practice of pseudoscience: A reply to Bloodstein. *Journal of Speech Language & Hearing Research, 42*, 913–914.

Supernaturalism. [Online]. 14 January 2003. Available: http//www.unnu.com/hewhome/attractions/philosophy/Supernaturalsim.html

Teesson, K., Packman, A., & Onslow, M. (2003). The Lidcombe Behavioural Data Language of Stuttering. *Journal of Speech, Language and Hearing Research, 46*, 1009–1015.

Thompson, M. (1995). *Teach yourself philosophy*. Chicago, IL: NTC Publishing Group.

Thompson, R. F. (1967). *Foundations of physiological psychology*. New York: Harper & Row.

Travis, L. E. (1957). The unspeakable feelings of people, with special reference to stuttering. In L. E. Travis (Ed.), *Handbook of speech pathology* (pp. 916–946). New York: Appleton-Century-Crofts, Inc.

Travis, L. E. (1978). The cerebral dominance theory of stuttering: 1931–1978. *Journal of Speech and Hearing Disorders, 43*, 278–281.

Travis, L. E. (1986). Postscript 5: Emotional factors. In G. H. Shames & H. Rubin (Eds.), *Stuttering then and now* (pp. 117–122). Columbus, OH: Charles E. Merrill.

Van Hooft, S., Gillam, L., & Byrnes, M. (1995). *Facts and values: An introduction to critical thinking for nurses*. Sydney, Australia: Maclennan & Petty.

Van Riper, C. (1963). *Speech correction: Principles and methods*. Englewood Cliffs, NJ: Prentice-Hall.

Van Riper, C. (1982). *The nature of stuttering* (2nd Ed.). Englewood Cliffs, NJ: Prentice-Hall. [First published 1971.]

Warburton, N. (1999). *Philosophy: The basics* (3rd Ed.). New York: Routledge.

Webster, R. W. (1977). Concept and theory in stuttering: An insufficiency of empiricism. In R. W. Rieber (Ed.), *The problem of stuttering*. New York: Elsevier.

Webster, W. G. (1985). Neuropsychological models of stuttering – I. Representation of sequential response mechanisms. *Neuropsychologia, 23*, 263–267.

Webster, W. G. (1986a). Neuropsychological models of stuttering – II. Interhemispheric interference. *Neuropsychologia, 24*, 737–741.

Webster, W. G. (1986b). Response sequence organisation and reproduction by stutterers. *Neuropsychologia, 24*, 813–821.

Webster, W. G. (1987). Rapid letter transcription performances by stutterers. *Neuropsychologia, 25*, 845–847.

Webster, W. G. (1988). Neural mechanisms underlying stuttering: Evidence from bimanual handwriting performance. *Brain and Language, 33*, 226–244.

Webster, W. G. (1989a). Sequence initiation performance by stutterers under conditions of response competition. *Brain and Language, 36*, 286–300.

Webster, W. G. (1989b). Sequence reproduction deficits in stutterers tested under nonspeed response conditions. *Journal of Fluency Disorders, 14*, 79–86.

Webster, W. G. (1990a). Evidence in bimanual finger tapping of an attentional component to stuttering. *Behavioral Brain Research, 37*, 93–100.

Webster, W. G. (1990b). Concurrent cognitive processing and letter sequence transcription deficits in stutterers. *Canadian Journal of Psychology, 44*, 1–13.

Webster, W. G. (1991). Task complexity and manual reaction times in people who stutter. *Journal of Speech and Hearing Research, 34*, 708–714.

Webster, W. G. (1993). Hurried hands and tangled tongues: Implications of current research for the management of stuttering. In E. Boberg (Ed.), *Neuropsychology of stuttering* (pp. 73–127). Edmonton, Canada: The University of Alberta Press.

Webster, W. G. (1997). Principles of human brain organization related to lateralization of language and speech motor functions in normal speakers and stutterers. In W. Hulstijn, H. F. M. Peters, & P. H. H. M. van Lieshout (Eds.), *Speech production: Motor control, brain research, and fluency disorders* (pp. 119–139). Amsterdam, The Netherlands: Elsevier.

Webster, W. G. (1998). Brain models and the clinical management of stuttering. *Journal of Speech-Language Pathology and Audiology, 22*, 220–230.

White, P. A. (1990). Ideas about causation in philosophy and psychology. *Psychological Bulletin, 108,* 3–18.

WHO (1977). *International Classification of Diseases.* Geneva: World Health Organisation.

Wingate, M. (1964). A standard definition of stuttering. *Journal of Speech and Hearing Disorders, 29,* 484–489.

Wingate, M. (1976). *Stuttering theory and treatment.* New York: Irvington Publishers, Inc.

Wingate, M. (1983). Speaking unassisted: Comments on a paper by Andrews et al. *Journal of Speech and Hearing Research, 48,* 255–263.

Wingate, M. (1988). *The structure of stuttering: A psycholinguistic analysis.* New York: Springer-Verlag.

Wingate, M. (1994). Comments on Postma & Kolk's "The covert repair hypothesis: prearticulatory repair processes in normal and stuttered disfluencies" (1993). *Journal of Speech and Hearing Research, 37,* 581.

Wingate, M. (1997). *Stuttering: A short history of a curious disorder.* Westport, CT: Bergin & Garvey.

Wingate, M. (2001). SLD is not stuttering. *Journal of Speech, Language, and Hearing Research, 44,* 381–383.

Wingate, M. (2002). *Foundations of stuttering.* San Diego, CA: Academic Press.

Wynn, C., & Wiggins, A. (1997). *The five biggest ideas in science.* New York: John Wiley & Sons.

Yairi, E. (1997). Disfluency characteristics of childhood stuttering. In R. F. Curlee & G. M. Siegel (Eds.), *Nature and treatment of stuttering: New directions* (2nd Ed., pp. 49–78). Needham Heights, NJ: Allyn & Bacon.

Yairi, E., & Ambrose, N. (1992a). A longitudinal study of stuttering in children: A preliminary report. *Journal of Speech and Hearing Research, 35,* 755–760.

Yairi, E., & Ambrose, N. (1992b). Onset of stuttering in preschool children: Selected factors. *Journal of Speech and Hearing Research, 35,* 782–788.

Yairi, E., & Ambrose, N. (1999). Early childhood stuttering I: Persistence and recovery rates. *Journal of Speech, Language and Hearing Research, 42,* 1097–1112.

Yairi, E., & Ambrose, N. (2001). Longitudinal studies of childhood stuttering: Evaluation of critiques. *Journal of Speech, Language, and Hearing Research, 44,* 867–872.

Yairi, E., Ambrose, N., & Cox, N. (1996). Genetics of stuttering: A critical review. *Journal of Speech and Hearing Research, 39,* 771–784.

Yairi, E., & Lewis, B. (1984). Disfluencies at the onset of stuttering. *Journal of Speech and Hearing Research, 27,* 154–159.

Yaruss, J. S. (1997). Clinical implications of situational variability in preschool children who stutter. *Journal of Fluency Disorders, 22,* 187–203.

Yaruss, J. S. (2000). The role of performance in the demands and capacities model. *Journal of Fluency Disorders, 25,* 347–358.

Yaruss, J. S., LaSalle, L., & Conture, E. (1998). Evaluating stuttering in young children: Diagnostic data. *American Journal of Speech-Language Pathology, 7,* 62–76.

Zebrowski, P. M. (1991). Duration of the speech disfluencies of beginning stutterers. *Journal of Speech and Hearing Research, 34,* 483–491.

Zuriff, G. E. (1985). *Behaviorism: A conceptual reconstruction.* New York: Columbia University Press.

Author index

Subject index